Gimson's
PRESIDENTS

By the same author

The Desired Effect
Boris: The Making of the Prime Minister
Gimson's Kings & Queens: Brief Lives of the Monarchs since 1066
Gimson's Prime Ministers: Brief Lives from Walpole to May

Gimson's
PRESIDENTS

BRIEF LIVES
from
WASHINGTON to TRUMP

BY ANDREW GIMSON

illustrated by

Martin Rowson

◨ SQUARE PEG

1 3 5 7 9 10 8 6 4 2

Square Peg, an imprint of Vintage,
20 Vauxhall Bridge Road,
London SW1V 2SA

Square Peg is part of the Penguin Random House group of companies
whose addresses can be found at global.penguinrandomhouse.com

Penguin
Random House
UK

First published by Square Peg in 2020

Penguin.co.uk/vintage

A CIP catalogue record for this book is available from the British Library

ISBN 9781529110012

Typeset in 10.25/15 pt Quadraat by Jouve (UK), Milton Keynes

Printed and bound in Great Britain by Clays Ltd, Elcograf S.p.A.

Penguin Random House is committed to a sustainable future for our
business, our readers and our planet. This book is made from Forest
Stewardship Council® certified paper.

For Holly Brewer and Roland Stephen

With experience enough in subordinate offices to have seen the difficulties of this, the greatest of all, I have learned that it will rarely fall to the lot of imperfect man to retire from this station with the reputation and the favour which bring him into it.

THOMAS JEFFERSON, PRESIDENT 1801–09,
FIRST INAUGURAL ADDRESS

I am loath to close. We are not enemies, but friends. We must not be enemies. Though passion may have stretched it must not break our bonds of affection. The mystic chords of memory, stretching from every battlefield and patriot grave to every living heart and hearthstone over this broad land, will yet swell the chorus of the Union, when again touched, as surely they will be, by the better angels of our nature.

ABRAHAM LINCOLN, PRESIDENT 1861–65,
FIRST INAUGURAL ADDRESS

What a melancholy spectacle it was, from George Washington down to the last incumbent; what vexations, what disappointments, what grievous mistakes, what very objectionable manners!

HENRY ADAMS, GREAT-GRANDSON OF
JOHN ADAMS, PRESIDENT 1797–1801,
AND GRANDSON OF JOHN QUINCY ADAMS,
PRESIDENT 1825–29, IN DEMOCRACY:
AN AMERICAN NOVEL, 1880

I did not care a rap for being shot. It is a trade risk, which every prominent public man ought to accept as a matter of course.

THEODORE ROOSEVELT, PRESIDENT 1901–09, AFTER BEING SHOT IN MILWAUKEE ON 14 OCTOBER 1912 WHILE CAMPAIGNING FOR A THIRD TERM

I sit here all day trying to persuade people to do the things they ought to have sense enough to do without my persuading them . . . That's all the powers of the president amount to.

HARRY S. TRUMAN, PRESIDENT 1945–53, QUOTED BY RICHARD E. NEUSTADT

I would build a great wall, and nobody builds walls better than me, believe me, and I'll build them very inexpensively, I will build a great, great wall on our southern border. And I will have Mexico pay for that wall. Mark my words.

DONALD TRUMP, PRESIDENT 2017–, PRESIDENTIAL ANNOUNCEMENT SPEECH 16 JUNE 2015

CONTENTS

INTRODUCTION

My spirits always rise on visiting America, not because it is so modern, but because it is so traditional. Here is an eighteenth-century republic of exceptional vitality, the greatest and most successful attempt ever made to build and maintain a free government on a continental scale.

This book sets out to show, in a chain of forty-four biographical sketches, how the United States got from George Washington to Donald Trump. Is Trump part of the American tradition, or a dreadful aberration? Few of the politicians and journalists who condemn him have read enough history to be able to answer that question. At the end of this volume I give my own answer.

It is a tremendous story, but large tracts of it are unknown even to most people versed in American history. Washington, Jefferson, Lincoln, the current President and perhaps half a dozen others, most of them within living memory, take almost all the light going, leaving at least thirty holders of the office, if not in darkness, at least in deep shadow. Who can name the eight presidents before Lincoln, or – except for Grant, famous as a soldier rather than a politician – the eight presidents after him? Historians focus on the inspiring figures, to the exclusion of the rest.

And because the president is head of state as well as head of the executive, a tone of pompous reverence often descends on those who write about him (not yet about her, though that can only be a matter of time). The noble cadences of the Declaration of Independence prepare us for the history of the republic as a morality tale, as edifying in its way as Parson Weems's *Life of Washington* (see page one). Evidence which detracts from this view of history is downplayed, and the educated classes were unprepared for the arrival of Trump.

Readers may wonder how an Englishman can write this book. Alistair Cooke, celebrated reporter of America to the British in the second half of the twentieth century, warned in 1972 of 'the delusion which is universal among Englishmen, that Americans are Englishmen gone wrong'. In my youth (I was born in 1958) I yielded to that delusion, but I hope by now I have got over it.

This is undeniably an encounter with America by an outsider. But the history of democracy in America is the universal inheritance of all who value freedom. We pore over it as the founding fathers studied Rome, hoping to understand how republican government works. A visitor may, moreover, be struck by things the inhabitants of a country have ceased to notice, and no Englishman is a complete outsider in the United States, a country with a reverence for the past which often surpasses what is found in the United Kingdom. We share Magna Carta, the common law and the English language, and for a few years we shared George III, a king of such Hanoverian obstinacy that he lost the American colonies.

Before embarking on this work, I wrote brief lives of the forty English and British kings and queens since 1066, and brief lives of the fifty-five British prime ministers since 1721. As in those books, brevity has trumped comprehensiveness. I have not attempted to give a full account of the various political transactions in this period, or to offer more than a few allusions to the development of the party system. The focus here is on temperament, not doctrine.

The book is dedicated to two friends beneath whose hospitable roof I have often stayed, Holly Brewer, Burke Chair of American History at the University of Maryland, and her husband, Roland

Stephen, whom I have known since we studied at Cambridge University in the late 1970s. They did not see the text before it went to press, so should not be blamed for any errors of fact, judgement or taste I may have made. My thanks are due to Martin Rowson for his brilliant drawings; my agent, Andrew Gordon, for his infallible guidance; Edward Fox, David and Debbie Owen, Robert Chote, William Franklin, Michael Crick, Thomas Kielinger, Susan Clarke, Bruce Clark and Jonathan Aitken for early encouragement and the loan or gift of books; Andrew Mackinlay for reciting a line by Vachel Lindsay about president Andrew McKinley which impelled me to discover the poem; Rowan Yapp, Mireille Harper, Kris Potter, Fran Owen and Mari Yamazaki at Square Peg for their editorial genius; and above all my wife, Sally Gimson, who has listened to various anecdotes about American presidents which she indicated were not amusing enough to include in this book.

Andrew Gimson, Gospel Oak, December 2019

A BRIEF NOTE ON PRESIDENTIAL ELECTIONS

Presidential elections have taken place every four years since 1788, with polling day fixed by a law of 1845 as the first Tuesday after 1 November. Washington was inaugurated on 30 April 1789, and subsequent inaugurations were held on 4 March, or the following day if that was a Sunday, until 1937, when inauguration day was moved to 20 January (with the same provision for avoiding Sunday).

Donald Trump is described as the 45th president, but is actually the 44th person to have held that office, because Grover Cleveland, president 1885–89 and 1893–97, is counted as both the 22nd and the 24th president.

GEORGE WASHINGTON

Lived 1732–99; president 1789–97

Whatan enigma is posed by George Washington, who founded a nation and revealed almost nothing of himself. Even his contemporaries found him admirable but opaque, and to posterity he can seem as lifeless as his image graven upon Mount Rushmore.

His modern biographers make him less enjoyable to read about by dismissing as pernicious drivel the one story of his upbringing every schoolchild used to know, for once heard it cannot be forgotten. According to Parson Weems (whose *Life of*

Washington appeared soon after its subject's death, and enjoyed a vast sale), at the age of about six George was given a hatchet, of which he was 'immoderately fond'.

> One day in the garden, where he often amused himself hacking his mother's pea-sticks, he unluckily tried the edge of his hatchet on the body of a beautiful young English cherry-tree, which he barked so terribly, that I don't believe the tree ever got the better of it. The next morning the old gentleman [Washington's father] finding out what had befallen his tree, which, by the by, was a great favourite, came into the house, and with much warmth asked for the mischievous author, declaring at the same time, that he would not have taken five guineas for his tree. Nobody could tell him any thing about it. Presently George and his hatchet made their appearance. *George*, said his father, *do you know who killed that beautiful little cherry-tree yonder in the garden?* This was *a tough question;* and George staggered under it for a moment; but quickly recovered himself: and looking at his father, with the sweet face of youth brightened with the inexpressible charm of all-conquering truth, he bravely cried out, 'I *can't tell a lie, Pa; you know I can't tell a lie. I did cut it with my hatchet.'*

Weems, a hucksterish clergyman who was determined to sell books, knew just what his readers wanted: vivid anecdotes about their greatest national hero, coated in sugary religiosity and demonstrating that virtue would be rewarded with earthly success, for Washington's father exclaims with delight that the courage to be honest '*is more worth than a thousand trees, though blossomed with silver, and their fruits of purest gold*'.

All nations feel the need for founding myths, which may or may not be the literal truth but become part of how they see themselves. To smash such images is to impoverish our understanding of the past. The Romans looked back to Romulus and Remus, the English to King Alfred and the cakes, the Scots to Robert the Bruce and the spider, the Swiss to William Tell and the apple, and the Americans contemplated with profound satisfaction George Washington and the cherry tree.

He was born in Westmoreland County, in the Colony of Virginia, in February 1732. The Washingtons were an old-established family of English gentry, their coat of arms three mullets and two bars – three stars and two stripes – which somewhat surprisingly is not reckoned to be the inspiration for the flag of the United States, though it did become the emblem of the District of Columbia. George's great-grandfather arrived in Virginia in 1657, acquired land by marriage and farmed tobacco using slave labour. The family's and colony's links with England remained so close as to seem indissoluble. George's father, Augustine, was sent to the famous school at Appleby, in Westmorland in the north of England, where he in turn sent his oldest two sons, born to his first wife, who died young.

George, the first of the six children born to Augustine's second wife, was only eleven when his father died. There was probably too little money to send the boy away to school. The most notable relic of his education is a list which he copied out in his admirably clear hand of 110 'Rules of Civility & Decent Behaviour in Company and Conversation', beginning: 'Every Action done in Company, ought to be with Some Sign of Respect, to those that are Present.'

These rules have been treated by some historians as a joke or an irrelevance, an attitude which renders Washington incomprehensible, for here was a man who attached supreme importance to proper behaviour. Manners matter because they show what kind of a person you are, and the precariousness of his family's situation made it all the more important that he conduct himself as a gentleman, for whom any display of ambition would be a painful and demeaning vulgarity. Woodrow Wilson understood this when he wrote: 'The real Washington was as thoroughly American as Jackson or Lincoln. What we take for lack of passion in him was but the reserve and self-mastery natural to a man of his class and breeding.'

Washington's actions reveal a man of exceptional energy and boldness, who never rested on his laurels but spent his whole life in pursuit of land and yet more land, and ended his days as one of the greatest landowners in America. At the age of thirteen he began training as a surveyor, a profession which required a good grasp of mathematics and trigonometry, and three years later he seized the chance to take part in an expedition to map the vast property of Lord Fairfax, 8,100 square miles in extent and stretching into the Shenandoah Valley on the far side of the Blue Ridge.

His older half-brother Laurence, to whom he was close, sickened and in 1752 died, and left him the Mount Vernon estate, named after a British admiral and situated in a commanding position on the Potomac River. The situation is worthy of a patrician. George was by now six foot two inches tall, remarkably strong, an excellent horseman who loved foxhunting, and was a graceful dancer who enjoyed going to dances, and sighed after a 'Low land beauty', but being a gentleman left us no details.

Washington took his brother's place as an officer in the Virginia militia, and was almost at once sent west by Robert Dinwiddie, Governor of Virginia, in command of an expedition charged with wresting control of the Ohio Country, the immense region south of the Great Lakes, from the French. At the age of twenty-one, this intrepid young man pushed himself to the forefront of the imperial rivalry between Britain and France, and before long, as Horace Walpole wrote, 'The volley fired by a young Virginian in the backwoods of America set the world on fire.'

Here was Colonel Washington's school of war. He discovered

he enjoyed danger and could instil courage in those who followed him. He worked out by the most arduous experience the best tactics for those remote and inhospitable forests, trained his men accordingly and set about winning over the Indians, who understood forest warfare better than anyone. Perhaps most important of all, he found that defeat need not be final, if you kept your head, retreated in good order and persevered. In 1755 he saw General Braddock, the British commander to whom he was acting as aide-de-camp, cut down by the French and their Indian allies, and became a hero by extricating the remnant of the force.

Four years later, Washington came home victorious, set about enlarging the small house at Mount Vernon into a mansion, and at the age of twenty-six married a rich young widow, Martha Dandridge Custis, who already had two children. Just before this prudent and happy match, he wrote to Sarah Cary Fairfax, wife of his friend George William Fairfax. Washington had been in love with Sarah for some years, acted in amateur theatricals with her, and now told her: 'I profess myself a Votary to Love . . . the World has no business to know the object of my Love, declared in this manner to – you.' He was in the grip of strong emotion but brought it under control. The year before he died, when Sarah was living as a widow in England, he wrote to her that no later events 'have been able to eradicate from my mind, the recollection of those happy moments, the happiest in my life, which I have enjoyed in your company'.

He and Martha had no children, but their steadily more imposing house, which as its final touch would acquire while he was president a grand, simple, lofty colonnade facing the river and done apparently to his own design, was filled with the wider family and with visitors. With the help of 144 gallons of rum, punch, cider and wine, distributed to voters before they cast their ballots, he was elected in 1758 to the House of Burgesses, whose members had since 1619 constituted Virginia's ruling class. He was an independent country gentleman, taking his place and fulfilling his obligations in a society led by people like himself.

Washington could imagine no higher form of existence, and was excited by the vast acreage which might be acquired to the west, where it seemed Virginia might one day stretch to the Pacific Ocean. He was a passionate improver of Mount Vernon, rising early to ride round his farms and give instructions, doubling the size of the estate to 6,500 acres, increasing the number of slaves to well over a hundred, introducing the most advanced agricultural techniques from England in an attempt to make his crops pay, persisting through every setback caused by poor soil, bad weather and unfavourable terms of trade set in London, and adding a distillery and an iron foundry to his other ventures. He was energetic too in his pleasures: in 1769 he writes in his diary, 'Went up to Alexandria to a Barbecue and stayed all Night.' Grander figures in Virginia, such as George Mason, might think of him as a parvenu surveyor, but that attitude was becoming harder and harder to sustain.

After the defeat of France, Britain and her thirteen North American colonies drifted into mutual misunderstandings which ended in a war between themselves. For the triumphs gained over the French, consolidated at the Treaty of Paris in 1763, came at an alarming cost to the British Exchequer. In London it seemed reasonable to ask the colonists to contribute to the cost of their own defence; in the colonies that was seen as taxation without representation, which was an intolerable attack on their ancient liberties. A decade later, a band of colonists dramatised their defiance by hurling a cargo of tea into Boston Harbor.

At Westminster, Edmund Burke warned his fellow parliamentarians that the Americans were freeborn Englishmen, to whom the tea tax, however moderate the rate, was a monstrous imposition: 'No man ever doubted that the commodity of tea could bear an imposition of three pence. But no commodity will bear three pence, or will bear a penny, when the general feelings of men are irritated, and when two millions of men are resolved not to pay.' Sensible people on both sides, including Washington, believed until a late stage that the dispute could be settled without going to war. They had reckoned without the Hanoverian intransigence of George III.

Twelve of the thirteen colonies sent delegates, Washington one of the seven from Virginia, to the First Continental Congress, which met in Philadelphia in the autumn of 1774 and vainly petitioned the King for the redress of grievances. By May 1775, when the Second Continental Congress met, the first shots had been fired at Lexington and Concord, and reinforcements for the British garrison in Boston were said to be on their way from London. In a hint to the delegates that his services were available, Washington was the only delegate to attend in uniform, the blue and buff of the Virginia militia. In June 1775 John Adams of Massachusetts, who knew it was vital to bind the southern states into the arduous struggle now unfolding, proposed Washington as the general who should command 'all the continental forces raised for the defence of American liberty'.

Washington slipped from the room when this happened. The following day, in a three-paragraph address to Congress, he declared 'with the utmost sincerity, I do not think myself equal to the Command I am honoured with', and added that he would 'serve without pay' while keeping an exact account of his expenses. Whenever he took on great responsibilities, right up to the presidency, he protested his unfitness for them. A gentleman does not grab at honours or boast of his abilities. He declares these by his behaviour. He made his will, and sent it with a letter of tender solicitude to his wife.

Benjamin Rush, an ardent and distinguished patriot, said of Washington: 'He has so much martial dignity in his deportment that you would distinguish him to be a general and a soldier among 10,000 people. There is not a king in Europe that would not look like a valet de chambre by his side.' The patriots, or in British terms the rebels, were proud of their leader. At the start of July, he took command of the 15,000-strong militia besieging a regular British force of less than half that number in Boston.

Washington complained that 'Order, Regularity and Discipline' were lacking in his troops. They were also in dire need of food, ammunition, artillery, medicine, uniforms, blankets, tents and money to pay their wages. Yet in March 1776, after hauling captured cannon 300 miles from Fort Ticonderoga and placing them by night on Dorchester Heights overlooking Boston, they forced the British to evacuate the town and sail away. This success was followed by defeat that summer at New York, where superior British forces chased out Washington, who had no experience of operating on this scale, seems to have suffered from over-confidence, was fortunate not to be trapped by a professional army which had total command of the sea, and found his own army disintegrating as his men fell sick, deserted or returned home at the end of their stipulated period of service. 'Our only dependence now,' he wrote to his cousin Lund Washington on 10 December 1776, 'is upon the Speedy Enlistment of a New Army. If this fails us, I think the game will be pretty well up.'

Yet a fortnight later, on Christmas night, Washington led a raid in a snowstorm across the half-frozen Delaware River and overwhelmed a British garrison of 1,500 Hessians in Trenton. This daring exploit restored the patriots' morale and was later commemorated in a famous painting by Emanuel Leutze, showing the dauntless Washington standing in a small boat amid the ice floes. Like Weems's biography, the picture contains numerous implausibilities, but expresses to perfection how Americans came to regard their national hero.

With remarkable stamina, Washington kept going for eight

and a half years, waging war not only with the British but with Congress for proper supplies. Early encouragement came in October 1777, when General Burgoyne, advancing with a large force of redcoats down the Hudson towards New York, was forced to surrender at Saratoga, a battle in which Washington played no part, though he contributed some of his best commanders and troops. The lowest point for the Continental Army came in the winter of 1777–78, which the British spent in comfort in Philadelphia, then the largest city in North America, while Washington and his men shivered twenty miles away at Valley Forge, ill-fed, ill-clad, ill-housed and ill-paid.

But their general commanded respect. The French admired him, and after Saratoga came in on the American side, Washington formed a close bond with the Marquis de Lafayette, a young French nobleman who joined his staff and became a kind of surrogate son to him. In London, Pitt the Elder, who had led Britain to victory against France, warned the House of Lords: 'America . . . is not a wild and lawless banditti, who having nothing to lose, might hope to snatch something from public convulsions; many of their leaders . . . have a great stake in this great contest: the gentleman who conducts their armies, I am told, has an estate of four or five thousand pounds a year.'

In 1781 the opportunity arose to conduct a joint operation with 8,000 French troops and the French West Indies fleet, which had temporarily deprived the British of command of the seas. Washington marched south from New York with 9,000 troops of his own, handled his mighty allies with perfect tact, and together with the French forced General Cornwallis, who himself had fewer than 8,000 men, to surrender at Yorktown, on the shores of Chesapeake Bay. For the British there could be no recovery from this disaster, though hostilities dragged on until peace was made in 1783.

In December of that year Washington said farewell to his

officers in Fraunces Tavern in New York. He and they wept. Fears that he would behave like a latter-day Julius Caesar or Oliver Cromwell, a military leader who at the end of a victorious war seized power for himself, proved groundless. He went home to Mount Vernon, conducting himself like a latter-day Cincinnatus, the hero of the Roman Republic who was called from the plough to save his country and went back to his farm having done so.

Washington claimed to see himself as 'a private citizen of America, on the banks of the Patowmac . . . under my own Vine and my own Fig-tree, free from the bustle of a camp and the intrigues of a court'. But so many visitors took advantage of his Virginian hospitality that he described the house as 'a well-resorted tavern', and he could never be inactive. Years of frustrating negotiations with Congress had already convinced him the new republic would have to develop a strong national government, or else go to rack and ruin. Shays' Rebellion, by backwoodsmen in Massachusetts in the autumn of 1786, prompted him to exclaim in angry alarm, 'We are fast verging to anarchy and confusion!' His fellow Virginian James Madison persuaded him that the Constitutional Convention, to be held in Philadel-phia in the summer of 1787, had a realistic chance of devising a better form of government, so Washington agreed to chair it. According to the South Carolina delegate Pierce Butler, 'Many of the members cast their eyes towards General Washington as President; and shaped their Ideas of the powers to be given to a President, by their Opinion of his Virtue.'

At the Fourth of July ceremony in Wilmington, Delaware in 1788 a toast was drunk to 'Farmer Washington – may he like a second Cincinnatus, be called from the plough to rule a great people'. For once the new constitution, with its skilful separ-ation of powers between the different branches of government, had been ratified by eleven of the thirteen states (only North Carolina and Rhode Island stood out against it), someone was needed to fill the new post of president, and who better than Washington?

He expressed both public and private reluctance to take on the burden. At the age of fifty-seven, his health was less robust, and he had lost all but one of his teeth, so had to wear a brace, equipped first with cows' teeth and then with a set made out of hippopotamus tusk, constructed by a leading dentist in Philadelphia, but so painful he had to take laudanum. In the stiff, unamused portraits of him, his mouth set in a rigid line and his cheeks looking slightly stuffed, it is more than possible he was suffering from acute toothache.

'My movements to the chair of Government will be accompanied with feelings not unlike those of a culprit who is going to the place of his execution,' he told his old friend and fellow veteran Henry Knox, the Boston bookseller who had hauled the cannon from Ticonderoga. But this absence of vainglory just intensified the conviction that Washington was the right man for the job. In April 1789 he heard at Mount Vernon that he had received all 69 votes cast in the Electoral College, and set out on an eight-day journey through cheering crowds to New York. At Philadelphia a laurel crown was lowered upon his head from a triumphal arch as 20,000 people watched him ride on a white horse across the Schuylkill River. He was not a king, but was taking the place of a king, and the reverence with which he was regarded had to be kept in bounds, for there was something uncomfortably royalist in it, a departure from republican simplicity.

He was sworn in at Federal Hall in New York, adding after the oath, 'So help me God,' words it became customary for each new president to utter. Here was a man who could impart to American constitutional practice the sacred, sacerdotal, somewhat ponderous tone which the new nation needed. In his first inaugural address he said, 'the preservation of the sacred fire of liberty, and the destiny of the Republican model of Government, are justly considered as *deeply*, perhaps as *finally* staked, on the experiment entrusted to the hands of the American people'.

Not everyone was impressed by Washington's demeanour during the inauguration. According to William Maclay, a senator from Pennsylvania, 'This great man was agitated and embarrassed more than ever he was by the leveled cannon or pointed musket. He trembled, and several times could scarce make out to read, though it must be supposed he had often read it before.'

We have no examples of Washington being witty, or even trying to be witty. Nor was he learned in the way that his immediate successors, John Adams – now serving under him as vice president – and Thomas Jefferson, were. He was clear, judicious, pragmatic, trustworthy and authoritative, a man accustomed to having every reasonable request obeyed. In the councils of war he so frequently held as commander of the Continental Army, he had shown his genius for identifying and promoting gifted younger colleagues such as Alexander Hamilton and getting them to make the case for whatever course of action they thought should be followed, before he said what would be done. No leader has been better at using the talents of those around him, while himself remaining somewhat above the fray, employing, as Adams put it, 'the gift of silence'.

And this approach he now brought to government. He appointed a cabinet of remarkable men, including Hamilton to run the Treasury and Jefferson as secretary of state, responsible for foreign affairs. The new federal government was awash with debt, its paper virtually worthless. Hamilton devised a bold scheme to lay the foundations of national prosperity by funding the debt not only of the federal government but of the states too, with repayments to be made in gold. There were evident unfairnesses in this scheme: it bailed out the most improvident states, and put money in the hands of northern financiers who had bought up other people's debt.

Washington backed Hamilton to the hilt, but the southern states, which envisaged an agrarian future for America, were dismayed by a plan which would strengthen the power of the federal government and of bankers. The proposals only went through Congress after a deal between Hamilton and Jefferson, the price being the establishment of the national capital, not in New York or Philadelphia, but on a southern plot of land situated on the Potomac, only sixteen miles upstream from Mount Vernon. Philadelphia, which had hoped to become the capital, was awarded the consolation prize of serving in that role for ten years from 1790, while the new government buildings were erected. New York, which had started constructing a grand presidential mansion for Washington, lost out altogether and was very cross, with its newspapers voicing the first public criticisms of him.

The federal government was now credit-worthy and, as Hamilton had predicted, the country started to prosper. The passing, with Washington's approval, of the Bill of Rights, guaranteeing freedom of religion, assembly and speech, helped reconcile the states to the establishment of a stronger central power. But another great if tacit concession, indefensible in terms of either liberty or equality, had been made to the southern states. Slavery remained intact, with no path set towards emancipation. If this had not been so, the southern states would have refused to ratify the constitution, and the new nation would not have been born.

With the benefit of hindsight, we can see that the United States had from its birth a fatal flaw which led towards the disaster of the Civil War. But the moral question is not just hindsight. The inconsistency between proclaiming the freedom of white Americans, while keeping African Americans as slaves, was plain at the time. As Dr Johnson put it, 'how is it that we hear the loudest yelps for liberty from the drivers of Negroes?'

Lafayette had proposed to Washington as early as 1783 that slaves be freed in Virginia and settled as tenant farmers further west. 'I shall be happy,' Washington replied, 'to join you in so laudable a work.' Nothing happened, but by 1786 Washington had resolved not to buy any more slaves himself and hoped legislation could be passed 'by which slavery in this Country may be abolished by slow, sure, & imperceptible degrees'. That he did not achieve, and in February 1790, when the aged Benjamin Franklin, one of the greatest figures in the American Revolution, signed a Quaker petition for the gradual abolition of slavery, President Washington did nothing to help, but agreed the whole subject should be put off until 1808. In his will, Washington left categorical instructions that all his and his wife's slaves be freed after his death, which was more than any other of the founding fathers from Virginia did.

By 1792 a deep feud had opened between Hamilton and Jefferson, and both of them told Washington that, in order to hold the country together, he must serve a second term. With even greater reluctance than usual, Washington agreed to carry on, and was for a second time elected unanimously, being inaugurated in March 1793. He was not a modern man, and refused to turn himself into a party politician. He was a man of the eighteenth century, who believed faction was a wholly destructive force, and could not share Jefferson's enthusiasm for the French Revolution.

The President agreed with Hamilton that it was vital to stay on good terms with the British, who remained the country's main trading partner. At the end of 1793, Jefferson resigned as secretary of state and retired to Monticello. But he continued to foment attacks on Hamilton and Washington in the press. The Jay Treaty with Britain, named after the envoy, John Jay, who negotiated it, averted an Anglo-American war, but on terms which were furiously assailed for failing to uphold American interests.

In 1796 Jefferson wrote to Washington denying that he had played any part in the campaign of vilification waged against him. Washington replied that he knew Jefferson had described him as 'a person under a dangerous influence' – Hamilton – and that as president he had striven to save the country from 'the horrors of a desolating war' but had been misrepresented in the press 'in such exaggerated and indecent terms as could scarcely be applied to a Nero; a notorious defaulter; or even to a common pick-pocket'. Soon afterwards, the notorious Mazzei letter, written by Jefferson himself and containing this denunciation of the President, became public:

In place of that noble love of liberty and republican government which carried us triumphantly through the war, an Anglican monarchical aristocratical party has sprung up, whose avowed object is to draw over us the substance, as they have already done the forms, of the British government . . . It would give you a fever were I to name to you the apostates who have gone over to these heresies, men who were Samsons in the field and Solomons in the council, but who have had their heads shorn by the harlot England.

Correspondence between Mount Vernon and Monticello, which had continued on innocently agricultural topics, now ceased, and Washington prepared to deliver one last, magnificent apologia, in which with barely suppressed anger he would justify himself and his policy. He sent the draft he had written of his Farewell Address, plus the version Madison had composed for him to use at the end of his first term, to Hamilton and instructed him that the final text must be in a 'plain style' which would give the lie to the idea that the President, now retiring from public life, had harboured monarchical ambitions. The text, which was printed in the newspapers rather than delivered as a speech, occupies sixteen pages in John Rhodehamel's collection of Washington's writings, and its urgency and force can only be conveyed in the original words, which are all too often reduced to a bland paraphrase:

> I have already intimated to you the danger of Parties in the State, with particular reference to the founding of them on Geographical discriminations. Let me now take a more comprehensive view, and warn you in the most solemn manner against the baneful effects of the Spirit of Party, generally . . .
>
> The alternate domination of one faction over another, sharpened by the spirit of revenge natural to party dissention, which in different ages and countries has perpetrated the most horrid enormities, is itself a frightful despotism. But this leads at length to a more formal and permanent despotism. The disorders and miseries, which result, gradually incline the minds of men to seek security and repose in the absolute power of an Individual: and sooner or later the chief of some prevailing faction more able or more fortunate than his competitors, turns this disposition to the purposes of his own elevation, on the ruins of Public Liberty . . .
>
> It opens the door to foreign influence and corruption, which find a facilitated access to the government itself through the channels of party passions . . .
>
> Why, by interweaving our destiny with that of any part of Europe, entangle our peace and prosperity in the toils of European Ambition, Rivalship, Interest, Humour or Caprice?

With these tremendous warnings to his compatriots, the first President left the stage and retired in March 1797 to Mount Vernon. Unlike Napoleon Bonaparte, who was about to make himself First Consul and then Emperor of France, Washington knew when to stop. The following year he was for the last time in danger of being recalled to public life when his successor President Adams, without seeking his permission, appointed him commander-in-chief at a moment when war with France seemed likely. But luckily the crisis subsided.

On 12 December 1799 Washington mounted his horse and, despite a storm of snow, sleet and hail, made his usual five-hour tour of his farms at Mount Vernon. He reached home wet and cold, and dined without changing because he did not wish to keep his guests waiting. His good manners killed him. The following day he was merely hoarse, but in the early hours of 14 December he woke his wife to say he had a pain in his throat and could hardly breathe. He had developed a severe respiratory infection. His doctors bled him, taking five pints of blood, which was the orthodox treatment. That night he died while taking his pulse.

He was buried four days later in the family vault at Mount Vernon. He was buried too beneath a mountain of superlatives. The best epitaph was coined by his fellow Virginian and hero of the Revolutionary War, Henry 'Light-Horse Harry' Lee, who described him, in an address at the four-and-a-half-hour memorial service held later that month in Philadelphia, as 'first in war, first in peace, and first in the hearts of his countrymen'. The society which by slow degrees, for it ran out of money, erected the Washington Monument in Washington DC, intended that it 'should blend stupendousness with elegance'. But although that obelisk was for a few years in the 1880s, until overtaken by the Eiffel Tower, the highest man-made structure in the world, like most things which seek to impress by mere size, it seems almost wilfully unimaginative.

JOHN ADAMS

Lived 1735–1826; president 1797–1801

J ohn Adams had the unenviable task of following a hero, and after serving for a single term was defeated by a genius. But although Washington and Jefferson, the tall Virginians, attracted much of the fame which might have accrued to this tubby New Englander, they could not deny him the virtue of being his own man, tenacious, ambitious, querulous and one of the most considerable intellects to form the American Revolution. Here was a founding father more candid than either of them, who despite being touchy to the point of persecution mania, never allowed himself to be browbeaten, and once exclaimed: 'Thanks to God that he gave me stubbornness when I know I am right.'

There spoke Adams' Puritan forefathers, who in 1638 left England and settled at Braintree, outside Boston. In the winter, when there was no work on their farm, Adams' father made shoes:

> My father was an honest man, a lover of his country, and an independent spirit and the example of that father inspired me with the greatest pride of my life . . . My father, grandfather, great grandfather, and great, great grandfather were all inhabitants of Braintree and all independent country gentlemen. I mean officers in the militia and deacons in the church . . . The line I have just described makes about 160 years in which no bankruptcy was ever committed, no widow or orphan was ever defrauded, no redemptor intervened and no debt was contracted with England.

So wrote Adams while serving as vice president under Washington. As a boy, he fell in love with farming, but his father insisted he learn Latin and go to Harvard, after which he made his way as a lawyer. He developed a thriving practice, continued to till the land, married the redoubtable Abigail Smith, argued in print that British liberties had existed 'even before Parliament existed', added that 'no freeman should be subject to any tax to which he has not given his own consent', in 1770 had the courage to defend the British soldiers accused of the Boston Massacre in which five men had died, in the same year was elected to the Massachusetts legislature, was chosen to be one of his state's delegates to the Continental Congress in Philadelphia, and in 1776 urged Jefferson to draft the Declaration of Independence, telling him (by Adams' own account), 'You can write ten times better than I can.'

But words poured from Adams too. He was an early advocate

of the break with Britain, and it was his speech, the greatest of his life, which persuaded Congress to take the momentous step of voting for independence. According to Jefferson, Adams had 'a power of thought and expression that moved us from our seats'. The die was cast, but success depended on enlisting France's help, and Congress, to Abigail's horror, recognised her husband's talents by appointing him a commissioner to that country. He left her to run the farm and care for three young children, and sailed with their oldest boy, John Quincy Adams, who was ten, through a terrible winter storm from Boston to Bordeaux.

In Paris he found his fellow envoy, the aged Benjamin Franklin, an established star with a European reputation, but shockingly familiar with the fashionable ladies, and indolent in the performance of official duties. Franklin for his part saw what Adams was like: 'He means well for his country, is always an honest man, often a wise one, but sometimes and in some things, absolutely out of his senses.'

For the next ten years Adams served as an American envoy in Paris, where he became good friends with his colleague Thomas Jefferson; in Amsterdam, where on his own initiative he obtained Dutch loans at a critical moment; and in London. His cantankerous honesty might have been expected to disqualify him for the profession of diplomacy, but his seriousness and ability to think his way to the heart of a problem carried him through. Abigail joined him in Paris, where she was shocked but charmed by French culture: 'To be out of fashion is more criminal than to be seen in a state of nature, to which the Parisians are not averse.'

In London, Adams was the first minister to represent the newly independent United States, was vilified by the British press, but had a successful audience with George III, telling the king that he hoped to restore 'the old good nature and the old good humour between people who, though separated by an ocean and under different governments, have the same language, a similar religion, and kindred blood' – the earliest of many efforts to assert the existence of a special relationship between the two countries.

Adams wrote in praise of the British constitution, describing it as 'the most stupendous fabric of human invention' in all history, words for which he knew he would be denounced at home. 'I tell him they will think in America that he is setting up a king,' Abigail said.

On returning home in the summer of 1788, he found himself the favourite to serve as vice president. But while Washington obtained all 69 votes in the Electoral College, Adams suffered the humiliation of coming second with only 34 votes. He was unaware that Alexander Hamilton had behind the scenes been campaigning against him, apparently in order to ensure Washington's pre-eminence.

And Washington was indeed pre-eminent, greeted with rapture on his arrival to be sworn in. Adams did not even play second fiddle to the President: that role was taken by Hamilton. The Vice President chaired the Senate, a role in which he contrived to make a fool of himself, for he intervened with his own opinions, which was not how a chairman should behave, and became obsessed with the question of titles, which to most people seemed unimportant.

Adams had been away from America for too long to understand public opinion, including the preference, in the new republic, for plain forms of address. When he proposed that Washington be called 'His Majesty the President', he opened himself to ridicule, and the joke went round that Adams should be called 'His Rotundity'. Jefferson was now secretary of state, but never consulted him about foreign affairs and was clearly (though he issued specious denials) fomenting the view that Adams was a monarchist, and mad. Nor did Washington consult Adams much.

Like the President, the Vice President could not bear the development of party politics, which had poisoned the atmosphere. Relations between Hamilton and Jefferson were soon so embittered that both men implored Washington to seek re-election. Hamilton also wanted Adams to carry on, in order to avert the election of a candidate from the other side, and at the election of 1792 helped arrange a more convincing victory for him than four years before.

'My country in its wisdom contrived for me the most insignificant office that ever the invention of man contrived or his imagination conceived,' Adams wrote to Abigail, a verdict with which later vice presidents have concurred. But by the beginning of 1796, Adams was seen as Washington's heir apparent, and in the autumn of that year he ran against Jefferson, with the two candidates remaining at home, as was then the custom, while the press abused or boosted them. The *Aurora* claimed Adams, 'champion of kings, ranks, titles', was intent on arranging a hereditary succession for his eldest son, John Quincy, who had already embarked on an impressive diplomatic career. But by the narrow margin of 71 to 68 votes, Adams emerged the victor over Jefferson. Adams wrote to Abigail, describing his own inauguration, overshadowed by the departure of Washington: 'A solemn scene it was indeed, and it was made affecting to me by the presence of the General, whose countenance was as serene and unclouded as the day. He seemed to enjoy a triumph over me. Methought I heard him say, "Ay! I am fairly out and you fairly in! See which of us will be the happiest!"'

Adams was not happy during his presidency. It is hard to avoid the thought that, despite his many admirable qualities, he lacked an instinctive feel for politics. At his moment of maximum power he made the error of deciding to keep Washington's cabinet, who were loyal to Hamilton rather than himself. The new President lacked not just Washington's air of authority, but his gift for handling men. And while as Vice President he had been scrupulously loyal to Washington, and had often used his casting vote in the Senate to get the President's business through, Jefferson, the new Vice President, was not loyal, and was opposed to him on the great question of how to deal with revolutionary France, with whom an undeclared state of war existed, with the French preying on American shipping and expelling an American peace envoy from Paris.

Adams announced he would make a renewed attempt 'to adjust all our differences with France by amicable negotiation', while at the same time building up the American navy, of which he is justly regarded as the founder. His opponents accused him of leading the country to war, and a French diplomat reported being told by Jefferson that 'Mr Adams is vain, irritable, stubborn, endowed with excessive self-love, and still suffering pique at the preference accorded Franklin over him in Paris.' Abigail, who had by now arrived at her husband's side in Philadelphia, remarked darkly that they were 'in perils by false brethren'.

In the spring of 1798 news arrived from France that the peace mission had failed, with the American envoys refusing to pay the enormous bribes demanded by three agents of Talleyrand, the French Foreign Minister, referred to in the envoys' dispatches as X, Y and Z. American opinion was outraged by the XYZ affair, as it came to be known, war fever swept the country, and Congress passed the Alien and Sedition Acts, which empowered the President to expel foreigners suspected of being enemy agents and to shut down any newspaper which sought 'to stir up sedition'. According to Adams, justifying the Alien Act in a letter to Jefferson written fifteen years later, 'French Spies then swarmed in our Cities and in the Country. Some of them were intolerably, turbulent, impudent and Seditious.'

In another sign that he was putting the country on a war footing, Adams appointed Washington commander-in-chief of the

American army. Washington insisted on Hamilton as his deputy, and the latter, seen by Abigail as 'a second Bonaparte', planned to make great conquests in Spanish America with this army, himself at its head. Meanwhile Jefferson tried to thwart the Alien and Sedition Acts, which he regarded as a monstrous assault on liberty, by promoting states' rights. Adams himself was exhausted and despondent, telling Abigail, 'I am old, old, very old and never shall be well.' The couple learned to their sorrow that their second son, Charles, had deserted his wife, gone bankrupt and was dying of alcoholism. Abigail spoke tenderly of the 'Poor, poor, unhappy wretched man', but his father called him 'a mere rake, buck, blood, and beast' and added, 'I renounce him.'

Yet Adams did not give up working for peace. In October 1799 he again dispatched commissioners to France, and in May 1800 he at last sacked two members of his Cabinet, telling one of them that Hamilton, who had been born in the West Indies, was an 'intrigant . . . a man devoid of every moral principle, a bastard . . . a foreigner'. Hamilton's army was disbanded, and peace with France was at last concluded in October 1800. Hamilton took revenge with a pamphlet in which he condemned Adams' 'disgusting egotism' and his record in government. From an electoral point of view, the split between Adams and Hamilton was disastrous, for they were supposed to be on the same side, both of them Federalists, preparing to take on Jefferson, the Republican candidate.

It was a dirty fight. The idea that the spring of American politics ran pure in the early years, and was only polluted later, is unhistorical. James Callender, a scurrilous Scottish journalist, chucked mud at both Hamilton, whom he accused of financial corruption and adultery (Hamilton admitted the latter but not the former), and Adams, whom he assailed not just as a warmonger and a monarchist, but as a 'repulsive pedant'. Callender was prosecuted under the Sedition Act and given a nine-month prison sentence.

Adams moved to Washington, almost none of which had yet been built, in 1800. The President's House, as it was then known, stood unfinished in a rutted field, but in November he moved in and wrote to Abigail, 'May none but Honest and Wise Men ever rule under This Roof.' When Abigail joined him, she used the unplastered audience room to dry her laundry. But their stay there was short. Adams lost the presidential election of December 1800, the result of which was not known until February 1801. He used the brief time left to him to appoint a new Chief Justice, John Marshall, a staunch Federalist who served for thirty-four years and became the greatest holder of that office, entrenching the Supreme Court's power to interpret the Constitution. Adams filled many other posts too – his 'midnight judges', as his enemies called the judicial appointments – and at four in the morning on 4 March 1801, the day of Jefferson's inauguration, left Washington by the public stagecoach, an act seen as graceless even by his admirers.

He enjoyed a quarter-century of retirement on his farm near Boston, and was eventually reconciled by letter with Jefferson, the two men conducting a lengthy correspondence. In 1825 Adams had the pleasure of hearing that his eldest son, John Quincy, had been elected president. The following year he died, aged ninety, on the Fourth of July, remarking to his assembled family and doctors: 'Thomas Jefferson survives.' This, however, was wrong, for Jefferson had died some hours earlier. Adams had suggested, in a letter to a friend, his preferred epitaph: 'Here lies John Adams, who took upon himself the responsibility of the peace with France in the year 1800.'

THOMAS JEFFERSON

Lived 1743–1826; president 1801–09

T homas Jefferson was one of the most brilliant presidents, and also one of the most perplexing. By drafting the Declaration of Independence, he won a fame which will endure as long as people care about liberty, and by making, while president, the Louisiana Purchase, he doubled the size of the United States. Yet as Henry Adams remarks in his history of Jefferson's presidency, 'As a leader of democracy he appears singularly out of place.' For this apostle of American democracy and enthusiast for the French Revolution could not bear to show

26

himself in crowds, was a poor orator and guarded his privacy as jealously (though not as successfully) as Washington. His tastes were those of a liberal European nobleman, and his unsurpassed ability to express high ideals opened him to the charge of hypocrisy when some of his low manoeuvres became known.

Born into Virginia's land-owning class, he was early identified, at the College of William and Mary in Williamsburg, as a man of intellectual promise. He acquired an insatiable love of books, set up as a lawyer, was elected for Albemarle County to Virginia's House of Burgesses, and married a beautiful widow, Martha Wayles Skelton. He was six feet two inches tall, with red hair and a gangling frame. As they played duets, she on the harpsichord, he on the violin, they would sing. Only two of their six children survived infancy, and Martha herself died in 1782, after ten years of marriage, having extracted from Jefferson a promise that he would not marry again, for she could not bear the thought of her children coming under the dominion of a stepmother.

While still in his twenties, Jefferson designed and built Monticello, his grand Palladian house on a hilltop. He was a compulsive home improver, who could not live anywhere without instituting changes, and loved to design gadgets, some of which, like the dumb waiter and the revolving door, allowed him to see less of his slaves. He made tremendous efforts to improve Virginia by rendering the state's laws more enlightened, and was soon drafting *A Summary View of the Rights of British America*, in which he contended that Americans possessed the natural right to govern themselves, for, after all, 'America was not surrendered to William the Norman, nor its lands surrendered to him or to any of his successors.' He was deeply anti-clerical, and one of his proudest achievements was writing and seeing into law the Statute of Virginia for Religious Freedom.

In 1776, his 'happy talent for composition' led Congress, including writers as distinguished as Benjamin Franklin and

John Adams, to entrust to Jefferson the drafting of the Declaration of Independence. With omniscient brio he composed what he later called 'an expression of the American mind', asserting the first principles which justified rebellion:

> We hold these truths to be self evident: that all men are created equal; that they are endowed by their Creator with certain inalienable rights; that among these are life, liberty, and the pursuit of happiness; that to secure these rights, governments are instituted among men, deriving their just powers from the consent of the governed; that whenever any form of government becomes destructive of these ends, it is the right of the people to alter or to abolish it, and to institute new government . . .

Jefferson proceeded to condemn George III as a tyrant, and to blame him for slavery: 'He has waged cruel war against human nature itself, violating its most sacred rights of life and liberty in the persons of a distant people who never offended him, captivating and carrying them into slavery in another hemisphere, or to incur miserable death in their transportation hither.'

The passage about slavery was struck out by Congress for, according to Jefferson, South Carolina and Georgia objected to it, and some northerners who had been 'pretty considerable carriers' of slaves were 'a little tender' on the subject too. Some other minor changes were made, very painful to the author, who preferred the way he had put things. On 4 July 1776 Congress adopted, as the Americans' battle cry, the Declaration of Independence.

Jefferson played no part in the actual battles, for although an excellent horseman, he was by no means a soldier. In 1779 he was elected Governor of Virginia, and two years later suffered the indignity of being chased out of Monticello by British redcoats, an inquiry into his conduct only averted by the surrender soon afterwards of General Cornwallis at Yorktown. The following year, Jefferson was plunged into profound gloom by the death of his wife. He nevertheless managed, in response to a French correspondent, to compose his one book, *Notes on the State of Virginia*.

From 1784 Congress prevailed on him to serve for five years as an American envoy in Paris. Here Jefferson gorged himself on books, and also loved buying paintings, sculptures, furniture and scientific instruments. He became a devotee of French food and wine, good friends with his fellow envoy, John Adams, and enjoyed an amorous friendship with Maria Cosway, the spirited wife of an English painter. In his early forties, Jefferson broke his wrist while vaulting a fence to impress Maria, and she received the longest of all his letters, the so-called 'Dialogue between Head and Heart', in which he sang her beauties and those of Monticello. In Paris he soon after began a long affair, productive of several children, with Sally Hemings, a slave from Monticello who had accompanied his younger daughter across the Atlantic. Sally was the half-sister of his own late wife, with whom she shared a father.

In 1789 Jefferson witnessed the earliest and most hopeful stages of the French Revolution, and returned home convinced it was a continuation of the American Revolution. This mattered, for Washington prevailed on him to become Secretary of State, charged with the conduct of foreign relations. The President and the Treasury Secretary, Alexander Hamilton, were determined to remain on friendly terms with Great Britain, America's main trading partner. Jefferson was appalled by the policy of the 'Anglomanes', as he called them, which he thought was preparing the ground for the reintroduction of 'a monarchy bottomed on corruption', and favoured instead an alliance with revolutionary France.

The news from Paris became discouraging, especially after

the massacres of September 1792, but Jefferson was not a man to be put off by bloodshed, and maintained an attitude of ruthless insouciance. As he had already declared in 1787, during Shays' Rebellion in Massachusetts, 'The tree of liberty must from time to time be refreshed with the blood of patriots and tyrants. It is its natural manure.' Jefferson took the view, which even his friend and successor James Madison regarded as excessive, that people have the right to remake their constitution every nineteen years.

Bitter factional strife broke out between Jefferson and Hamilton and their respective supporters. This was the start of party politics in the United States, the two sides becoming known as Republicans and Federalists, and was pursued by means as disreputable as anything seen in more recent times. Jefferson did not attack Hamilton directly, but urged Madison to do so on his behalf: 'For God's sake, my dear sir, take up your pen, select the most striking heresies, and cut him to pieces in the face of the public.'

In May 1793 an envoy from France, Edmond Charles Genêt, arrived in Charleston, in South Carolina, and in a direct challenge to Washington's declaration that the United States would remain 'impartial' in the war that had broken out between Britain and France, attempted in the most tactless way to stir up popular pro-French feeling. This was profoundly embarrassing to Jefferson, who at the end of the year resigned as secretary of state and retired to Monticello, which he tore down and rebuilt on a larger scale.

His friendship with John Adams, now vice president, had been wrecked. A sense of how poisonous the atmosphere had become can be gained from Adams' reaction, in a letter to his son John Quincy, to Jefferson's retirement:

Ambition is the subtlest beast of the intellectual and moral field. It is wonderfully adroit in concealing itself from its owner, I had almost said from itself. Jefferson thinks by this step to get a reputation of an humble, modest, meek man wholly without ambition or vanity. He may even have deceived himself into this belief. But if a prospect opens, the world will see and he will feel that he is as ambitious as Oliver Cromwell though no soldier.

In the presidential election of 1796, the first without Washington, Jefferson ran against Adams and lost by the narrow margin of three Electoral College votes. This meant, under the curious system used in the first years of the United States (it was changed in 1804), that Jefferson became Vice President. Adams in that office had been loyal to Washington, but Jefferson found it impossible to be loyal to Adams. After the passing during the 'quasi-war' with France in 1798 of the Alien and Sedition Acts, which he regarded as an intolerable attack on the constitution, he secretly prevailed on Madison to draft the Virginia Resolution against these laws, and himself did the same for Kentucky. If this attempt to develop the doctrine of states' rights had worked, it could have destroyed the Union, and before many years elapsed the same argument was being employed by the defenders of slavery.

In 1800 Jefferson ran again for the presidency, beat Adams, but tied with his own running mate, Aaron Burr, a gifted but untrustworthy buccaneer from New York who two years later was to kill Hamilton in a duel. The House of Representatives, which had the task of resolving the deadlock, held thirty-five tied votes. Hamilton regarded Jefferson, despite their differences, as the lesser of two evils, and swung the thirty-sixth his way.

In his first inaugural address Jefferson extended an olive branch to his opponents: 'Every difference of opinion is not a difference of principle. We have called by different names brethren of the same principle. We are all Republicans, we are all Federalists.' But how was he to dramatise the change from Adams the monarchist to himself, the apostle of freedom and equality? How was he to do away with the power of banks, and make the country a larger version of Virginia, where there were no cities? For Jefferson, the pursuit of agriculture (in which he took a close interest) was 'more likely to make us a numerous and happy people than the mimicry of an Amsterdam, a Hamburg, or a City of London'.

He began with an ostentatious refusal to stand on ceremony, which continued throughout his presidency. While Washington had bowed to visitors, Jefferson introduced the modern custom of shaking them by the hand. In 1803, when Anthony Merry arrived in Washington to serve as British envoy, he recorded with horror how he was met by Jefferson: 'I, in my official costume, found myself at the hour of reception he had himself appointed, introduced to a man as president of the United States, not merely in undress, but *actually standing in slippers down at the heels*, and both pantaloons, coat and under-clothes indicative of utter slovenliness and indifference to appearances.'

The deliberateness of the insult was confirmed few nights later, when the Merrys were invited to dine at the President's House. Jefferson not merely invited the envoy of a hostile power, France, on the same evening, but instead of taking Mrs Merry in to dinner, insisted on giving his arm to Dolley Madison, wife of James Madison, the new Secretary of State, despite her protest at such a breach of decorum.

But much though Jefferson enjoyed insulting the British, he was also a pragmatist. One of the most acute portraits of him was written by his enemy Hamilton, who in 1801 made this case for him:

> I admit that his politics are tinctured with fanaticism; that
> he is too much in earnest with his democracy . . . But it is
> not true, as is alleged, that he is an enemy to the power of

the Executive . . . He is as likely as any man I know to temporise, to calculate what will be likely to promote his own reputation and advantage; and the probable result of such a temper is the preservation of systems, though originally opposed, which, being once established, could not be overturned without danger to the person who did it.

So Jefferson, who in theory wanted to get rid of America's fledgling navy, actually used it to crush the Barbary pirates, a triumph responsible for the words 'to the shores of Tripoli' in the anthem of the US Marine Corps. And although he was devoted to the idea of decentralised power and a small and frugal central government, he realised departures from these principles must be made if the new nation was to be defended.

He strengthened America, and exceeded his authority as president, by seizing the moment when Napoleon was ready to sell off France's possessions in the New World. Jefferson's Louisiana Purchase stretched so far beyond Louisiana that it doubled the size of the United States, at a cost of four cents an acre. The President dispatched Lewis and Clark to explore the continent all the way to the Pacific. But he did not avert the spread of slavery into Louisiana, nor did he even free, in his will, his slaves at Monticello, with the exception of the few who were his own descendants, his children by Sally Hemings.

Not long after his inauguration, Jefferson suffered appalling embarrassment at the hands of James Callender, the muck-raking Scottish journalist who had been imprisoned for defaming John Adams. Callender, who had by now served his sentence, asked the President to make him postmaster in Richmond, Virginia. When Jefferson refused and tried to buy him off with the derisory sum of fifty dollars, Callender turned on him. He revealed that Jefferson had been paying him to defame Hamilton and Adams, and he printed all the scandal he could about his former patron, including the Sally Hemings story: 'It is well known that the man *whom it delighteth the people to honour*, keeps and for many years has kept, a concubine, one of his slaves . . . By this wench Sally, our President has had several children . . . The AFRICAN VENUS is said to officiate as housekeeper at Monticello.'

Jefferson remained silent in the face of these scurrilities, which was certainly his least bad option. There was nothing to be gained from pointing out that the 'African Venus' was actually three-quarters white. The story was taken up with relish by the Federalist press, and by the poet Thomas Moore, who alluded to Aspasia, mistress of Pericles in ancient Athens:

> The weary statesman for repose hath fled
> From halls of council to his Negro's shed;
> Where, blest, he woos some black Aspasia's grace,
> And dreams of freedom in his slave's embrace.

Reverential biographers long refused to believe the story, but DNA analysis of Sally Hemings' descendants has confirmed its truth. The gutter press is rude, but quite often right. Callender soon afterwards drowned in the James River, in three feet of water from which he had apparently been unable to save himself because he was blind drunk.

Jefferson condemned slavery, but was no prophet of a multi-racial society. In his *Autobiography*, composed in old age, he wrote of the slaves: 'Nothing is more certainly written in the book of fate, than that these people are to be free; nor is it less certain that the two races, equally free, cannot live in the same government. Nature, habit, opinion have drawn indelible lines of distinction between them.' The first part of this, up to the words 'to be free', is inscribed on the Jefferson Memorial in Washington DC, dedicated by Franklin Roosevelt in 1943. The second, less politically correct part is omitted. In a sense, this is entirely fitting, for

Jefferson made enormous efforts to suppress those parts of his record which did not square with his lofty notion of himself.

At the election of 1804 Jefferson won a second term, which went less well than the first. The Royal Navy was behaving in an intolerably high-handed way, boarding American ships in order to recapture British seamen who had opted for an easier life on American merchant vessels, and to force Americans into British service. Jefferson convinced himself he could avoid war, yet make the British behave, by imposing a trade embargo: 'Our commerce is so valuable to them that they will be glad to purchase it, when the only price we ask is to do us justice.' Successive embargoes unfortunately caused more harm to the Americans than to the British. The policy did not live up to Jefferson's expectations, and the extreme measures taken to enforce it, including the deployment of troops, turned him into a worse oppressor of civil liberties than Adams. But the embargoes did at least avert war.

In 1808 Jefferson declined to stand for a third term, thus entrenching the custom begun by Washington of serving no more than eight years, which was to survive unbroken until Franklin Delano Roosevelt. Jefferson was able to pass on the presidency to his friend James Madison, and remained, in retirement, an influential figure, the Sage of Monticello. He founded the University of Virginia and designed splendid buildings for it, but impoverished himself by his princely hospitality. His words continue to inspire high-minded liberals, but his defence of revolutionary violence has been interpreted with disastrous literalness by terrorists such as the Oklahoma bomber, Timothy McVeigh, who in 1995 murdered 168 people by blowing up a federal building. Jefferson died on the fiftieth anniversary of the adoption by Congress on 4 July 1776 of his immortal Declaration of Independence.

JAMES MADISON

Lived 1751–1836; president 1809–17

James Madison possessed sublime authority on paper, but not in person. He had the intellectual self-confidence and gifts of exposition needed to play a decisive role in framing his country's constitution. But these abilities were an inadequate basis for leading the new republic, and he was an at times pitifully weak president, who displayed such ineptitude as a war leader that the British were able to burn down the main public buildings in Washington DC. He was only five foot four inches tall, the shortest of all the presidents, a frail and bookish scholar clad in black, but had the attractive quality of not taking himself too seriously, which is one reason why he left office as popular as when he entered it.

He lived and died at Montpelier, his family's estate in Virginia, studied at the College of New Jersey, now Princeton University, and read voluminously on the history and theory of how to create a free government. Madison was too frail to fight, but like his friend and neighbour Thomas Jefferson showed an outstanding ability to master the arguments for independence. By 1787, when the Constitutional Convention met in Philadelphia, he was prominent in the politics of Virginia. He persuaded George Washington to preside over the convention, himself spoke on no fewer than 71 of the 86 days of debate, was acclaimed by his fellow delegates as the best prepared and most resourceful contributor on all contentious questions, became one of the 39 signers of the new constitution, and left this famous account of the great Benjamin Franklin, at the age of 81 the oldest person to take part in that ceremony:

Whilst the last members were signing it, Doctor Franklin, looking towards the President's chair, at the back of which a rising sun happened to be painted, observed to a few members near him, that painters had found it difficult to distinguish in their art a rising from a setting sun. I have, said he, often and often in the course of the session, and the vicissitudes of my hopes and fears as to its issue, looked at that behind the President without being able to tell whether it was rising or setting; but now at length I have the happiness to know that it is a rising and not a setting sun.

The constitution had to be ratified by the thirteen states, whose support was far from certain, for under it they would lose many of their powers. Alexander Hamilton enlisted Madison to help write The Federalist Papers, in which the case for the new dispensation was made. 'If men were angels, no government would be necessary,' Madison wrote, but as it was, 'ambition must be made to counteract ambition' by means of a system of checks and balances. He upheld the creation of a strong central government by arguing that it would 'secure the national councils against any danger from . . . a rage for paper money, for an abolition of debts, for an equal division of property, or for any other improper or wicked project'. Like the other signers, Madison saw the connection between property rights and freedom.

In his home state of Virginia he carried ratification by a narrow margin against powerful opposition. Madison served from 1788 in the US House of Representatives, where he took the lead in passing the Bill of Rights, the first ten amendments to the Constitution, which by guaranteeing individual rights helped render that document acceptable. He had a genius for working with others in committee, and is regarded as the Father of the Constitution, though he himself said it 'ought to be regarded as the work of many heads & many hands'. Washington, while taking his first cautious steps in 1789 as president, treated Madison as a valued adviser.

But Madison, like Jefferson, approved of the French Revolution and was soon at odds with Hamilton and Washington, whom he accused of selling out to the British and conspiring to turn the United States into a monarchy. Things came to a head in 1796, when Madison did all he could to thwart ratification of the Jay Treaty with Britain. Washington defeated these efforts and never trusted him again.

On a more cheerful note, Madison's eye was caught by a merry young widow, Dolley Payne Todd. She was twenty-six and had returned with her small son to live with her mother, who kept a boarding house in Philadelphia. Madison, who was forty-three and sharing a room in another house with two future presidents,

Jefferson and James Monroe, asked Senator Aaron Burr from New York, a lodger in Dolley's establishment, to introduce him to her. She called her admirer Little Jemmy and they were married a few months later. Dolley became the greatest Washington hostess of her day, famed for her turbans and her love of dancing, relieving her pale and reticent husband of the burden of making people feel welcome.

In 1801, when Jefferson was elected president, he made Madison his secretary of state and closest adviser, and on leaving office eight years later nominated him as his successor. A fellow Virginian, John Randolph of Roanoke, objected to the choice of Madison: 'We ask for energy, and we are told of his moderation; we ask for talent, and the reply is his unassuming merit; we ask what were his services in the cause of Public Liberty, and we are directed to the pages of the *Federalist*.'

Dolley held the first inaugural presidential ball, attended by Washington Irving, who described in a letter to a friend how he

emerged from dirt & darkness into the blazing splendour of Mrs Madison's Drawing room. Here I was most graciously received—found a crowded collection of great and little men, of ugly old women, and beautiful young ones—and in ten minutes was hand and glove with half the people in the assemblage. Mrs Madison is a fine, portly, buxom dame—who has a smile & pleasant word for every body. Her sisters, Mrs Cutts & Mrs Washington are like the two Merry Wives of Windsor—but as to Jemmy Madison—ah! poor Jemmy! he is but a withered little apple-John.

Madison began his presidency badly by appointing a set of inadequate men to important positions, and continued badly by failing to sack them once their inadequacy became undeniable. He also continued to believe, in the face of overwhelming evidence to the contrary, that a trade embargo would dissuade the British from press-ganging American sailors. In 1812 he shared the widespread view that now was the ideal time to seize Canada from the British, who were at full stretch in their long war against Napoleon. Jefferson, still a strong influence, was of the same opinion: 'The acquisition of Canada . . . will be a mere matter of marching.'

A week after the United States declared war on Britain, Napoleon invaded Russia. The feebleness of America's land forces was soon exposed. In Canada they only got as far as the village of York, capital of Upper Canada, on the site of the present-day Toronto, which they burned to the ground. At sea, however, the Americans won a string of famous victories, thanks to their wonderful new frigates, and at the end of 1812 these helped Madison to gain, by a narrow margin, a second presidential term.

But even at sea superior British numbers began to tell, and in 1814 Admiral George Cochrane sailed into Chesapeake Bay, mounted a raid on Washington and brushed aside an ill-handled American force at Bladensburg, only six miles short of the Capitol. Madison galloped about on his horse, brave but from a military point of view of doubtful value. Dolley, at home in the presidential mansion, was warned to flee the advancing redcoats, but refused to leave in her beloved carriage until she had got the portrait of Washington by Gilbert Stuart cut from its frame and taken away for safe-keeping. She and her husband were only reunited after a desperate night in Virginia during which they were unable to find each other.

The British entered the executive mansion, drank 'Jemmy's health' in the President's wine, ate the meal which was awaiting Madison, and then burned down his house in reprisal for the burning of York. They also burned down the Capitol. But at Washington's house, Mount Vernon, sixteen miles down the Potomac, they set a guard and made sure the property of their late, highly esteemed adversary survived intact. The invaders proceeded next to attack Baltimore, but there they were repulsed. The Star-Spangled Banner was written by Francis Scott Key in celebration of the huge flag, now a prized exhibit in the Museum of American History in Washington DC, which continued to flutter above Fort McHenry during the defence of that port.

At the end of 1814 the British agreed to make peace, but in January 1815, before the news reached the United States, Andrew Jackson, a future president, won a famous victory at New Orleans. So the war ended on a high from Madison and his compatriots' point of view, especially as New England, which had strongly opposed the whole venture, had not gone through with its threat to secede from the Union and make a separate peace with the British. Louis Sérurier, the French representative in Washington, noted that 'the war has given the Americans what they so essentially lacked, a national character founded on a glory common to all'.

Madison saw out his term and retired to Montpelier, where he found himself short of money, for farming in Virginia did not pay, and Dolley's spendthrift son by her first marriage had mismanaged the estate. Dolley herself continued to throw large parties. Although Madison had always worried about his health, he lived to the age of eighty-five. He also worried about his reputation, which he tried to improve by doctoring his papers. After his death, Dolley moved back to Washington, where she had almost nothing to live on, but survived to the age of eighty-one and instructed her successors in the presidential mansion in the arts of entertainment.

JAMES MONROE

Lived 1758–1831; president 1817–25

James Monroe is overshadowed by his fellow Virginians Thomas Jefferson and James Madison, but although he had a less brilliant mind, was in many ways a better president. His judgement was sounder and he was an accomplished conciliator, shown in his handling both of foreign powers and of his own countrymen. Early in his first term he toured New England, something none of the Virginian presidents had bothered to do after Washington in 1789, since from their point of view it was hostile territory. A Boston newspaper, the *Columbian Centinel*, hailed this evidence of a new 'era of good feelings', and the phrase stuck as a description of Monroe's presidency.

He was born in 1758 on the family farm in Westmoreland County, Virginia, attended school with John Marshall, who would become Chief Justice of the Supreme Court, and after studying for a short time at the College of William and Mary volunteered on the outbreak of the Revolutionary War for service as a lieutenant with the Continental Army. In Leutze's famous picture of Washington crossing the Delaware on the night of 25 December 1776, the eighteen-year-old Monroe can be seen standing behind the commander-in-chief, holding the American flag, though in reality he had already crossed the river with an advance party. He was wounded the next day at the Battle of Trenton, and had his life saved by a local doctor, John Riker, who stemmed the bleeding after insisting on coming along with the troops as 'I may be of help to some poor fellow.' John Trumbull, whose painting of the Capture of the Hessians at Trenton shows Monroe lying wounded on the ground, said the bullet which struck him down later raised him to the presidency.

Monroe's status as a veteran did him no harm, and on a tour of inspection of the military posts in the north and east made early in his presidency he recalled his past by dressing as he would have done when a Revolutionary officer, in a blue military coat of homespun, light-coloured breeches and a cocked hat. During the Revolutionary War he gained the good opinion of Washington and the friendship of the Marquis de Lafayette, the celebrated French nobleman who served with the Continental Army.

But Monroe raised himself to the presidency by four decades of increasingly distinguished public service. After studying law under the guidance of Jefferson, who became his lifelong friend and mentor, he entered politics first in Virginia and then from 1790 as a member of the Senate. He was the first president from Virginia not to marry a widow. While attending Congress in New York he fell in love with and in 1786 married Elizabeth Kortright, a handsome young woman from a wealthy New York family. He was twenty-seven, she seventeen, and together they had two daughters, and a son who died in infancy.

In 1794 Washington dispatched Monroe to serve as minister to France, where Elizabeth became known in Parisian society as *la belle américaine*. She with great pluck rescued Lafayette's wife, who was being held under sentence of death, by hiring a carriage, a form of transport at that time banned in Paris, driving to the prison, demanding to see her, and after their meeting announcing loudly that she would be back to see her again tomorrow morning. Madame Lafayette, who was due to be executed that afternoon, was instead released as a token of Franco-American friendship. Monroe himself managed to obtain the release of his friend Thomas Paine, propagandist of the American Revolution, who was likewise languishing in a Parisian prison. The Monroes nursed him back to health, but he repaid their hospitality by penning a bitter attack on Washington. The President was displeased by the unbounded enthusiasm Monroe showed for the French Revolution, and recalled him.

Monroe became Governor of Virginia, but was restored to diplomatic life by Jefferson, who in 1803 sent him back to Europe. In Paris he helped to negotiate with Napoleon the Louisiana Purchase. In London, at his first state dinner Monroe found himself placed at the foot of the table between the representatives of two tiny German states. 'James Monroe doesn't care where he eats his dinner,' he later recalled, 'but to find the American minister put at the bottom of the table between two little principalities no bigger than my farm in Albemarle made me mad.' The Russian minister saw how cross he was, and mollified him by proposing a toast 'to our latest-comer, the President of the United States'. Lord Holland, a distinguished British figure, said of Monroe that 'he was plain in his manner and somewhat slow in his apprehension; but he was a diligent, earnest, sensible, and even profound man'.

In 1811 Monroe became secretary of state in Madison's otherwise very weak Cabinet. The War of 1812 then began so badly that Monroe, who had opposed it, had to become secretary of war too. With energy and shrewdness he began to put American forces on a proper footing, and by the time Madison stepped down he had emerged as the outstanding candidate to succeed him. He was elected almost unopposed, by 183 votes to 34 in the Electoral College, and was sworn in by his old classmate John Marshall, the ceremony for the first time taking place outdoors because there had not been time to rebuild the Capitol following its destruction in 1814 by the British. Monroe's simple republican manners made a favourable impression, but his wife was considered standoffish, and was compared unfavourably to Dolley Madison.

Like Washington, Monroe took the conventional pre-democratic view that political parties or factions are extremely harmful. He was determined to govern in the interests of the whole nation, and struck an optimistic note in his inaugural address, delivered on 4 March 1817: 'During a period fraught with difficulties and marked by very extraordinary events the United States have flourished beyond example. Their citizens individually have been happy and the nation prosperous . . . On whom has oppression fallen in any quarter of our Union?' To which it could be retorted that about 1.5 million slaves were oppressed, and so were very large numbers of native Americans, who were being driven westwards by an unstoppable tide of settlers.

Monroe went on to declare: 'With the Indian tribes it is our duty to cultivate friendly relations and to act with kindness and liberality in all our transactions. Equally proper is it to persevere in our efforts to extend to them the advantages of civilisation.' But the advantages of civilisation were extended in a series of brutal wars. From 1816 to 1819 General Andrew Jackson, a future president, waged war against the Seminole tribe, who lived in Florida, then still a Spanish possession. The Cabinet picked by Monroe was more formidable than its predecessor, and included John Quincy Adams, a man of extensive diplomatic experience, as secretary of state. He negotiated the purchase of Florida by the United States, whereupon the Seminole were confined to a reservation.

In 1819 Missouri applied to join the Union as a slave state. During the earliest years of the United States it had been possible to hope that slavery would dwindle and could at length be abolished, for in Virginia it had become uneconomic, as Washington, Jefferson, Madison and Monroe all knew to their cost. But the invention in 1793 by Eli Whitney of the cotton gin, which could extract cotton from seeds far faster than had been done by hand, revolutionised the industry and led to a vast increase in slavery across the South, with Britain providing an insatiable market for raw cotton.

Missouri threatened to upset the balance between the slave and the free states, for it lay almost entirely to the north of the line then separating the two. From Monticello Jefferson saw how grave the peril was: 'This momentous question, like a fire-bell in the night, awakened and filled me with terror.' After much dispute, a compromise was reached. Missouri was allowed to enter the Union as a slave state, but so, to balance it, was the free state of Maine, and it was agreed that in future slavery would be prohibited north of latitude 36 degrees and 30 minutes, which meant north of the southern boundary of Missouri.

In December 1823, Monroe declared in his annual address to Congress that 'the American continents, by the free and independent condition which they have assumed and maintain, are henceforth not to be considered as subjects for colonisation by any European powers'. The aim was to prevent Russian incursions in the far west of North America, and attempts by Spain and Portugal to regain control of their rebellious colonies in South America. The policy was devised by George Canning, the British Foreign Secretary. Adams, who distrusted the British, urged Monroe to turn it into a purely American initiative, for as he wrote in his diary: 'It would be more candid, as well as more dignified, to avow our principles explicitly to Russia and France, than to come as a cock-boat in the wake of the British man-of-war.'

So although British warships were needed throughout the nineteenth century to prevent other European powers from meddling in the Americas, the policy had been declared by the American president and was a sign of American independence. It became known, about twenty years after his death, as the Monroe Doctrine, and is a fitting memorial to an under-rated president. Monrovia, the capital of Liberia, was also named after him, for he had supported moves to repatriate freed slaves to that newly founded African state. The policy never worked, for most African Americans wanted to make their future in the United States, so Monroe had not solved the slave problem. But since everyone else had found it insoluble too, he can hardly be blamed for that.

In old age Monroe was, like previous presidents, hard up, engaged in humiliating wrangles with Congress about the reimbursement of expenses incurred many years before on government business, and after his wife's death in 1830 went to live with one of his daughters and her husband in New York, where in 1831 he died.

JOHN QUINCY ADAMS

Lived 1767–1848; president 1825–29

John Quincy Adams was an inept president but a brilliant diplomat. Like his father, John Adams, the second president, he served only one term because in a partisan period he refused on principle to be partisan. Nor would he have known how to charm people into following him even if he had tried: as he himself wrote with only a touch of exaggeration, 'I am a man of reserved, cold, austere, and forbidding manners.' He inspired respect for his intellect, industry and inflexible sense of right and wrong, but disgust for his prissiness and his habit of drawing up lists of enemies who 'conspired together [and] used up their faculties in base and dirty tricks to thwart my progress in life'.

He was born in 1767 and at the age of seven saw and heard in the distance, from Penn's Hill above the family farm at Braintree near Boston, one of the early engagements in the Revolutionary War, the Battle of Bunker Hill, in which his father's good friend Dr Joseph Warren was killed. When he was ten, John Quincy accompanied his father on a diplomatic mission to Europe and demonstrated his astonishing gift for learning languages. His career of public service started at the precocious age of fourteen, when he served as secretary to the American envoy in St Petersburg, to whom his command of French was useful.

His mother, the formidable Abigail Adams, poured out a stream of good advice to him, exhorting him to 'adhere to those religious sentiments and principles which were early instilled into your mind, and remember that you are accountable to your Maker for all your words and actions'. The boy was condemned to a life of moral seriousness and public service, unless he cracked up, which was a distinct possibility. Abigail's brother succumbed to alcoholism, so did John Quincy's two younger brothers, and so did two of his own sons.

He studied at Harvard, qualified as a lawyer, under the pseudonym Publicola defended his father in print against attacks from Thomas Jefferson, and at the age of twenty-six began a distinguished career as the representative of the United States in various European capitals. While in London he met and married Louisa Johnson, the elegant and intelligent daughter of the American consul, not informing his own mother until it was too late for her to advise against the match. For Abigail 'was troubled by the fear that Louisa might not be made of stern stuff enough, or brought up in conditions severe enough, to suit a New England climate, or to make an efficient wife for her paragon son', as Henry Adams, grandson of John Quincy, later wrote.

From 1801 John Quincy had a spell as Senator for Massachusetts, during which he enraged the Boston Brahmins, the leading figures in the town, by abandoning the Federalist cause. To them he was a traitor, but he told them, 'My sense of duty shall never yield to the pleasure of party.' He was welcomed into the opposing camp by James Madison and sent as American minister to Russia, where he was soon on friendly terms with Tsar Alexander I. Adams distressed his wife by insisting they leave their two older boys, aged eight and six, to be brought up in New England. He was transferred in 1815 to London, and played a successful role in the peace negotiations which ended the War of 1812 on terms surprisingly favourable to the United States.

In 1817 the newly elected President James Monroe invited him to become secretary of state. Adams was by now the outstanding candidate for that office, three of whose holders – Jefferson, Madison and Monroe – had gone on to become president. And Adams duly became a great secretary of state. It was in his nature to drive a hard bargain, his conviction that he knew best was in the sphere of diplomacy often correct, and circumstances were propitious for the assertion of American power. He arranged for the transfer of Florida, where General Andrew Jackson with his usual disregard for legal niceties had led various American incursions, from an enfeebled Spain to the United States. Adams also got Madrid to recognise, under the Transcontinental Treaty, a southern American boundary which stretched all the way to the Pacific Ocean.

And he wrote what became known as the Monroe Doctrine, according to which European powers were to keep out of the Americas. George Canning, the British Foreign Secretary, had put this forward as an Anglo-American project. But Adams, with his usual ineffable earnestness, thought Canning had 'a little too much wit for a Minister of State' and persuaded Monroe that it was better to proceed without the British.

In 1824, as Monroe's second term drew to a close, it was by no means clear who would succeed him. There were four candidates, Adams, Jackson, William Crawford and Henry Clay. Jackson finished top of the poll, some way ahead of Adams but well short of a majority in the Electoral College, so the election went to the House of Representatives. Here Clay acted as kingmaker by throwing his weight behind Adams, who won on the first ballot.

Jackson and his supporters reckoned they had been robbed, felt even more furious when Adams conferred the office of secretary of state on Clay, and accused the two men of making a 'corrupt bargain'. John Randolph of Roanoke described the alliance of Adams and Clay as 'the coalition of Blifil and Black George – the combination, unheard of till then, of the puritan with the blackleg'. This was amazingly rude, for the allusion was to the novel *Tom Jones* by Henry Fielding, in which Blifil is an odious hypocrite and Black George a disreputable gamekeeper. Clay challenged Randolph to a duel. Neither man was hurt, but the whole thing was an embarrassment to the upright Adams.

So from the start the new president was in a weak position, a point he acknowledged in his inaugural address, delivered on Friday 4 March 1825: 'Less possessed of your confidence in advance than any of my predecessors, I am deeply conscious of the prospect that I shall stand more and oftener in need of your indulgence.'

Adams nevertheless had ambitious plans for his presidency. He expressed his faith in 'progressive improvement' as 'the purpose of a superintending Providence'. His noble plan was to open up the country's vast reserves of land by building roads and canals, employing the resulting wealth to fund great educational and scientific programmes in order to create an informed and high-minded citizenry. His opponents ridiculed this scheme and were more skilful and better organised than he was, and also more in tune with the desire of settlers to grab what land they could for themselves. Adams pointed out that Europe already had 130 observatories for studying the stars, while America had none, but he could not get Congress to pay for one. He did, however, have the pleasure of opening the Erie Canal, completed during his term in office.

He worked himself immensely hard. When he found he was not getting enough done by rising at five in the morning, he rose at 4.15 instead. In the summer months he invigorated himself by going very early in the morning for a bathe in the Potomac. On one occasion, when the canoe in which he was crossing the river capsized, he was thrown into the water fully clothed, his sleeves 'hung like 52-pound weights upon my arms', and he nearly drowned as he swam to the shore, after which he made his way back to the White House 'half dressed', having lost his coat and waistcoat. Such engaging touches of absurdity make it hard not to feel some affection for him.

But the presidential campaign of 1828 was one of the dirtiest in American history. Jackson's supporters spread gross calumnies about Adams, including the absurd claim that while in St Petersburg he had procured a beautiful American girl for the Tsar and had kept a harem of concubines for himself. All this was so painful for Adams that for some months he stopped keeping his diary.

When his miserable four years in the White House were over, he returned at the age of sixty-two to Massachusetts. Louisa had enjoyed herself no more than he did, and two of their sons now ran definitively off the rails. One of them seems to have committed suicide by jumping off the side of the steamship which was carrying him to his father, to whom he would have to confess getting a servant girl pregnant. The other died of an unknown illness. Adams seemed to have only a sad retirement to look forward to, but to his surprise some local citizens suggested he run for the House of Representatives. This offer he was not too grand to accept, on the understanding that he would be free to say whatever he wanted. He became the only former president ever to sit in the House, and when it tried to suppress debate on slavery by refusing to accept petitions on the subject, he waged an eight-year campaign to have the 'gag rule' overturned. An English visitor, Harriet Martineau, saw Adams fighting this battle:

> While hunted, held at bay, almost torn to pieces by an outrageous majority . . . he preserved a boldness and coolness as amusing as they were admirable. Though he now and then vents his spleen with violence when disappointed in a favourite object, he seems able to bear perfectly well that which it is the great fault of Americans to shrink from, singularity and blame. He seems, at times, reckless of opinion; and this is the point of his character which his countrymen seem, naturally, least able to comprehend.

The best thing about the second Adams was that, like his father, he did not run with the crowd, and at length his campaign was crowned with success, making him once more a respected figure. He worked to the end, for it was not in his nature to do anything else, and at the age of seventy-six was delighted to attend the opening of the first observatory in the United States, on a hill outside Cincinnati where he delivered a two-hour oration on the history of astronomy to a crowd of 3,000 people. At the age of eighty he collapsed in the House and was carried to the Speaker's room, where two days later he died.

ANDREW JACKSON

Lived 1767–1845; president 1829–37

Andrew Jackson was the kind of man with whom it was inadvisable to pick a quarrel in a tavern if you did not want to end up dead. He is one of the most vivid personalities in this book, and marked a startling change from his six predecessors, all of whom acknowledged their debt to the European ruling classes.

Jackson was the first frontiersman to reach the top in American politics, and expressed himself with a biblical ferocity inherited from his Ulster Presbyterian forebears but adapted to local conditions. So he warned one of his adversaries that his creed was 'An Eye for an Eye, Toothe for Toothe and Scalp for Scalp'. He was tough, fearless, patriotic, loyal and a born leader of men, but also touchy, quarrelsome, ignorant, vindictive and a born killer. Historians confuse matters by making him an apostle of democracy, and Jackson certainly expressed and turned to political advantage the resentments of backwoodsmen who felt they were looked down on by the folks in Washington DC. But he himself was a natural autocrat.

His parents were recent immigrants from Ulster who had settled at Waxhaw on the border of North and South Carolina. His father died before he was born and his mother told him when he burst into tears at the age of six that girls cry and boys fight. He served as a boy soldier in the Revolutionary War and at the age of fourteen was captured by the British and ordered to clean an officer's boots. Jackson refused to obey, and received a deep cut across his head and hand from the officer's sword.

Both his older brothers died in the war, as did his mother from an infection contracted while nursing the wounded. Jackson hated the British, but without any corresponding love of the French. He gambled away a small inheritance from his grandfather, qualified as a lawyer and went west to the recently founded town of Nashville, where at the age of twenty-one he obtained the post of public prosecutor.

From 1796 he served briefly as congressman and then senator for the newly created state of Tennessee. He set up as a planter and created an estate called the Hermitage, near Nashville, where he grew cotton, bred racehorses, built a Greek Revival house, and at his death in 1845 owned 110 slaves. When one of his slaves ran away, he offered a reward of fifty dollars for his recapture 'and ten dollars extra for every hundred lashes a person will give to the amount of three hundred'.

In 1791 he married Rachel Robards, née Donelson, unaware

that her first husband had failed to complete the formalities needed to divorce her. They regularised things a few years later by going through a second ceremony, and Jackson always flew into a fury when anyone aspersed her name.

Charles Dickinson, a brilliant shot, referred while drunk to the Jackson 'adultery', so Jackson picked a quarrel with him about the payment of a forfeit in a horse race. In the resulting duel, fought at eight paces, Jackson decided to let Dickinson fire first, hoping that speed would be the enemy of accuracy, but was hit in the chest. The bullet, though partially checked by his coat, broke two of his ribs and was so close to his heart that it could never be removed, and in years to come caused him much pain. Jackson then took aim at Dickinson, but the hammer of his pistol stuck at half-cock. Their seconds conferred and decided Jackson could have another go if he insisted. He did insist and hit Dickinson, who bled to death.

In local society, Jackson's reputation suffered from this cold-bloodedness. But his cold-bloodedness also helped to make his name as a commander of Tennessee's militia. He had an intuitive eye for his opponents' weaknesses, and massacred hundreds of Creek Indians, whose lands were taken by white settlers. Jackson's troops nicknamed him Old Hickory in tribute to his toughness and powers of endurance. When a dead Indian woman was found with a living baby in her arms, Jackson adopted the orphan boy and raised him as his own until the child's death from tuberculosis at the age of sixteen. Like many cruel men, he had a streak of sentimentality. He and Rachel had no children of their own.

In 1815 Jackson won a famous victory over regular British troops at New Orleans, and became a national hero. His opponent, Edward Pakenham, who perished in the battle, was singularly incompetent, but General Jackson showed a remarkable ability to improvise a defence and bring down a lethal hail of fire on the advancing redcoats. He followed this up with illegal attacks on the Seminole Indians in Florida, which was still in Spanish hands. During one of these expeditions he conducted a summary trial of two British officers who were inciting the Indians to resist the Americans, and had the pair executed by firing squad. Such high-handedness suited John Quincy Adams, who as secretary of state regularised the takeover by the United States of Florida. But Jackson now found himself in a position to run for the presidency in the election of 1824, which certainly did not suit Adams, who referred to his opponent as 'the brawler from Tennessee'.

Jackson topped the poll with 41 per cent of the vote – not a winning margin, but very clearly ahead of Adams, on 31 per cent, and a mark of the General's popularity, especially in the west and the south. Henry Clay, who came third with 13 per cent, described him as 'ignorant, passionate, hypocritical, corrupt and easily swayed by the basest men who surround him'. This view was shared by many members of the political class, and when the election went to the House of Representatives for its decision, Clay ensured that Adams won on the first ballot. Jackson wrote of Clay: 'So you see the Judas of the West has closed the contract and will receive the 30 pieces of silver. His end will be the same. Was there ever witnessed such bare-faced corruption?'

With the vindictiveness that was a deep part of his character, Jackson began almost at once to campaign for victory in 1828. He and Martin Van Buren, who became his most valued lieutenant, assembled a mighty coalition of all those who felt angry with the uncharming and independent-minded Adams. Van Buren built the political organisation which became the Democratic Party. The campaign was described in a piece of doggerel as 'Between J. Q. Adams, who can write / And Andy Jackson, who can fight.' It was the dirtiest in American history, with each side hurling mud at the other. Jackson's opponents circulated a pamphlet about his 'youthful indiscretions', accusing him of fourteen fights in which he 'killed, slashed, and clawed various American citizens'.

The General won a decisive victory by promising to 'cleanse the Augean stables' of Washington. By the time he took office, Rachel had died of a heart attack, which he blamed on his opponents, who 'had maligned that blessed one who is now safe from suffering and sorrow, whom they tried to put to shame for my sake!' The President wore mourning for his inauguration. The mob which at his invitation came to Washington to celebrate his victory was less restrained. It invaded the White House, smashed the furnishings and could only be induced to leave by the provision of free punch on the lawn.

Jackson had promised to reform Washington, but in practice this meant that more office holders, most of them perfectly competent, were sacked in the first year of his presidency than in the whole forty years since Washington, and replaced with his own supporters. The process was dignified with the term 'rotation of offices', but the spoils system had been born. Jackson presided over this plunder, or party patronage, and assembled around himself a kitchen cabinet of unelected advisers who could be counted on to be loyal. It included a number of journalists who, like the President, were adept at harnessing the new force of public opinion. Adams observed that 'every editor of a scurrilous and slanderous newspaper is provided for'.

Jackson had an instinctive gift for throwing opponents off balance by waging campaigns no sane man would have undertaken. One of the first was in defence of Peggy O'Neill, the beautiful and notorious daughter of a tavern keeper in Washington. Her first husband had committed suicide while serving with the navy in the Mediterranean, nobody quite knew why, and Senator John Eaton, who had long boarded at the tavern in question and hoped to be offered a post, asked Jackson whether marrying

Peggy would constitute an obstacle to promotion. The President, who saw in her a woman as unjustly maligned as his own recently deceased wife, said that on the contrary Eaton must marry her if he loved her. This he proceeded to do, whereupon official Washington said: 'Eaton has just married his mistress, and the mistress of eleven dozen others.'

'She is as chaste as a virgin,' Jackson informed the Cabinet, but respectable matrons led by Floride Calhoun, wife of Vice President John Calhoun, refused to receive 'Pothouse Peg'. One might dismiss the affair as a storm in a teacup, but since it enabled Van Buren to supplant Calhoun as Jackson's heir apparent, it had serious consequences. Van Buren, whose own wife was long dead so could not be offended, ingratiated himself with Jackson by calling on Peggy and by devising the solution to the problem, which was for the entire Cabinet to resign. Clay said of Peggy, 'Age cannot wither nor time stale her infinite virginity.'

This scandal was followed by Jackson's 'War on the Bank', his attack on the Bank of the United States. Jackson hated paper money and banks, as did many of his supporters. As a young man he had been wiped out when he accepted some paper which turned out to be worthless. In the west, which was full of debtors and speculators, the Bank was known as 'the Monster', dreaded agent of the 'money power' preying on them from the cities of the north-east.

In 1832 Congress renewed the Bank's charter, with Clay, Calhoun and Daniel Webster all speaking in favour. Jackson observed that these three great orators were 'always on the losing side'. He vetoed renewal of the charter, denounced attempts 'to make the rich richer and the potent more powerful', got himself re-elected for a second term on an anti-Bank ticket and then destroyed the Bank by withdrawing federal deposits. He replaced it with nothing, and soon after his second term ended business was plunged into a severe depression. The United States did not acquire a sound banking system until the foundation of the Federal Reserve in 1913. Jacksonian populism had done grave damage to the people, but remained popular as long as Jackson himself was in charge.

When John Marshall, Chief Justice of the Supreme Court, defended the Cherokee Indians against maltreatment by the state of Georgia, Jackson said: 'John Marshall has made his decision. Now let him enforce it.' Here was a president who could be relied on to side with the plunderers of Indian lands. But when John Calhoun, in South Carolina, asserted that a state had the right to declare an act of the federal government null and void where the relevant power had been usurped from the state, Jackson reacted with fury.

Calhoun declared that South Carolina would defy the high tariffs imposed by Washington, which protected northern industries but damaged southern farmers. Jackson retorted that 'Disunion by force is *treason*' and mobilised the army to defeat nullification, as it was called. Clay proposed, as a compromise, a set of tariff reductions which Calhoun felt obliged to accept. Southern secession was averted.

Jackson's brutality was endorsed by electoral success, and he has many admirers among later presidents. Theodore Roosevelt said of him: 'With the exception of Washington and Lincoln, no man has left a deeper mark on American history; and though there is much in his career to condemn, yet all true lovers of America can unite in paying hearty respect to the memory of a man who was emphatically a true American.'

The day after he stepped down as president, Jackson was asked if he had any regrets, and replied: 'I didn't shoot Henry Clay and I didn't hang John C. Calhoun.' He returned to his house outside Nashville, where in 1845 he died. Alfred, one of his slaves, was asked if he expected Jackson to get into to heaven on Judgement Day, and is supposed to have said: 'If General Jackson takes it into his head to git to heaven, who's gwine to keep him out?'

MARTIN VAN BUREN

Lived 1782–1862; president 1837–41

Martin Van Buren was famous for not giving straight answers. The term 'vanburenish' was coined to mean suavely evasive, and when asked whether the sun rises in the east, he is supposed to have replied: 'I presume the fact is according to the common impression, but as I sleep until after sunrise, I cannot speak from my own knowledge.' He was a pioneer of machine politics, and reached the top by manipulating Andrew Jackson, but had no idea what to do once he got there.

Van Buren was born in his father's tavern at Kinderhook, a

Dutch settlement on the east side of the Hudson River about twenty miles south of Albany, the capital of New York state. He left school at the age of fourteen, made his way as a lawyer and a politician, and married Hannah Hoes, a childhood friend and distant cousin, with whom he conversed in Dutch. She died in 1819 after twelve years of marriage, leaving him with four sons. Dapper, dandyish Van Buren never remarried.

He constructed and dominated the Albany Regency, which from 1822 controlled the turbulent and complicated politics of New York state. He saw earlier than most of his competitors that the future belonged to political machines which could harness public opinion while buying loyalty to themselves through the distribution of public offices. Politics, in other words, could be made to pay.

From 1821 he served as senator in Washington, where he opposed John Quincy Adams and threw in his lot with Andrew Jackson, for whom he built the alliance of northern and southern politicians which became the Democratic Party. After Jackson won in 1828, he rewarded Van Buren by making him secretary of state. The Peggy Eaton affair erupted, and Van Buren stole a march on his better-known rivals by supporting the President's ruling that this scandalously attractive woman, who had entertained an unknown number of the customers in her father's tavern and was regarded as a prostitute by the older and perhaps less attractive wives of other Cabinet members, was as pure as the driven snow.

In the words of Jackson's biographer, James Parton, writing in 1860, 'The political history of the United States for the last thirty years dates from the moment when the soft hand of Mr Van Buren touched Mrs Eaton's knocker.' He called on her and told her in confidence that he regarded Jackson as the greatest man he had ever known. This report reached the lonely, ailing President's ear, and pleased him exceedingly. Van Buren became Jackson's heir, and in 1836, with the help of the Democratic machine, was swept into the presidency.

At his inauguration he was overshadowed by his predecessor, who elicited fervent cheers from the crowd. 'For once the rising sun was eclipsed by the setting sun,' as Senator Thomas Hart Benton put it. Van Buren was unwise enough to remark how prosperous the country was. A few weeks later the storm broke. The panic of 1837 was the worst crash in American history until 1929. The banks collapsed, and so did huge numbers of other businesses. The price of cotton, staple crop of the southern states, halved, and seven years of depression set in.

Economists still debate the exact causes of the slump, but Jackson's War on the Bank plainly had something to do with it, and Van Buren, who was Jackson's favoured son, took the blame. He was helpless, for he had no idea how to respond to the disaster. His other achievements – keeping out of war with Mexico, and with Britain over Canada – counted for little, and because he liked to do things in style, he was accused of wallowing in luxury, dining with gold forks off silver plates while others starved.

He stood again in 1840, but the opposition was unsporting enough to field a war hero against him, the victor of Tippecanoe, General William Henry Harrison. The campaign songs were unkind:

> Let Van from his coolers of silver drink wine
> And lounge on his cushioned settee.
> Our man on his buckeye bench can recline,
> Content with hard cider is he,
> The iron-armed soldier, the true-hearted soldier,
> The gallant old soldier of Tippecanoe.

This was a great age for campaign songs, another of which went: 'Van! Van! / Is a used up man.'

One of his sons, John Van Buren, coined the election slogan 'Vote early and vote often', but people did not vote often enough for Van Buren. He was called by many not especially encouraging nicknames, including the Red Fox of Kinderhook and the Flying Dutchman. His partisans pushed 'OK', standing for Old Kinderhook. OK had recently been coined in Boston as a shortened form of 'oll korrect', meaning 'all right', and was imprinted on the popular imagination by the Van Buren campaign in 1840. It did not, however, save Van Buren. He returned home to Kinderhook, ran in vain for the Democratic Party nomination in 1844, stood in 1848 for the Free Soil Party but obtained only 10 per cent of the vote, and died at last in 1862, having voiced his support for Abraham Lincoln at the start of the Civil War.

WILLIAM HENRY HARRISON

Lived 1773–1841; president 1841

William Henry Harrison is the most fleeting figure in this book, president for a month before dying of pneumonia, or possibly as a result of drinking bad water. His contemporaries regarded him as a mediocrity, and he had no time to prove them wrong. His father, who had signed the Declaration of Independence and became governor of Virginia, wished him to study medicine, but he decided to go west and fight Indians. By the age of twenty-seven, he was governor of the Territory of Indiana, which extended far beyond the present-day state.

In the War of 1812 he defeated the Indians at Tippecanoe, and a combined British and Indian force at the Battle of the Thames. Harrison served thereafter in Congress for Ohio, but made no impression and retired to his estate at North Bend, on the Ohio just below Cincinnati, where he supplemented his meagre income by serving as clerk of the Hamilton County Court.

When the Whig Party – a coalition of anti-Jackson forces – held its convention at Harrisburg in 1840, the outstanding candidate for the presidential nomination was Senator Henry Clay, who had warned, correctly, that Jackson's War on the Bank would end in disaster. But the party decided it would be safer to go with General Harrison, about whom nobody knew anything much, except that he had a creditable war record and had been a competent enough presidential candidate four years before.

Nicholas Biddle, president of the bank attacked by Jackson, who hoped for a revival of that institution in the event of a Whig victory, made the following plea to Harrison's handlers: 'Let him say not one single word about his principles or his creed – let him say nothing – promise nothing. Let no committee, no convention – no town meeting ever extract from him a single word about what he thinks now or will do hereafter. Let the use of pen and ink be wholly forbidden as if he were a mad poet in Bedlam.'

Here was the prospectus for a vacuous campaign. But what then would the election be about? A Baltimore newspaper attacked Harrison as the 'log cabin' and 'hard cider' candidate. It was true he lived on the site of a log cabin and was reputed to drink cider rather than wine with his meals, but he had been born into the ruling class of Virginia and had long since built a house modelled on his family's old place. The Whigs were shrewd enough to exploit this misleading description of their candidate. Although they wished to appeal to people like Biddle by promising better economic management, their election parades were dominated by images of cabins and barrels. They dubbed their candidate Old

Tip, in reference to his famous victory at Tippecanoe, and sang songs comparing him to 'Mat' Van Buren:

> Old Tip he wears a homespun coat
> He has no ruffled shirt-wirt-wirt
> But Mat he has the golden plate
> And he's a little squirt-wirt-wirt.

Harrison's supporters squirted tobacco juice through their teeth as they finished the last line.

The economy was in such a bad way that Harrison could hardly avoid romping home to a convincing victory, but as soon as he was elected, he began to betray alarming signs of wanting to be his own man. He refused to deliver the inaugural address Senator Daniel Webster composed for him, and instead wrote a windy oration of his own in praise of Roman virtue and warning against demagogues like Caesar and Cromwell, by whom he was understood to mean Jackson. He showed it to Webster, who spent a day trying to remove some of its worst excesses, and arrived late and exhausted for dinner. When his landlady asked him if anything had happened, he replied: 'Madam, you would think something had happened, if you knew what I have done. I have killed seventeen Roman proconsuls as dead as smelts!'

Harrison's inaugural address, delivered on 4 March 1841, was 8,445 words long, much the longest ever given. For almost two hours he spoke without hat or overcoat in bitterly cold weather in order to demonstrate that although, at the age of sixty-eight, he was the oldest president to take office (a record he would keep until Ronald Reagan) and his listeners were stamping their feet in a vain attempt to keep warm, he himself was tough as nails. Before his inauguration, hordes of office seekers had besieged Harrison, who in the words of one observer was 'elated by their pressure on him' but also broken by it. Harrison's wife, who might have helped to protect him, had not yet joined him in Washington, for she was herself ill. Instead the news was brought to her at North Bend that on 4 April 1841 he had died. But his name lived on in public life, for his grandson, Benjamin Harrison, was to serve as president from 1889 to 1893.

JOHN TYLER

Lived 1790–1862; president 1841–45

Johnn Tyler was determined to back his own judgement, both when defying the attempts of the Whigs to order him around, and when marrying, against the advice of friends, a woman thirty years younger than himself. By insisting on taking over the presidency after Harrison died, he established that the vice president had the right to do this, a point on which the constitution was unclear.

Charles Dickens, who visited the United States in 1842 and was disgusted by many aspects of American politics – 'despicable trickery at elections; under-handed tamperings with public officers; cowardly attacks upon opponents, with scurrilous newspapers for shields, and hired pens for daggers' – approved of Tyler: 'at a business-like table covered with papers, sat the President himself. He looked somewhat worn and anxious, and well he might; being at war with everybody—but the expression of his face was mild and pleasant, and his manner was remarkably unaffected, gentlemanly, and agreeable. I thought that in his whole carriage and demeanour, he became his station singularly well.'

Tyler, born in Virginia in 1790, regarded himself as a follower of Thomas Jefferson, and was throughout his career a staunch defender of states' rights and of the landed, agrarian, slave-owning class of country gentlemen to which he himself belonged. He qualified as a lawyer, was elected like his father before him as governor of Virginia, and in Washington served in both the House of Representatives and the Senate. Here he fell out with President Jackson, whom he accused of making excessive use of federal powers.

In 1840 the Whigs, a disparate party united only by their opposition to Jackson and to Jackson's successor Martin Van Buren, adopted the mediocre William Harrison as their presidential candidate and offered the vice-presidential candidacy to the infinitely more gifted and talented Senator Henry Clay. But Clay, smarting at his rejection for the top job and intending to control the administration from the Senate, ignored the offer. The Whigs turned to the tall, courteous, patrician Tyler, for it suited them to have a southerner on the ticket to balance Harrison's pull with western voters. Tyler's political opinions were of no interest to them. He looked the part, and that was enough.

After Harrison's inauguration, Tyler went home to Williamsburg, Virginia, where he is said to have been playing knucks, a form of marbles, with his sons on the path up to his house when he received the news of the President's death. He went at once to

Washington and had himself sworn in as the new president, pre-empting congressional opposition and setting a precedent which has endured. He kept Harrison's Cabinet but did not allow himself to be tricked into accepting the principle of one man one vote around the Cabinet table, and warned its members that they could not dictate to him.

Clay nevertheless presumed he could control Tyler, and get him to agree to the creation of a Third Bank of the United States to replace the one wrecked by President Jackson. But when Clay called on the new president and declared, 'I demand a bank *now!*' Tyler replied: 'Then, sir, I wish you to understand this – that you and I were born in the same district, and have breathed the same natal air. Go you now, then, Mr Clay, to your end of the avenue, where stands the Capitol, and there perform your duty to the country as you shall think proper. So help me God, I shall do mine at this end of it, as I think proper.'

The two men never spoke again, and Tyler repeatedly vetoed banking bills which he regarded as an infringement of states' rights. Nor would he accept the high tariffs on imports which were part of his party's programme. The Whigs regarded this as treachery, and were beside themselves with rage. They dubbed him 'His Accidency', and Clay derided him as 'a president without a party'. Except for the Secretary of State, Daniel Webster, who had convinced himself that it was his duty to fix the border between Canada and Maine in negotiation with the British, the entire Cabinet resigned. Once the Ashburton Treaty had settled the border, Webster too went, and Tyler in due course appointed John C. Calhoun, another great exponent of states' rights, secretary of state. Calhoun hoped to guarantee the security of slavery 'throughout the whole of this continent'. The administration was now entirely southern, an ominous sign of a divided nation.

Tyler, aged fifty-one when he took office, was the youngest president so far. His first wife, Letitia, who had given birth to

JOHN TYLER · 71

eight children, died in 1842, after several years of failing health and twenty-nine years of marriage. Her widower, who felt himself to be still in his prime, started to court Julia Gardiner, a beautiful and spirited twenty-two-year-old debutante from New York. In February 1844 she was among a party of dignitaries taken by Tyler down the Potomac on the navy's most advanced frigate, which had an enormous gun known as the Peacemaker. The gun blew up, and her father, John Gardiner, was among those killed.

Soon after this accident, Tyler married Julia. The age gap between them led to a certain amount of adverse comment, with John Quincy Adams denouncing in the pages of his diary the 'indecency' of this modern version of 'the old fable of January and May'. The couple went on to have seven children. In February 1845 Julia threw a farewell party for 3,000 people in the White House, at which Tyler joked, 'They cannot say now that I am a *President without a party!*'

In an age of rabid party strife Tyler displayed the self-assurance of a southern gentleman who was determined to rise above mere faction. In 1844 neither the Whigs nor the Democrats would have him as their candidate, but he hoped that by promoting the annexation of Texas, he could keep himself in contention. This manoeuvre failed, but three days before the end of his presidency Tyler succeeded in annexing Texas to the United States by the unusual method of a joint resolution of Congress, which required only simple majorities in both houses, rather than the unobtainable two-thirds of the Senate. John Quincy Adams said this turned the constitution into 'a menstruous rag'.

Tyler and his wife retired to his plantation in Virginia, which he renamed Sherwood Forest, the haunt in England of Robin Hood, a jocular reference to Tyler's status as an outlaw from the Whig Party. He lived until 1862 and supported the Confederacy at the start of the Civil War. At the time of writing two of his grandsons are still alive, one of whom resides at Sherwood Forest. The grounds contain a cemetery for the Tyler family's pets, including this epitaph written by the President:

Here lie the bones of my old horse, 'General',
Who served his master faithfully
For twenty-one years,
And never made a blunder.
Would that his master could say the same!

JAMES K. POLK

Lived 1795–1849; president 1845–49

James K. Polk was the first 'dark horse' presidential candidate to emerge from a blocked Democratic convention. He was an obscure political operator of whom his opponents enquired in a satirical spirit, 'Who is James K. Polk?' But his personality was so insipid, humourless and unmemorable that even at the time few people felt like answering the question.

One of his predecessors, John Quincy Adams, remarked that Polk had 'no elegance of language' and 'no felicitous impromptus'. Yet by advocating a bold policy of westward expansion Polk defeated the celebrated Henry Clay in the election of 1844, and by an astute mixture of force and diplomacy he proceeded to enlarge the territory of the United States more dramatically than anyone except Thomas Jefferson with the Louisiana Purchase.

Polk was born in North Carolina into a farming family who soon afterwards moved to Tennessee. His name is a shortened form of Pollock, his forebears having arrived from Ireland in the late seventeenth century. His middle name was Knox, for his mother was related to John Knox, the fiery Edinburgh Calvinist. A self-mortifying sense of duty permeated Polk's outlook, and while president he wrote in his diary: 'Though I occupy a very high position, I am the hardest-working man in this country.'

As a child he was so sickly that farming was out of the question. At the age of seventeen, strapped to a table and with no anaesthetic except brandy, he underwent a surgical operation, said to have been for gallstones but more likely to have been for the removal of a bladder stone. His health improved, and he was able to study mathematics and classics at the University of North Carolina, after which he qualified as a lawyer and became obsessed by politics.

First in Tennessee and then as a member of the House of Representatives, Polk was a follower of Andrew Jackson. Because of his small stature and cogent campaign speeches, he was known as the Napoleon of the stump. In 1839 he left Washington and became governor of Tennessee, but there was something about him which repelled people, and in both 1841 and 1843 he failed to win re-election.

Then came the Democratic convention in 1844 in Baltimore, where the front-runner Martin Van Buren, president 1837–41, was punished for coming out against the annexation of Texas, and proved unable in repeated ballots to obtain the necessary two-thirds majority. Polk, the summit of whose hopes was to be vice president under Van Buren, instead became, as someone who strongly approved of taking Texas, the beneficiary of a stampede which made him the Democratic nominee.

Nobody had realised he could get that far, and when news of his victory was conveyed from Baltimore to Washington over the telegraph just devised by Samuel Morse, there was a widespread assumption that the new technology must have malfunctioned. Polk was written off as a nonentity, but proceeded to win a narrow victory over Clay, the Whig candidate, who took a more nuanced view of the perilous issue of slavery, and recognised it could become enflamed if Texas, as a state where slavery was allowed, were admitted to the Union.

Polk had no close friends apart from his wife, Sarah. They had no children, but she helped him with his political work, and as hostess in the White House supplied the charm which he lacked. Perhaps because he was so small and had so little presence, she encouraged the playing of 'Hail to the Chief' to signal his arrival. This had been done from time to time under previous presidents, but now became the custom.

In his inaugural address Polk endorsed the annexation of Texas, just carried out by his predecessor, John Tyler, and claimed, 'Our title to the country of Oregon is clear and unquestionable.' The British disagreed, and since they were powerful, Polk negotiated with them. His maximum claim of all Oregon up to the border with Alaska (then in Russian hands), was expressed in the slogan 'Fifty-four, forty, or fight', but a compromise was reached on the 49th Parallel, which remains the border between the United States and Canada. Mexico was weak, so Polk in 1846 provoked a war, by 1848 had won it and under the resulting peace treaty not merely pushed the southern border of the United States to the Rio Grande, but gained New Mexico, Arizona and, most valuable, California, where in 1849 a gold rush broke out.

Two future presidents were among the many who questioned the morality of the Mexican War. Abraham Lincoln, newly elected to the House of Representatives, accused Polk of starting hostilities out of thirst for 'military glory . . . that serpent's eye which charms to destroy', and said 'the blood of this war, like the blood of Abel, is crying to Heaven against him'. Ulysses S. Grant, who fought as a junior officer, wrote in his memoirs: 'I do not think there was ever a more wicked war than that waged by the United States on Mexico. I thought so at the time, when I was a youngster, only I had not moral courage enough to resign.'

But the spirit of the age was summed up by John O'Sullivan, editor of the *Democratic Review*, who in the summer of 1845 wrote of 'our manifest destiny to overspread the continent allotted by Providence for the free development of our yearly multiplying millions'. The phrase 'manifest destiny', with its connotations of justice and inevitability, entered the language, expressing the self-declared right of the United States to take possession of the whole of North America. Polk was an efficient agent of this process. But he was an unpopular president, not just because of his unattractive personality, but also perhaps from a suppressed sense of shame at his rapacity. No serious politician proposed to hand back the gains of the Mexican War, but it was hard to pretend it had been an edifying episode.

In his diary Polk described telling some people how he coped, as president, with so much handshaking:

I told them that I had found that there was great art in shaking hands, and that I could shake hands during the whole day without suffering any bad effects from it. They were curious to know what this art was. I told them that if a man surrendered his arm to be shaken, by some horizontally, but others perpendicularly, and by others again with a strong grip, he could not fail to suffer severely from it, but that if he would shake and not be shaken, grip and not be gripped, taking care always to squeeze the hand of his adversary as hard as he squeezed him, that he suffered no inconvenience from it. I told them also that I could generally anticipate when I was to have a strong grip, and that when I observed a strong man approaching I generally took advantage of him by being a little quicker than he was and seizing him by the tip of his fingers, giving him a hearty shake, and thus preventing him from getting a full grip upon me.

Polk was a cold and capable man, who seldom allowed an opponent to get a grip upon him. But only fifteen weeks after he stepped down as president, he died at the age of fifty-three, his health broken by overwork.

ZACHARY TAYLOR

Lived 1784–1850; president 1849–50

Zachary Taylor became a hero of the Mexican War at the right moment to be adopted by the Whigs as their candidate in the presidential election of 1848. His military record was impressive, his manner charmingly unpretentious, but he had no experience of politics, and when a visitor to his tent tried to toast him as the next president he is supposed to have replied: 'Stop your nonsense and drink your whisky.'

Soon, however, he persuaded himself that he could be the people's candidate, 'untrammelled by party schemes'. Like General

Harrison, whom the Whigs propelled to victory in 1840, General Taylor possessed no discernible programme and died before he could show what he could do. His plea to Congress to avoid the perilous subject of slavery was unrealistic.

He was born in Virginia but brought up in Kentucky. From his father, who fought under Washington, he inherited a taste for soldiering and for farming. He spent forty years as a regular army officer, constantly on the move so never voting in elections. He found a wife, Peggy Smith, who was willing to share these rigours with him, and together they had six children, of whom two died young. His troops nicknamed him Old Rough and Ready, for he had an aversion to wearing uniform, or smartness of any kind, and was often mistaken for a farmer by new recruits. During the Mexican War of 1846–48, a junior American officer, Adolph Engelmann, offered this description of his commander in a letter home: 'Taylor is short and very heavy, with pronounced face lines and grey hair, wears an old oil cloth cap, a dusty green coat, a frightful pair of trousers and on horseback looks like a toad.'

General Taylor led his men through a series of hard-fought engagements against gallant opponents, winning famous victories at Palo Alto, Monterrey and Buena Vista. These triumphs enchanted the American public but dismayed President Polk, who could not bear to see someone else become a plausible presidential contender. Polk tried starving Taylor of men and supplies, but shortages just brought out the best in the brave and resourceful general.

In 1848 the Whigs met in Philadelphia, adopted Taylor as their candidate and wrote to him in Baton Rouge to tell him so. They omitted to prepay the postage, and the general refused to pay it too, so for some weeks he was unaware of his victory. A second letter eventually reached him, and in his reply accepting the nomination he confused matters by declaring, 'I am a Whig, but not ultra Whig.'

The great men of the Whig Party, Henry Clay and Daniel Webster, were disgusted that its choice had fallen on 'a swearing, whisky-drinking, fighting frontier colonel', as Webster called him. Taylor nevertheless won the election, helped by divisions between his opponents, some of whom came out against slavery while others temporised. The new president charmed people by grazing his horse, Whitey, on the White House lawn. The great question of whether slavery would be extended into the vast new territories conquered from Mexico was unavoidable. Taylor nevertheless urged Congress to avoid the issue, declaring as late as December 1849, 'we should abstain from the introduction of those exciting topics of a sectional character which have hitherto produced painful apprehensions in the public mind'.

Clay and Webster ignored this futile plea, as did Calhoun, the champion of the southern states, and these three mighty orators dominated the greatest debates the Senate has ever known. Taylor, though a slaveholder himself, held that California should not be admitted to the Union as a slave state. When southerners denounced him, and said they would secede if California came in as a free state, Taylor replied: 'Then I will command the army in person and hang any man taken in treason.' It seems he was also preparing to veto the compromise devised by Clay and supported by Webster.

We shall never know how the crisis would have played out if Taylor, with his honest, courageous, unflappable but unsubtle responses, had survived in office. On 4 July 1850, which was a boiling hot day, the sixty-five-year-old President officiated for hours at the laying of the foundation stone for the Washington Monument. He fortified himself by consuming large quantities

of iced water, cherries in iced milk, raw fruit, cucumbers and cab-
bages. The tough campaigner who had survived so many battles
in Mexico perished five days later of gastroenteritis, or possibly of
cholera, in the District of Columbia. Southerners reckoned he
had been poisoned because he was going to veto Clay's compromise, but in 1991, when his remains were disinterred and tests
carried out on his fingernails and hair, no traces of arsenic were
found.

MILLARD FILLMORE

Lived 1800–74; president 1850–53

Millard Fillmore was out of his depth as president, and is mentioned fleetingly, or passed over in silent embarrassment, by most historians. He looked the part, a tall, dignified figure, which is one reason why the Whigs chose him as General Taylor's running mate. They were also confident he would do as he was told. And the explanation for Fillmore's nullity, the sense of surpassing vacuousness which he conveyed, is that he did indeed do as he was told, so could not become his own man.

He was born into poverty in a log cabin in the western part of New York state, which was then still a frontier region. As a boy he laboured on his family's failing farm, and at the age of fifteen was set to learn the trade of wool carder. Four years later he started at the New Hope Academy, where he was taught by Abigail Powers, who was only two years older than himself. With her encouragement, he developed an invincible love of reading, and seven years later they were married.

Fillmore rose in the world. He established himself as a lawyer in the town of Buffalo, became a protégé of the New York power broker Thurlow Weed, served briefly in the New York state assembly and from 1833 in the US House of Representatives. Fillmore was a handsome, energetic and popular figure, but failed to gain election as governor of New York when he stood in 1844. As vice president from 1849 he suffered the humiliation of being totally ignored by President Zachary Taylor, and was lonely too, for his wife detested Washington and stayed in New York. But Fillmore presided skilfully over Senate debates, and no less a figure than Henry Clay regarded him as 'able, enlightened, indefatigable and . . . patriotic'.

Taylor's sudden death in 1850 came as a dreadful shock. Fillmore suffered a sleepless night and looked exhausted when he was sworn in as the new president. Unlike Taylor, he supported the so-called Compromise, a package of bills relating to slavery to which Clay was devoting one last great rhetorical effort in the Senate. For although Fillmore opposed slavery, he treated it more as a political than a moral problem, and held that 'we must endure it, and give it such protection as is guaranteed by the constitution, till we can get rid of it without destroying the last hope of free government in the world'.

As part of the Compromise, in September 1850 he signed into law the Fugitive Slave Act, which made it much harder for slaves to escape to the north, by weighting the whole judicial system against them. The President regarded this as a necessary concession to the slave lobby, which in return was obliged to accept the admission to the Union of California as a free state. He failed to foresee, or to feel, the abhorrence which the act would rouse among northern abolitionists, or the fatal effect which passing and enforcing it would have on his own authority.

The contempt in which he was held is conveyed by a story which did the rounds in Washington soon after he became president. Fillmore was said to have decided he must have a carriage. 'Old Edward' Moran, a White House attendant, took him to see a handsome equipage which was going cheap because the owner was leaving Washington.

'This is all very well, Edward,' Fillmore said, 'but how would it do for the President of the United States to ride around in a second-hand carriage?'

'But, sure,' the old retainer replied, 'your Ixcellency is only a sicond-hand prisident.'

Fillmore's touch in foreign policy was happier. He made Daniel Webster secretary of state, and sent Commodore Perry to open up Japan to American trade, an event which presaged the collapse of the traditional order presided over by the Shogun, and was foreseen in a Japanese song of the time:

> Through a black night of cloud and rain,
> The Black Ship plies her way –
> An alien thing of evil mien –
> Across the waters grey.

The Whigs, who were doomed as a party because of their divisions over slavery, declined to adopt Fillmore as their candidate for the election of 1852. His wife, Abigail, who had installed the beginnings of a library in the White House, caught a chill at the inauguration in March 1853 of Franklin Pierce and died of pneumonia at the end of the month. Their daughter Mary, who had helped to animate their White House receptions, died soon after of cholera.

The grieving Fillmore went to Europe, where he declined the offer of an honorary degree from Oxford, for he explained, 'I have not the advantage of a classical education, and no man should, in my judgement, accept a degree he cannot read.' Oxford performs its honorary degree ceremonies in Latin, but many recipients have proved less modest than Fillmore, who also feared he might be ridiculed by the students: 'They would probably ask who's Fillmore? What's he done? Where did he come from? And then my name would, I fear, give them an excellent opportunity to make jokes at my expense.'

On returning to the United States, he stood in the presidential election of 1856 as the candidate for the Know-Nothings, a new anti-Catholic and anti-Irish party whose members were instructed, when asked about its principles, to reply: 'I know nothing.' He came third, but his declining years were eased by marriage to a wealthy widow.

President Truman took a dim view of the means by which Fillmore had risen in the world: 'he started toadying to the rich, which he continued to do all the rest of his life, including when he was president. As a result, he was never any kind of leader. He did just what he was told, and what he was told was not to do anything to offend anybody. Which, of course, meant that he ended up by offending everybody.' Fillmore has since passed into oblivion, so no longer offends anyone.

FRANKLIN PIERCE

Lived 1804–69; president 1853–57

F ranklin Pierce was one of the most handsome men ever to
become president, but fell far below the level of events. He
enjoyed a lifelong friendship with Nathaniel Hawthorne,
who soon after the publication of his masterpiece *The Scarlet Letter*
took on the task of writing Pierce's campaign biography, in which
he omitted the convivial candidate's propensity to drink too
much, and tried to present inertia as the masterful steering of
affairs: 'He has in him many of the elements of a great ruler.
His talents are administrative, he has a subtle, subtle facility of

making affairs roll onward according to his will, and of influencing their course without showing any trace of his action.'

That was wishful thinking. Pierce was a doughface, as northern politicians who backed the south's position on slavery were known. He was the disastrously malleable tool of southern interests, one of the succession of weak presidents who allowed things to go from bad to worse.

He was born in New Hampshire, where his father was a prominent local figure and encouraged him to go into politics. Pierce met Hawthorne at Bowdoin College in Maine, qualified as a lawyer and enjoyed a swift but unremarkable ascent within the Democratic Party. He served from 1837 to 1842 in the Senate, from which he resigned because his wife, Jane – the pious daughter of a former president of Bowdoin – could not bear life in Washington, which entailed heavy drinking in which Pierce joined with enthusiasm.

Perhaps because he did not find life as a lawyer in Concord, the capital of New Hampshire, altogether satisfying, Pierce volunteered for service in the Mexican War, where in 1847 he served as a brigadier general in the advance on Mexico City. His opponents afterwards attempted, rather unfairly, to cast doubt on his courage in that campaign. He had fainted not from fear, but because his horse broke its leg and fell on him.

In 1852 the Democrats went through thirty-three ballots without being able to agree on a presidential candidate. Senator Bradbury of Maine, another of Pierce's old friends from Bowdoin, persuaded the Virginians to bring Pierce's name into play, and on the forty-ninth ballot he was chosen as the compromise candidate. Pierce greeted the news with surprise, as did most people. His son Bennie, who was eleven years old and the only survivor of three children, told his mother in a letter: 'I hope he won't be elected for I should not like to be at Washington and I know you would not either.'

Pierce was elected: in the autumn of 1852 he defeated the Whig candidate, General Winfield Scott, who had been his commanding officer in Mexico. But in January 1853 he, Jane and Bennie were travelling on a train which crashed, dashing out the boy's brains in full view of his horrified parents. The couple survived the disaster without physical injury, but never really recovered from the loss of their son.

Jane felt unable to attend the inauguration, at which Pierce attempted to strike a confident note: 'The policy of my Administration will not be controlled by any timid forebodings of evil from expansion.' But expansion was perilous, for it brought with it the question of whether the new territories would allow slavery. In Europe Pierce's diplomatic agents made a cack-handed attempt to buy Cuba from Spain on condition that slavery was not abolished on the island first. This project was dear to the slave-owning south, but scandalised wider public opinion when it became known, and Pierce had to abandon it.

More troublesome still was the Territory of Nebraska, which Senator Stephen A. Douglas of Illinois wanted to open up by building a railway. Under Douglas's Kansas-Nebraska Act of 1854, he proposed that the settlers be allowed to decide for themselves whether or not to allow slavery. Since the region lay entirely to the north of the line laid down in 1820 as the northern limit of slavery, this required the repeal of the Missouri Compromise Act. Pierce went along with all this at the behest of Jefferson Davis, the forceful southern leader whom he had made secretary of war. Bleeding Kansas, the bloody conflict of 1854–61 between settlers determined to have slavery and those determined to avert it, was the result of this policy.

In Washington too, bitter enmities led to violence. In May 1856 Senator Charles Sumner of Massachusetts declared that what was happening in Kansas was 'the rape of a virgin territory' and accused Senator A. P. Butler of South Carolina of having 'chosen a mistress who . . . though polluted in the sight of the world, is chaste in his sight – I mean the harlot, slavery'. Two days later, Butler's nephew Congressman Preston S. Brooks attacked Sumner in the Senate, beating him so badly with his cane that the Senator did not return to his desk for two years. Butler was hailed in the south as a hero, and hundreds of people presented canes to him. Each side by now found the other intolerable, and Pierce was reduced to the status of an impotent spectator. His support for the south had encouraged it to overplay its hand, on the mistaken assumption that it would always be able to find northern allies.

Pierce wanted to run again in 1856, but the Democrats would not have him. During the Civil War he made himself unpopular in his home state of New Hampshire by criticising Abraham Lincoln, and not until fifty years after his death was a statue erected of him there. Harry Truman, contemplating the series of inadequate presidents before the Civil War, dismissed Pierce as 'a complete fizzle'.

JAMES BUCHANAN

Lived 1791–1868; president 1857–61

James Buchanan was a weak and vacillating president, who promised to preserve the Union, but had no idea how to cope with the forces which were destroying it. We cannot know whether a strong and decisive figure would have averted the Civil War, but Buchanan was chosen as the Democratic Party candidate because he was weak and feeble. He had never 'uttered a word which could pain the most sensitive Southern heart', as the *Richmond Enquirer* put it, and was averse to getting into an argument with anyone. His inoffensiveness made him electable, but also meant that when the great test of 1860–61 arrived he was useless.

He was the last president born in the eighteenth century, the last to wear a stock and the only one never to marry. His parents were Presbyterians, his father an emigrant from Ireland who kept a store and speculated in property, his mother the daughter of a Pennsylvania farmer. James, one of eleven children, qualified as a lawyer, began a profitable legal career and got engaged to a young woman called Ann Coleman. Her family was the richest in the town of Lancaster, Pennsylvania, and regarded him as not good enough for her. She broke off the engagement and soon afterwards died, it was said by suicide. Buchanan, grief-stricken, wrote to her father asking for permission to see her corpse and walk as a mourner at her funeral. After Buchanan's own death forty-four years later, this letter was found among his papers. It had been returned to him unopened.

In 1856, when he was running for president, he was falsely accused by the elder James Gordon Bennett, editor of the *New York Herald*, of having tried to hang himself while fleeing from the vengeful brother of his fiancée. It was said he had been cut down but his neck had been left permanently twisted. The truth was that he carried his head tilted to one side because one of his eyes was stronger than the other.

Buchanan prospered both as a lawyer and as a politician, served from 1821 in the House of Representatives, and became a follower of President Andrew Jackson, who in 1831 appointed him minister to Russia, and thus avoided any further meetings with him, for this cautious lawyer was not really Jackson's type. On returning home, Buchanan was elected senator for Pennsylvania, and in 1845 was made secretary of state by President Polk, who said of him in his diary, 'Mr Buchanan is an able man, but in small matters without judgement and sometimes acts like an old maid.'

From 1853 to 1856 he was minister in London, which meant he escaped being drawn into the ferocious animosities roused by the question of whether Kansas should enter the Union as a slave or free state. He instead faced the tricky question of how to appear at Court after he received an order from Washington instructing American diplomats to wear 'the simple dress of an American citizen', devoid of gold lace. The solution which he eventually arrived at – which included a plain, black-hilted dress sword – produced, he reported, 'an arch but benevolent smile' from Queen Victoria.

While serving in Britain he visited Nathaniel Hawthorne, whom President Pierce had appointed to the lucrative post of American consul in Liverpool. Hawthorne wrote of Buchanan: 'He cannot exactly be called gentlemanly in his manners, there being a sort of rusticity about him; moreover, he has a habit of squinting one eye, and an awkward carriage of his head; but, withal, a dignity in his large person, and a consciousness of high position and importance, which gives him ease and freedom.' Buchanan was accompanied to Liverpool by his niece Harriet Lane, who acted as his hostess in London, and who according to Hawthorne was 'quietly conscious of rank, as much as if she was an Earl's daughter . . . I talked with her a little, and found her sensible, vivacious and firm-textured, rather than soft and sentimental.' She was to preside with great success over the Buchanan White House, which was reckoned a vast improvement on the gloomy atmosphere under his predecessor, President Pierce. Buchanan could manage the social side of things. It was the politics that defeated him.

Like Pierce, Buchanan was a 'doughface', a northerner who sided with the south. He had for decades taken the orthodox Jacksonian line that the duty of northern Democrats like himself was (as Buchanan once put it) to 'inscribe upon our banners hostility to abolition' of slavery. But unlike Jackson, who in 1832 was prepared to go to war rather than allow South Carolina to go its own way, Buchanan was desperate to avoid hostilities. Nor did he have the largeness of mind to see, let alone admit, that unreserved support for slavery was becoming unsustainable.

'The night is departing,' Buchanan assured his friends after winning the presidential election of 1856, 'and the roseate and propitious morn now breaking upon us promises a long day of peace and prosperity for our country.' He took office at the age of sixty-five, older than any of his predecessors except Harrison, and supposed that like George Washington he could bring peace to a divided nation. In his inaugural address he said he would support the Supreme Court, whatever it decided in the Dred Scott slavery case, which turned on whether a slave who had lived in a free state remained a slave.

Two days later, the court handed down a judgment which was a crushing victory for the south. No compromise was attempted. An owner who took his slaves into a free state retained possession of them in the same way as if he had taken his horses there. The abolitionists were up in arms, and the northern Democrats split from the southern Democrats, but Buchanan would not accept that they had a point. In October 1859 John Brown attempted, very ineptly, to incite a slave revolt at Harpers Ferry in West Virginia. Brown was captured, tried and executed, but as the song soon had it, his soul went marching on. He became an abolitionist martyr.

In November 1860, Abraham Lincoln was elected president with no support in the slave states, and almost four months to wait before his inauguration. On 3 December 1860, in his last annual address to Congress, Buchanan said: 'The long-continued and intemperate interference of the Northern people with the question of slavery in the Southern States has at length produced its natural effects. The different sections of the Union are now arrayed against each other, and the time has arrived, so much dreaded by the Father of his Country [Washington], when hostile geographical parties have been formed.'

The outgoing president denied the right of secession and warned that if it were allowed the Union would become 'a rope of sand', but on 20 December 1860 South Carolina became the first state to secede. Buchanan was bewildered. Although he thought what had happened was wrong, he also thought the federal government had no right to coerce South Carolina to stay in the Union. Governor Henry A. Wise of Virginia, who liked Buchanan and had campaigned for his nomination in 1856, said of him: 'He is simply paralysed by the immensity of the issues and the perils of the hour.'

Edwin Stanton of Ohio warned Buchanan: 'You are sleeping on a volcano. The ground is mined all around and under you and ready to explode, and without prompt and energetic action, you will be the last President of the United States.' Prompt and energetic action was just what Buchanan could not provide. His Cabinet started to disintegrate as its members, most of whom were southerners, left to join the secession. Buchanan brought in northerners, including Stanton as attorney general.

On the day Stanton was sworn in, 20 December 1860, Major Robert Anderson, who commanded the small federal garrison at Fort Moultrie in Charleston Harbor, South Carolina, moved his force on his own initiative to the altogether more defensible Fort Sumter. South Carolina protested that this broke an undertaking given only eleven days earlier by Buchanan, who had promised as long as the forts were not attacked, he would not send reinforcements. In early January an attempt was made to send men and supplies to Anderson, but the ship carrying them turned back when fired on from Charleston. By the start of February, six more states, Mississippi, Florida, Alabama, Georgia, Louisiana and Texas, had seceded. They believed that as independent states they had the right to do this, and that the Yankees were cowards and would not fight. It was said in the south that 'a lady's thimble will hold all the blood that will be shed'.

Buchanan suggested amending the Constitution so slavery was protected in the south. His proposal found no favour. Neither side wanted to fire the shots which would start a civil war, but neither was in any mood to back down, and in Fort Sumter Major Anderson's supplies were running low. This was the impossible situation Buchanan bequeathed to his successor.

Buchanan lived on for another seven years at Wheatland, his mansion in Lancaster, Pennsylvania. He said history would vindicate him, but he was wrong.

There is much material about him in *Memories of the Ford Administration*, a novel by John Updike about an adulterous academic trying and failing to write a biography of Buchanan. But for all Updike's gifts, he does not make us feel we get to know this shadowy and ineffectual president. Perhaps there was not so very much to know.

ABRAHAM LINCOLN

Lived 1809–65; president 1861–65

braham Lincoln rose from obscurity to become the most famous president since George Washington. His portrait was displayed in humble homes around the globe and his name conveyed an elevated morality. He is the greatest orator in this book and gave the most celebrated speech in American history, the Gettysburg Address. In the years leading up to the Civil War, and as leader of the North during the conflict, he again and again showed his sublime powers of advocacy, tempering righteousness with pragmatism, resolve with compassion, high seriousness with jokes. After his death at the hands of an assassin in April 1865, he was remembered as a saint and martyr who had given his life to save the Union and bring freedom to the slaves.

But Lincoln won the presidential election of 1860 with just under 40 per cent of the vote, and never lacked for critics who blamed him for precipitating the bloodiest war in American history. In the South he was seen as a tyrant and a monster who incited slaves to murder and rape his white brethren. In the North he attracted bitter criticism for exceeding his presidential powers and failing for over four years to win the war, and from many abolitionists for taking such slow and cautious steps towards emancipation.

These critics were generally unfair, indeed in many cases hysterical, but one should bear in mind that Lincoln was a deadly opponent. Few politicians have been better at choosing the time and place to fight, making his opponents look disreputable and incoherent, and allowing them to impale themselves on their own contradictions. Charles Francis Adams, American ambassador in London during the Civil War and son and grandson of the two Adams presidents, wrote in his diary that Lincoln 'and his chief advisers are not without the spirit of the serpent mixed in with their wisdom'.

He was born in a one-room log cabin with a dirt floor in Kentucky. His shiftless, illiterate, wandering father, Thomas, whose own father had been killed by an Indian while clearing land, scraped a laborious living as a farmer. When Abraham was seven and his sister nine, the family crossed the Ohio into Indiana, built a new cabin and cleared land for a farm in the forest. His beloved mother, Nancy, died soon after of milk sickness, or brucellosis, a disease caught from cows which had fed on poisonous plants in the woods. Thomas, unable to manage on his own, soon found another wife, Sarah Bush Johnston, a widow with three small children.

Abraham had nothing good to say about his father, so stayed silent about him, and declined to visit him when he was dying. But he got on wonderfully well with his stepmother, who brought order and affection to the household and treated all the children equally. He revelled in the tradition of telling stories round the fire, and became a master storyteller himself. He received almost no formal education, but walked miles to borrow the few books he could get his hands on and read with avidity the Bible, Shakespeare's plays, Aesop's fables, Robinson Crusoe, Pilgrim's Progress and Parson Weems's Life of Washington.

His speeches were the product of continuous thought and an immersion in some of the greatest works in the English language. He was a teetotaller who played no sport or musical instrument and by night would read if he was not telling stories to his companions. Though steeped in the Bible he belonged to no church, and when asked about his religion replied in the words of the man in Saint Mark's Gospel: 'Lord, I believe; help Thou mine unbelief.'

He grew to be six foot four inches tall, and by hard work immensely strong. Even as president, he was able to grasp the handle of an axe between his finger and thumb and hold it level with his shoulder at the end of his outstretched arm. Thomas hired him out to prosperous neighbours as a labourer who could turn his hand to anything. He dug wells, slaughtered hogs, ploughed, planted, weeded and harvested crops, felled trees, split logs into rails for fences, and helped his father clear yet another new farm in Macon County, Illinois. But he could not bear the thought of spending his life as a frontiersman. Twice he journeyed by flat boat down the great rivers which led to New Orleans. In 1832, when he was twenty-three, he joined a company in the Black Hawk War against the Indians, and was proud to be elected its captain, but saw no action.

While keeping an unsuccessful store in New Salem, on the Sangamo River, a tributary of the Illinois, which itself flows into the Mississippi, he came across and studied a copy of Black-stone's *Commentaries on the Laws of England*, a work of fundamental importance in the development of the American legal system. In 1834 his neighbours elected him, at the second attempt, to the Illinois legislature. The following year, his first known love, Ann Rutledge, whose father owned Rutledge's Tavern in New Salem, died of a fever, and he was prostrate with grief.

Politics and the law were his callings. In 1837 he set up as a lawyer in Springfield, Illinois. He prospered, for he was brilliant at seeing to the heart of a case and by homely analogy making it comprehensible to everyone, and he loved the gypsy life of the circuit court, which for six months of the year toured the state. In 1840 he met Mary Todd, from a well-to-do family in Kentucky, who was staying with her sister in Springfield. She wanted to marry a future president and was perspicacious enough to see that Lincoln might be the man. They got engaged, but he failed to turn up for the wedding, presumably because he had misgivings. They nevertheless got married in 1842, and were to have four sons, of whom three died young. From 1847 to 1849 he served in the House of Representatives, but his opposition to the Mexican War made him unpopular, and he failed to win re-election.

That could have been the last that was heard of him on the national stage. But in 1854 the Kansas-Nebraska Act repealed the Missouri Compromise of 1820, which had forbidden the spread of slavery into the greater part of the vast new territories acquired in the Louisiana Purchase. This concession to the South pro-voked outrage in the North. Lincoln agreed that the spread of slavery was intolerable. He had found his cause, and became the most formidable opponent of the chief architect of the Kansas-Nebraska Act, Senator Stephen A. Douglas of Illinois. In 1856 Lincoln left the Whigs and joined the Republican Party, founded two years earlier to oppose the extension of slavery, and in 1858 he ran against Douglas for the Senate. On accepting the

Republican nomination he delivered one of his most famous speeches, quoting words spoken by Jesus:

> 'A house divided against itself cannot stand.'
>
> I believe this government cannot endure, permanently half *slave* and half *free*.
>
> I do not expect the Union to be *dissolved* – I do not expect the house to *fall* – but I *do* expect it will cease to be divided.
>
> It will become *all* one thing, or *all* the other.
>
> Either the *opponents* of slavery, will arrest the further spread of it, and place it where the public mind shall rest in the belief that it is in course of ultimate extinction; or its *advocates* will push it forward, till it shall become alike lawful in *all* the States, *old* as well as *new* – *North* as well as *South*.

Lincoln assured his listeners that 'the victory is *sure* to come'. Douglas, a formidable orator known because of his diminutive stature as the Little Giant, proceeded to accuse him, in the seven debates they held in different places in Illinois from August to October 1858, of wanting 'to turn this beautiful State into a free negro colony', full of emancipated slaves who would move in from Missouri and live 'on a social equality with your wives and daughters'. Many white Americans had no intention of living on terms of equality with African Americans, and Lincoln retorted that he himself did not want that:

> I will say then that I am not, nor ever have been in favour of bringing about in any way the social and political equality of the white and black races [applause] . . . I do not understand that because I do not want a negro woman for a slave I must necessarily want her for a wife [cheers and laughter]. My understanding is that I can just let her alone. I am now in my fiftieth year, and I certainly never have had a black woman for either a slave or a wife.

Douglas won re-election by a narrow margin. Walking home on the dark, rainy night when the result was declared, Lincoln slipped in the mud but caught himself. He took this as a sign of what had just occurred: 'It is a slip and not a fall.'

He was right. The debates had made his name. He spoke with great success at the Cooper Union in New York, began to be spoken of as a possible presidential candidate for the Republicans, and supplied a studiously modest campaign biography – 'it must not appear to have been written by myself'. In May 1860, when the Republicans held their convention at the Wigwam, a vast new hall in Chicago, he waited at home in Springfield, as was then the custom, but his cousin John Hanks turned up with two fence rails which were, he said, among a lot of 3,000 which Lincoln had split thirty years before. Honest Abe, as he was already known, acquired a new nickname, the Railsplitter, in tribute to his origins as a labourer who had raised himself by his own exertions. Amid scenes of wild enthusiasm, he overtook and defeated the favourite, William H. Seward of New York, who had expressed an inconveniently extreme hostility to slavery.

The Republicans, with Lincoln as their candidate, won the presidential election of 1860 because the Democrats split into two halves, the North, which put up Stephen Douglas as its candidate, and the South, which fielded John C. Breckenridge. There was also a fourth candidate, John Bell, representing the shattered remnants of the Whig Party. Lincoln remained silent during the campaign, careful not to say anything which might spoil the favourable conjuncture of forces. He won with 1,866,452 votes, drawn almost entirely from the North: in ten of the southern states he did not receive a single vote. The two Democrats between them received 2,216,738 votes, but cancelled each other out. Bell came in last with just under 600,000 votes.

Lincoln received confirmation of his victory late on the night of 6 November 1860, when the news that he had carried New York, and therefore established an unassailable lead, reached him in the telegraph office at Springfield. But he had to wait until 4 March 1861 to be inaugurated. During this period he grew a beard and continued the practice he had established during the election campaign of saying almost nothing. He had no experience of high office, knew he would need all the help he could get, and assembled a Cabinet which included the more experienced figures he had beaten for the nomination: Seward as secretary of state, Salmon P. Chase as Treasury secretary, Edward Bates as attorney general. Mary meanwhile went shopping in New York, and began to run up large debts of which she told her husband nothing.

On 11 February 1861 Lincoln bade a sorrowful farewell to Springfield, which he would never see again, and set out on a twelve-day journey by special train to Washington, taking a roundabout route of 1,904 miles so that people in many different places could see him. As he neared Washington, he was warned by Allan Pinkerton, head of the Pinkerton National Detective Agency, of a plot to assassinate him as he passed through Baltimore. Lincoln, with some reluctance, accepted Pinkerton's advice to arrive incognito in Washington. The President Elect was then mocked for having sneaked into the capital, as it was falsely put about, hidden under a Scotch plaid cap and a military cloak.

Before leaving home he had prepared with great care a draft of his inaugural address, which declared that the Union was indestructible, secession was illegal and he would do whatever was needed to enforce the laws and hold or reclaim public property. Seward and others advised him that this was needlessly provocative, and would drive the key states which had not yet seceded, Virginia and Maryland, into the arms of the Confederacy. Lincoln toned the whole thing down, and ended with his conciliatory appeal to 'the better angels of our nature', quoted as one of the epigraphs at the start of this book, which he had rewritten and improved from a draft supplied by Seward.

Bismarck, the architect of German unification, declared in 1862 that the great questions of the day would not be decided through speeches and majority resolutions, but by blood and iron. Americans had found the previous year that even speeches as eloquent as Lincoln's could not decide the great question of their Union. Only a complete surrender by the new President, an acceptance that the seven states which had broken away to form the Confederacy could not be kept in the Union, would have satisfied the South. His speech was instead seen by a correspondent for the *Charleston Mercury* as 'the tocsin of battle' and 'the signal of our freedom', with Lincoln dismissed as 'the Ourang-Outang at the White House'.

In the harbour at Charleston lay Fort Sumter, held by a federal garrison under the command of Major Robert Anderson, who sent word that his supplies would be exhausted in about six weeks, and a force of 20,000 men would be needed to make the fort secure. Lincoln had promised to 'avoid bloodshed or violence . . . unless it be forced upon the national authority', but also to hold 'places belonging to the government', which included Fort Sumter. But he had nothing like the troops needed to do so, for the entire US Army consisted of 16,000 men, mostly stationed far away on the Indian frontier.

His advisers bombarded him with contradictory messages. Seward favoured the abandonment of Sumter, and by implication of the seven states which had already seceded. Lincoln, under intense pressure and new to military affairs, did not buckle. After listening to all the advice and making numerous requests for additional information, he decided to send a relief expedition from New York, carrying food but no arms or ammunition. On 12 April 1861 Confederate batteries opened fire on the fort, while the relief force lay powerless offshore. After thirty-four hours, Anderson surrendered. The war had begun, and the South had fired the first shots.

Both sides were confident of early victory. The North had a population of twenty million, while the Confederacy when it reached its full extent, thirteen states, had only nine million, including almost four million slaves. The disparity in economic power was even greater, for the North had much the greater industry. But the South believed that, man for man, their soldiers were far superior.

Lincoln called for 75,000 volunteers, and within days had 92,000. But this prompted Virginia to secede, and with Virginia went General Robert E. Lee, who had thirty-two years' service in the US Army and had been invited by Lincoln to command the Union forces. Lee was a Virginian, and could not bring himself 'to raise my hand against my relatives, my children, my home'. He was to become the Confederacy's greatest commander.

In July 1861 Confederate forces made a push for Washington, defeated the Unionists at Bull Run, but were too exhausted to follow up their victory by seizing the capital. After this alarming setback, Lincoln made General George B. McClellan his commander-in-chief, but was repeatedly infuriated by his refusal to follow up success.

The war became bloodier and bloodier. Over 600,000 men were killed, more than in all other wars fought by the United States, and many others were maimed, for medical treatment consisted very often of amputation. Many people had friends and relations fighting on both sides. Mary Lincoln, whose three half-brothers were killed fighting for the Confederacy, was suspected of sympathising with the enemy. In 1862 the Lincolns suffered the appalling blow of the death of their son Willie at the age of eleven.

One may feel tempted to envy Lincoln his fame, but even before his untimely death, it was bought at a terrible cost, for he was the man blamed more than any other for the war's duration and its setbacks. As he observed in 1862, after attacks in Congress for military blunders:

> If I were to try to read, much less answer, all the attacks made on me, this shop might as well be closed for any other business. I do the best I know how, the very best I can; and I mean to keep doing so until the end. If the end brings me out all right, what is said against me will not amount to anything. If the end brings me out wrong, ten angels swearing I was right would make no difference.

Even from fellow moralists Lincoln did not always receive support. In England, William Gladstone, who strove with titanic energy to apply Christian principles to political life, expressed in a speech at Newcastle in October 1862, while serving as Chancellor of the Exchequer, an admiration for the South and an assumption that it was on the way to victory, which went well beyond British government policy, but reflected what many members of the British ruling class thought:

> We know quite well that the people of the Northern States have not yet drunk of the cup and they are still trying to hold it far from their lips – which all the rest of the world see they nevertheless must drink of. We may have our own opinions about slavery; we may be for or against the South, but there is no doubt that Jefferson Davis and other leaders of the South have made an army; they are making, it appears, a navy; and they have made what is more difficult than either, they have made a nation.

The tragedy is that Gladstone was in many ways right: America was now divided into two nations. Lincoln persisted in trying to make it one again. The poet Walt Whitman noted his 'perfect composure and coolness'. Nathaniel Hawthorne met the President in March 1862 and wrote:

> The whole physiognomy is as coarse a one as you would meet anywhere in the length and breadth of the state; but withal, it is redeemed, illuminated, softened and brightened by a kindly though serious look out of the eyes, and an expression of homely sagacity, that seemed weighted with rich results of village experience. A great deal of native sense, no bookish cultivation, no refinement; honest at heart, and thoroughly so, and yet in some sort, sly – at least endowed with a sort of tact and wisdom that are akin to craft, and would impel him, I think, to take an antagonist in flank, rather than make a bull-run at him in front. But on the whole I like this sallow, queer, sagacious visage, with the homely human sympathies that warmed it; and, for my small share in the matter, would as lief have Uncle Abe for a ruler as any man that it would have been practical to have put in his place.

In September 1862 Lincoln began a Cabinet meeting by reading a humorous story by Artemus Ward. Nobody except the President laughed, and the Secretary of War, Edwin Stanton, was so enraged by this 'buffoonery' that he almost walked out.

'Gentlemen,' Lincoln said, 'why don't you laugh? With the fearful strain that is upon me night and day, if I did not laugh I should die, and you need this medicine as much as I do.' The President took a paper out of his top hat, where he had been accustomed since his days as a lawyer to keep important documents, and read it out: 'On the first of January in the year of our Lord 1863, all persons then held as slaves in any state or designated part of a state the people whereof shall then be in rebellion against the United States, shall be then, and thenceforth and forever free.'

Lincoln later told an artist who was painting a picture of the Emancipation Proclamation that he considered it 'the central act of my administration, and the great event of the 19th century'. The fears of the South had been confirmed, but only because it had gone to war. Under peacetime conditions it would have possessed for another century the votes in Congress needed to block the abolition of slavery, if that was what it still wished to do. Only as a result of the war was the 13th Amendment to the Constitution, abolishing slavery, passed in 1865. Lincoln had the acute feeling for public opinion which was required in order to hold the North together, and know how quickly to move on this question.

In July 1863 the Union won the two-day Battle of Gettysburg, the bloodiest fight of the whole war, after which the Confederacy had less chance than ever of eventual victory. The Gettysburg Address, delivered on 19 November 1863 at the inauguration of a cemetery for the Union dead, saw Lincoln distil to its essence the argument he had long expounded, namely that the North was the true guardian of the freedom and equality proclaimed eighty-seven years earlier by Thomas Jefferson in the Declaration of Independence. Here is the whole of this masterpiece, which took barely two minutes to deliver.

Four score and seven years ago our fathers brought forth on this continent, a new nation, conceived in Liberty, and dedicated to the proposition that all men are created equal.

Now we are engaged in a great civil war, testing whether that nation, or any nation so conceived and so dedicated, can long endure. We are met on a great battlefield of that war. We have come to dedicate a portion of that field, as a final resting place for those who here gave their lives that that nation might live. It is altogether fitting and proper that we should do this.

But, in a larger sense, we cannot dedicate – we cannot consecrate – we cannot hallow – this ground. The brave men, living and dead, who struggled here, have consecrated it, far above our poor power to add or detract. The world will little note, nor long remember what we say here, but it can never forget what they did here. It is for us the living, rather, to be dedicated here to the unfinished work which they who fought here have thus far so nobly advanced. It is rather for us to be here dedicated to the great task remaining before us – that from these honoured dead we take increased devotion to that cause for which they gave the last full measure of devotion – that we here highly resolve that these dead shall not have died in vain – that this nation, under God, shall have a new birth of freedom – and that government of the people, by the people, for the people, shall not perish from the earth.

Lincoln had become the preserver, one might say the second founder, of the United States, and in 1864 he was elected to serve a second term. He delivered his second inaugural in March 1865, ending with the plea, 'With malice toward none; with charity for all . . . to bind up the nation's wounds.' Just over a month later, General Lee surrendered to General Grant at Appomattox Court House in Virginia.

Five days afterwards Lincoln went to the theatre, one of his favourite ways, since his arrival in Washington, of relaxing from the burdens of high office. He was shot by Robert Booth, a vengeful Confederate actor, and died some hours later in a house across the street. Stanton, who was present, declared, 'Now he belongs to the ages.'

And so he did. Leo Tolstoy said of him:

Lincoln was a man of whom a nation has a right to be proud; he was a Christ in miniature, a saint of humanity, whose name will live thousands of years in the legends of future generations.

He was bigger than his country – bigger than all the Presidents together. Why? Because he loved his enemies as himself and because he was a universal individualist who wanted to see himself in the world – not the world in himself.

Most Americans feel to this day a deep affection for Honest Abe, and believe that he never delivered a low blow. Not the least of his qualities was his humility. He did not claim to have controlled events, but said that events had controlled him. He never got the chance to bind up the wounds left by the Civil War.

ANDREW JOHNSON

Lived 1808–75; president 1865–69

Andrew Johnson came closer than any other president to being impeached. Winning the peace was in many ways an even harder task than winning the war, and it is possible Lincoln himself would not have achieved it, but under a president as bigoted and irritable as Johnson, failure was almost certain. Unlike his predecessor, he had no insight into those who disagreed with him, no gift for tactful accommodation, no capacity to enunciate noble yet realistic goals, and no legitimacy springing from winning a presidential election.

Johnson often flew into a rage when he failed get his way, which made him look as if he was in the wrong even when he was pursuing a defensible course. He intended to readmit the secessionist states to the Union on lenient terms without any insistence on equal rights for the former slaves, but was incapacitated by a bitter dispute with Republican Radicals in Congress, who were intent on keeping the ruined southern Democrats prostrate and used racial equality as a club with which to beat them. In 1867, Congress launched impeachment proceedings against Johnson, who clung to office by a single vote.

He was born to illiterate, poverty-stricken parents in Raleigh, North Carolina, and said in later life: 'I have grappled with the gaunt and haggard monster called hunger.' When he was three, his father died, leaving his mother, a washerwoman, destitute. He never went to school and at the age of ten was apprenticed to a tailor, for whom he was contracted to work until the age of twenty-one, but from whom he ran away after five years. Fearing arrest, he crossed the mountains to Greeneville in eastern Tennessee. Here he was in luck, or made his own luck. The only tailor left town, and at the age of seventeen he nailed above the door of a two-room house a sign reading:

A. JOHNSON

TAILOR

On the day of his arrival a local girl, Eliza McCardle, a shoemaker's daughter, said to her classmates, 'There goes my beau!' Within a year, they were married. She taught him to read, and the business prospered, for he produced good clothes: 'My work never ripped or gave way.' All sixteen previous presidents had started out as soldiers or lawyers, as would most future holders of the office. Johnson was the first and so far only craftsman.

In his tailor's shop he held debates with his friends. He was a forceful speaker who loved to crush an opponent and was always ready to defend the poor against the rich, whom he described in a letter as 'God forsaken and hell deserving, money loving, hypocritical, back bighting [sic], Sunday praying scoundrels'.

There was no hypocrisy about Johnson. He was a populist who believed what he said; a Democrat who like President Andrew Jackson would meet fire with fire. He became an alderman and then mayor of Greeneville, and rose via the Tennessee state legislature to the House of Representatives and the Senate. While governor of Tennessee, he made a suit of clothes as a present for the governor of Kentucky, who was a blacksmith by trade and in return made him a set of fire irons.

Johnson's independent spirit was brought to nationwide attention in 1861 when he was the only one of the twenty-two senators from the secessionist states to side with the Union. This defiance was dangerous. While returning to Tennessee after Lincoln's inauguration he was dragged from a train and nearly lynched. He refused to be intimidated and 'appealed with burning words for the preservation of the Union', but his home state ignored him and in June 1861 voted to join the Confederacy. The following year, when parts of Tennessee had been recaptured, Lincoln made him the state's military governor.

Lincoln and the Republicans were by no means confident of winning the 1864 presidential election. They set out to improve their chances by renaming themselves the National Union Party, and making Johnson the vice-presidential candidate. The war then turned in the North's favour, Lincoln won with 55 per cent of the vote, and by the time his second term began, in March 1865, hostilities had almost ceased.

On the day of the inauguration, Johnson was ill, but was persuaded by Lincoln to attend and decided to fortify himself with some whisky. In a slurred voice he declared: 'I'm a-going for to tell you – here today, yes, I'm a-going for to tell you all, that I'm a plebeian! I glory in it, I am a plebeian! The people – yes, the people of the United States have made me what I am . . .' This might do as a stump speech in Tennessee, but delivered in the Senate Chamber in Washington, before he was sworn in as vice president, it was an embarrassment, and his enemies called him a drunken tailor, a label which despite remaining generally sober, he never shook off.

On the night of 14 April 1865 there came a great hammering on the door of Johnson's room at the Kirkwood House hotel in Washington. Lincoln had been shot. Johnson went to Lincoln's bedside, but left again after half an hour because Mrs Lincoln was upset by his presence. At 7.30 in the morning church bells began to toll. Lincoln was dead, and soon after ten Johnson was sworn in as the seventeenth president.

Some northern power brokers believed Lincoln's death was a blessing in disguise, for they feared he was going to be too soft on the South. Johnson, by contrast, had spoken of the need to treat the defeated enemy with the utmost severity. But his tune soon changed. For although he loathed the old southern ruling class, he saw that the South as a whole had been ruined by the war, and that it would be wrong to impose a Carthaginian peace. He therefore set out to get the southern states readmitted to the Union provided they accepted the abolition of slavery and took an oath of allegiance to the Union. Under these relatively easy conditions, they were allowed to elect members to the new Congress, which did not sit until December 1865.

Congress refused to accept those members. It accused the South of failing to enact full equality for former slaves, which was true. But this accusation became an excuse for the northern Radicals – as the hard-line Republicans led by Congressman Thaddeus Stevens were known – to keep the South powerless. They imposed military government on the Confederacy and far more rigorous conditions for readmission to Congress.

Johnson reacted badly to this defiance. He tried to rouse public opinion in his favour by undertaking a tour of the country, but got so angry with hecklers that he was the one who ended up sounding unreasonable and out of touch. The Radicals pressed home their seizure of power by winning the congressional elections of 1866 and passing the Tenure of Office Act, under which the president could not dismiss Cabinet members without the agreement of the Senate. Johnson declared this unconstitutional (many years later, the Supreme Court got round to agreeing with him) and sacked the Secretary of War, Edwin Stanton, who responded by barricading himself in his office.

Many northerners were appalled by Johnson's failure to protect the former slaves, known as freedmen, from attack by gangs of vigilantes. According to Congressman William Kelley of Pennsylvania, 'The sheeted ghosts of the two thousand murdered negroes in Texas, cry . . . for the punishment of Andrew Johnson.' Congress launched impeachment proceedings against Johnson, which failed by a single vote in the Senate to reach the two-thirds majority needed for a conviction. Although Johnson stayed in office, his authority was shot to pieces.

There is no doubt that he had made a complete hash of being president. His refusal to compromise with anyone who defied him rendered him unfit for an office in which it is necessary to build coalitions. In that respect he deserves his reputation as one of the worst presidents. But the policy for the South pursued by Congress after the Civil War was worse than what Johnson wanted to do. Carpetbaggers – northerners intent on making a quick buck – hastened south and enriched themselves with shameless rapacity from the public purse while going through the motions of implementing Reconstruction. So did the scallawags, southern white Americans who collaborated with the new regime.

The waste of public money was grotesque, corruption was rife, and the former slaves often ended up in a more pitiable condition than before the Civil War. So too did the poor, whose interests Johnson had always tried to defend. The Ku Klux Klan was founded as a response to Reconstruction, and attempted by a campaign of murder and intimidation to defeat the carpetbaggers, keep down the former slaves and reassert white supremacy.

Although Johnson went home to Greeneville humiliated, he did not retreat into silence. He instead managed at his third attempt, in 1874, to gain election to the Senate, the only former president ever to do so. When he entered the Chamber he found his desk covered in flowers and was greeted, after a moment of embarrassed silence, with a standing ovation. Four months later he died of a stroke.

ULYSSES S. GRANT

Lived 1822–85; president 1869–1877

U lysses S. Grant was the most successful American general since George Washington, but a president so blind to his subordinates' deficiencies that he stayed obstinately loyal to fraudsters. The enduring popularity he won on the battlefields of the Civil War, and his evident personal decency, gave him an irresistible claim to the White House. But there were, unfortunately, two Grants: the man of action, brave, tenacious and resourceful under fire, and the passive, confused, well-meaning civilian, too trusting to understand politics, hopeless in any question to do with money, unflappable even when he ought to be perturbed. He was magnificent in war and out of his depth in peace.

Hiram Ulysses Grant was born in a one-room house at Point Pleasant, on the Ohio River. As a boy he displayed a remarkable gift for breaking in horses. His father, a loud-mouthed tanner, was ambitious for him, and got him a place to train as an army officer at West Point, on the Hudson River. The provincial youth did not want to go, dreaded being teased for having initials which spelled 'hug', but found that owing to an error by the congress-man who nominated him, he had instead been enrolled at the college as Ulysses S. Grant, the name by which he would be known for the rest of his life. His fellow cadets nicknamed him Uncle Sam, or Sam for short.

He was a reticent young man and did not distinguish himself at West Point except by being the best horseman, able to clear jumps a foot higher than anyone else. But he completed the four-year course and saw much action as a lieutenant in the Mexican War of 1846–48, which he considered an immoral conflict, but where his comrades noted, as one of them put it, that 'nothing ever rattled him'. During this conflict he became acquainted with most of the officers who would become famous fifteen years later in the Civil War, including his greatest adversary, Robert E. Lee, who was an exemplary soldier, but of whom Grant, wrote in his memoirs: 'I . . . knew he was mortal; and it was just as well that I felt this.'

Peacetime soldiering bored him to tears, and he suffered from a lifelong craving for alcohol, leading to occasional bouts of binge drinking in between long periods of temperance. He mar-ried Julia Dent, the sister of a brother officer, and was devoted to her, but while cut off from her at a remote outpost in California was forced to resign his commission after getting drunk. He tried his hand at farming, on a property he called Hardscrabble, and failed. At the age of thirty-nine he was drinking too much and working for one of his younger brothers in a leather goods store in Galena, Illinois.

The outbreak in 1861 of the Civil War transformed his life. He volunteered immediately, and was given command of an unruly regiment, which he brought to order with almost miraculous rapidity. His men found they were in the hands of a professional who knew what he was doing. Grant was very quickly promoted, and exploited his opportunities with shrewdness and audacity, catching the Confederates off balance by moving against them faster than they thought possible. At Fort Donelson in February 1862, on the Cumberland River in the vital state of Kentucky, he delivered a famous ultimatum to his opponent: 'No terms except an unconditional and immediate surrender can be accepted. I propose to move immediately upon your works.'

Fort Donelson was the first victory won by the Union and prompted wild rejoicing. Grant took about 13,000 prisoners, a record at that time for a battle on the North American continent. He was suddenly famous, and Lincoln saw that unlike his other commanders, who found excuse after excuse to avoid closing with their supposedly too-powerful opponents, Grant would attack again and again until victory was attained. He expressed his strategic intuitions in his usual laconic style: 'Find out where your enemy is. Get at him as soon as you can. Strike him as hard as you can, and keep moving on.'

An officer who served under Grant, and admired him, said: 'He habitually wears an expression as if he had determined to drive his head through a brick wall, and was about to do it.' The human cost of his victories at Shiloh, Vicksburg and the Wilderness was terrible, he was disparaged by some as a mere butcher, but he knew the North could take such casualties and the South, in the end, could not. The struggle had developed into a grinding war of attrition. In March 1864 Lincoln made him commander of all the Union's forces, numbering over a million men. On 9 April 1865, Lee surrendered to him at Appomattox, and Grant told the exhausted Confederates they could take their horses and mules home for, if they could not get in a crop, they faced starvation.

His magnanimity in victory created an indelible impression, and his manners were attractively egalitarian. Lincoln said of him: 'He makes the least fuss of any man I ever knew.' Grant never puffed himself up, but would happily chat to obscure strangers as he walked through the streets of whichever town he happened to be in. He would be smoking a cigar, for a grateful public showered him with gifts, including cigars, horses and even houses.

On 14 April 1865 the Lincolns invited the Grants to go to the theatre with them. The Grants declined, for Mary Lincoln had a few weeks before been rude to Julia Grant. That night Lincoln was shot. The conspirators intended to kill Grant too, but he had left town. Andrew Johnson was sworn in as president and Grant continued as commanding general of the US Army. He ordered the use of federal troops to protect southern African Americans from lynch mobs, which the authorities in states such as Louisiana were doing nothing to control or punish.

Johnson tried to harness Grant's immense popularity and boost his own failing cause by making him secretary of war. The President believed Grant had agreed to accept the post, but Grant maintained he had only agreed to take it for an interim period, at the end of which he stood down. The isolated President felt badly let down. Grant, his reputation still buoyant, was invited in 1868 by the Republicans to run for the presidency. In his letter accepting the nomination, he said, 'Let us have peace.' This became a famous exhortation, for almost everyone wanted the rancour between the victorious North and ruined South to end. Grant declined to say how peace would be actually be achieved, and during the 1868 campaign stayed quietly at home, as was still the usual practice for presidential candidates.

Across the South the Ku Klux Klan mounted a campaign of murder and assault against black and white Republicans, in order to drive them away from the polls. President Johnson made no attempt to stop the intimidation, and the Democrats ran on an explicitly racist platform: 'This is a white man's country. Let white men rule.' Grant won a modest majority, 307,000 votes out of 5.7 million votes cast, over his Democrat opponent, Horatio Seymour. Almost all the 500,000 black voters came out for Grant.

In his inaugural address in March 1869, about which he had consulted no one, the new President declared: 'This office has come to me unsought; I commence its duties untramelled.' He had been elected because he was not a politician, and was, indeed, above politics, a hero in the North for winning the war, in the South for behaving with chivalrous generosity to the defeated Confederates. But now he had to be a politician, and he was not very good at it.

The first of the scandals which marred his presidency was an attempt by two shady financiers, Jay Gould and James Fisk, to corner the market in gold. They got to know Grant through his brother-in-law, entertained him royally in New York and persuaded him to tell the Treasury to stop its regular gold sales. Grant belatedly realised on Black Friday, 24 September 1869, when gold shot up in price, that something had gone badly wrong, and told the Treasury to start selling gold again. In the view of the young Henry Adams, who looked closely into the whole affair, 'The worst scandals of the 18th century were relatively harmless by the side of this, which smirched executive, judiciary, banks, corporate systems, professions, and people, all the great active forces of society, in one dirty cesspool of vulgar corruption.'

The next great scandal was the Crédit Mobilier affair, which came to light just before the presidential election of 1872. It was named after the corporation in Pennsylvania through which the promoters of the Union Pacific Railroad, a project benefiting from handsome federal support, paid themselves to get it built, in one year receiving dividends of 805 per cent. In order to avert inconvenient inquiries, a number of congressmen were encouraged to invest in Crédit Mobilier without having to put up any actual money.

Grant nevertheless won the election of 1872 with an increased majority, for his opponents were inept and nothing seemed to dent his own standing. In the South African American voters supported him overwhelmingly in what has been called the fairest presidential election held there until 1968. Grant certainly wished to protect them. He was, however, unable to avert some terrible massacres, for example at Colfax, Louisiana, where on Easter Sunday 1873 at least 73 and possibly as many as 300 former slaves were slaughtered. The officer sent to restore order found heaps of dead bodies, their brains blown out by being shot in the back of the head, dogs and birds of prey feeding on the corpses: 'We were unable to find the body of a single white man.' No one was punished for these murders.

The financial panic, or crash, of September 1873 inaugurated a depression which lasted for five years. In 1875 the Whiskey Ring, a massive tax fraud centred on St Louis, Missouri, was exposed, but Grant refused to believe that his secretary, Orville Babcock, was up to his neck in the affair. The President insisted on providing a deposition which helped Babcock to escape conviction.

In the southern states the failure of Reconstruction became more and more apparent. When Mississippi erupted in violence against black Republicans in September 1875, Grant declined to send troops to restore order, and the powerless Governor, Adelbert Ames, wrote to his wife that the white supremacists were now in charge: 'Yes, a *revolution* has taken place – by force of arms – and a race are disfranchised – they are to be returned to a condition of serfdom – an era of second slavery.'

The Republicans warned Grant that if he intervened in Mississippi, they would lose the elections in Ohio in October 1875. The North was no longer interested in protecting former slaves or ensuring that they enjoyed equal rights with other citizens. Nor could Grant make the moral case for integration or argue that it would make the nation stronger. Lincoln's house divided was still divided.

In the West Grant wanted to protect the Sioux, and told them so, but could not prevent gold prospectors from flooding into an area they regarded as sacred, the Black Hills in what is now South Dakota. Nor could Grant stop General Custer, whom he recognised as a cruel and self-promoting officer, from undertaking a reckless advance against a far larger force of Indian warriors. In June 1876 Custer and 263 men of the 7th Cavalry were slain at the Little Bighorn River in southern Montana.

Only in foreign affairs did Grant end his presidency with a relatively creditable record. In 1869 he had appointed the admirable Hamilton Fish as secretary of state, and the *Alabama* Claims, for compensation from Britain for supplying warships to the Confederacy, were put to arbitration, which went in favour of the United States.

After the end of his presidency, Grant and his wife Julia embarked on a two-year tour of the world during which they were received as honoured guests by everyone from Queen Victoria to the Emperor of Japan. He surprised a young Englishwoman by telling her, 'Venice would be a fine city if it were only drained.' Only in India, while being entertained by the Viceroy, Lord Lytton, was he reported to have got disgustingly drunk.

On returning home, Grant worried how he was going to support himself and his wife, for his gift had always been for losing money. He entered into a partnership in New York with a young financier called Frederick Ward who seemed to have the Midas touch. Ward turned out to be a fraudster. Grant lost everything, and was found to be suffering from cancer of the tongue. Worried he would leave Julia penniless, he secured a profitable contract from Mark Twain to write his memoirs, which in the last year of his life, while his agonising disease got worse, he managed to complete. Here is an example of his terse style, describing an incident at the Battle of Shiloh in 1862.

During this second day of the battle I had been moving from right to left and back, to see for myself the progress made. In the early part of the afternoon, while riding with Colonel McPherson and Major Hawkins, then my chief commissary, we got beyond the left of our troops. We were moving along the northern edge of a clearing, very leisurely, toward the river above the landing. There did not appear to be an enemy to our right, until suddenly a battery with musketry opened upon us from the edge of the woods on the other side of the clearing. The shells and balls whistled about our ears very fast for about a minute. I do not think it took us longer than that to get out of range and out of sight. In the sudden start we made, Major Hawkins lost his hat. He did not stop to pick it up. When we arrived at a perfectly safe position we halted to take an account of damages. McPherson's horse was panting as if ready to drop. On examination it was found that a ball had struck him forward of the flank just back of the saddle, and had gone entirely through. In a few minutes the poor beast dropped dead; he had given no sign of injury until we came to a stop. A ball had struck the metal scabbard of my sword, just below the hilt, and broken it nearly off; before the battle was over it had broken off entirely. There were three of us: one had lost a horse, killed; one a hat and one a sword-scabbard. All were thankful that it was no worse.

The book was a bestseller. Grant had given a last proof of his courage, ability and perseverance, and the public subscribed to build him a grand tomb in New York, overlooking the Hudson River. He is one of the most astonishing figures in American history, but he was not a good president.

RUTHERFORD B. HAYES

Lived 1822–93; president 1877–81

Rutherford B. Hayes was a man of ostentatious integrity, which is why in 1876 the Republicans made him their candidate. But he became known to his critics as Rutherfraud Hayes, and by other rude names, when he was declared victor in the most bitterly disputed presidential election in American history, so close and so disfigured by fraud that it took almost four months before the two sides could agree, in a bargain struck at Wormley's Hotel in Washington, who had won. The Republicans kept the presidency and the Democrats got total control of the South.

Hayes proceeded to declare, in his inaugural address, that 'he serves his party best who serves the country best'. He was a patient and courteous man, who intended to cleanse the civil service and raise the tone of public life, but his sententious insistence that he was above politics won him few friends. The Republicans hated him as a turncoat while the Democrats despised him as a fraud.

He was born in Delaware, Ohio. His father, who had moved there from Vermont, died of malaria two months before he was born, but he had a rich uncle who paid for his education, completed at Harvard Law School. Hayes set up as a lawyer in Cincinnati. He met Lucy Webb when she was only fifteen, 'not quite old enough to fall in love with' as he later put it, but married her when she was twenty-one and he was thirty. She was a capable and strong-minded woman, active in every kind of good work, and passionately committed to the abolition of slavery and abstention from alcohol, causes in which he became active.

When the Civil War broke out, he volunteered for the Union army, in which he served with distinction and was several times wounded. In 1864 he was nominated as a Republican candidate for Congress, and gave the correct reply for a soldier: 'I have other business just now. Any man who would leave the army at this time to electioneer for Congress ought to be scalped.' He was nevertheless elected, after which he served two terms as governor of Ohio. In 1875, following a short break from politics, the Republicans persuaded him to run for a third term as governor, and he won a narrow victory, appealing to Protestant voters by fanning anti-Catholic sentiment.

The front-runner for the following year's presidential nomination was Congressman James Blaine, hailed by his ally Robert G. Ingersoll as 'a plumed knight' who 'threw his shining lance full and fair against the brazen forehead of every traitor to his country and every maligner of his fair reputation'. But despite frequent use of his lance, the plumed knight could not shake off the charge that he had been involved in a shady transaction to do with a railroad in Arkansas. The Republicans cast around for a candidate to whom no hint of impropriety attached. They needed someone untouched by the scandals which had disfigured President Grant's eight years in office, and lighted on Hayes, who was almost as much of a dark horse as Polk and Pierce had been. The convention was held in Hayes' home town of Cincinnati, and in the seventh ballot he was nominated.

The Democrats chose Samuel J. Tilden from New York, who won the popular vote by a margin of 264,000 and established what looked like a winning lead in the Electoral College of 184 to 165. But twenty votes – from Louisiana, South Carolina, Florida and Oregon – had yet to be apportioned. The three southern states, where Democrats fought by every means to throw out the Republicans, each submitted two opposing sets of returns, creating the nightmare possibility that two rival presidents were about to be elected, and the country would once more descend into civil war. The dispute was put to a fifteen-strong commission, which voted on partisan lines, and since it contained eight Republicans to seven Democrats, Hayes was awarded all twenty disputed votes and declared the victor.

But how were the Democrats to be persuaded to accept what to them was a manifestly fraudulent result? Hence the conference at Wormley's Hotel, at which it was agreed that Hayes would withdraw the last federal troops from the South. His victory was only declared at four o'clock on the morning of 2 March, fifty-six hours before he was due to be inaugurated. He heard of it later that day while passing by train through Harrisburg on his way to Washington. He kept his side of the bargain, pulling the army out of Louisiana and South Carolina, where the Republican state governments at once collapsed and their governors returned north.

The Democrats had promised Hayes that they would respect

the rights of black voters, but no such thing happened, and as he himself admitted: 'My task was to wipe out the colour line, to abolish sectionalism . . . I am forced to admit the experience was a failure.' The Democrats showed no gratitude for receiving a free hand in the South and continued to argue that the president was an imposter, while the Republicans who had with enormous difficulty got this uninspiring figure elected were furious that he refused to do as they told him. His moral conceit rendered him unattractive to less pious politicians, and he was subjected, as a sympathetic observer put it, 'to a murderous cross-fire'.

Morning prayers were said at the White House, evening hymns were sung and alcohol was prohibited. The impetus for the last measure, deeply unwelcome to those obliged to sit through official dinners, was said to have come from the President's wife, who was nicknamed Lemonade Lucy. The Secretary of State, William M. Evarts, remarked after one banquet: 'It was a brilliant affair; the water flowed like champagne.' There was, however, some political advantage in Lemonade Lucy's stance. Many Republicans supported temperance, and she was presented with a sideboard by the Women's Christian Temperance Union. But Hayes was despised as a henpecked husband, and a White House steward sabotaged the ban by serving punch made from frozen Santa Croix rum concealed within oranges. According to a reporter, 'This phase of the dinner was named by those who enjoyed it "the Life-Saving Station".' After leaving office, the President claimed he had given instructions to flavour the oranges 'rather strongly with the same flavour that is found in Jamaica rum', and had been amused to see how this fooled his guests.

Hayes tried to reform the civil service, so that appointments were made on merit rather than as patronage distributed to cronies and collaborators. His attack on the spoils system, as it had been known since its first flourishing under President Jackson, enraged Senator Roscoe Conkling, an imperious dandy who controlled, in the 1,500 appointments to the New York Custom House, a fount of riches which paid for his political machine. Conkling complained in the Senate: 'When Dr Johnson defined patriotism as the last refuge of a scoundrel, he ignored the enormous possibilities of the word reform.' But public opinion was turning against such blatant corruption, and Hayes managed, despite fierce congressional resistance, to sack Conkling's right-hand man, Chester Arthur, from the post of collector at the Custom House.

Hayes kept his promise to serve only one term, not that anyone wanted him to carry on, and went home to Spiegel Grove, the mansion in Fremont, Ohio he had inherited from his rich uncle, where in 1893 he died.

JAMES A. GARFIELD

Lived 1831–81; president 1881

J ames Garfield was the last president to be born in a log cabin, the second to be assassinated and the fifth, after Polk, Pierce, Lincoln and Hayes, to come through as a dark horse. The 1880 Republican convention, held in Chicago, became deadlocked between the so-called Stalwarts, led by the domineering Roscoe Conkling, who wished to bring back Ulysses S. Grant for a third term, and the Half-Breeds, who were led by and promoted the candidacy of Garfield's friend, the redoubtable James G. Blaine. Garfield himself had no apparent desire to become president, and greeted his victory on the thirty-sixth ballot with the words, 'Get me out of here.'

He was right to be worried, for he was unable to heal the rift between the Stalwarts and the Half-Breeds, and four months after his inauguration he was shot in the waiting room of the Baltimore and Potomac Railroad Station in Washington by a crazed office seeker who supposed this was the way to unite the Republican Party. After lingering for seventy-nine days, Garfield died, a potent symbol of the need for reform of the spoils system.

He had been born in Orange, Ohio, where his parents, who were from New England, had cleared a farm. When he was two, his father was killed fighting a forest fire. Garfield from an early age worked at every kind of manual labour, and at length managed to work his way through Williams College, Massachusetts, and to acquire a good knowledge of Latin and Greek.

He married Lucretia Randolph, whom he had known since childhood and who like him belonged to the Disciples of Christ, a Presbyterian church in which he served as a lay preacher. He took his first steps in Ohio politics, where he campaigned vigorously for Lincoln in 1860, served with success in the Union army and in 1862 was himself elected to the House of Representatives.

Garfield was recognised as an excellent orator, and became a valued lieutenant to Blaine, the plumed knight, who had been on bad terms with Conkling ever since telling him in a debate in 1865: 'The contempt of that large-minded gentleman is so wilting, his haughty disdain, his grandiloquent swell, his majestic, supereminent, overpowering, turkey-gobbler strut has been so crushing to myself and to all the men of the House, that I know it was an act of temerity for me to venture upon a controversy with him.'

The words 'turkey-gobbler strut' were henceforward indissolubly attached to Conkling, and the ground was laid for the showdown between the two men at the convention in 1880. Garfield, told by his home state of Ohio to support another candidate,

John Sherman, spoke so well that Conkling passed him a note, written in the margin of a newspaper: 'I congratulate you on being a dark horse!' And so it turned out. Garfield won and fled the convention, which as a sop to the Stalwarts proceeded to make Conkling's right-hand man Chester Arthur the vice-presidential candidate.

Garfield suffered much embarrassment during the election, for the Democrats accused him of involvement in the Crédit Mobilier scandal, and the figure 329 – the number of dollars he was supposed to have received as a bribe – began appearing all over the place, on doors, fences, sidewalks and so forth. But he held successful meetings on his front porch at Mobile, Ohio, and won the popular vote by the slender margin of 7,018 votes, and the Electoral College by a more comfortable 214 to 155.

John Hay, who as a young man had worked for Lincoln, warned the President Elect that he lacked one thing, 'a slight ossification of the heart'. Garfield was too malleable to be able to impose his authority. He made Blaine secretary of state, hoped to appease Conkling by giving him something too, but accepted Blaine's veto on this plan and filled all the New York offices at his disposal with Blaine's people.

Grant, who had campaigned hard for Garfield, was furious to find his advice about appointments disregarded, and denounced him in the newspapers: 'Garfield is a man without backbone; a man of fine ability, but lacking stamina.' Conkling was incandescent with rage. He and his fellow New York senator resigned their seats, proposing to get themselves re-elected by the state legislature. A desperate battle broke out in Albany, the capital of New York state, between the Stalwarts, including Vice President Arthur, and the Half-Breeds.

While the Stalwarts were losing that fight, a maddened office seeker called Charles J. Guiteau, who had in vain applied to both Garfield and Blaine for the post of consul in Paris, took matters into his own hands. On 2 July 1881 he lay in wait for Garfield, who planned to travel by train to visit his old college in Massachusetts. The President, who was only forty-nine years old, was in holiday mood, and had that morning jumped over his bed in the White House when dared to do so by one of his sons. Guiteau shot him twice at close range from behind and shouted: 'I am a Stalwart! Arthur is now President!'

Garfield was taken to the White House. It seemed at first he might survive the attack. But his doctor, Willard Bliss, a man of the old school who did not believe in the new doctrine of antiseptic surgery, could not find one of the bullets and infected him by searching over and over again for it with unsterilised instruments. The nation followed the daily bulletins with deep concern. Dr Bliss excluded other doctors and professed himself confident. In August the President insisted on being moved from the heat of Washington to a cottage on the New Jersey shore. On 19 September 1881 he died. His assassin was hanged, after a long and lurid trial, in June 1882.

CHESTER A. ARTHUR

Lived 1829–86; president 1881–85

Chester Arthur's presidency was awaited with profound foreboding during the two and a half months it took James Garfield to die. The Vice President was known to be a henchman of Roscoe Conkling, and as recently as 1877 had been sacked by President Hayes from the post of collector of customs in New York after investigators found evidence of corruption. Boss Conkling was a byword for the shameless use of the spoils system, and it seemed reasonable to assume that Chet Arthur was just as bad. Great, therefore, was the astonishment when he turned out to support civil service reform.

Arthur cared about his reputation, and although he was a man of the world, he was also the son of a Baptist minister from Vermont. He broke with Conkling, whose rage breathes through his observation in 1883 to the *Cincinnati Commercial Gazette*: 'I have but one annoyance with the Administration of President Arthur, and that is, in contrast with it, the Administration of Hayes becomes respectable, if not heroic.'

Arthur had just signed into law the Pendleton Civil Service Reform Act, named after one of its sponsors, Senator George H. Pendleton. This provided for promotion by competitive exam rather than according to political affiliation, and although at first it only applied to about one in ten federal employees, spelled the beginning of the end for the funding of political parties from this source.

Although Arthur never stood for elective office, he knew from the inside how politics worked, and had demonstrated formidable abilities as the builder and operator of a party machine. In the 1850s he made his name as an attorney in New York, helped establish the Republicans there, and married Ellen Lewis Herndon, a Virginian with a beautiful singing voice and superior social connections. During the Civil War he was responsible for fitting out 200,000 soldiers from New York, an impressive administrative performance which was regarded as more valuable than anything he might have achieved at the front.

In 1868 he obtained, as a reward for having supported the election of President Grant, the job of running the New York Customs House. New York was the busiest port in the world, and Arthur's income of $50,000 a year was the same as the President's. He and Nell lived an elegant and moneyed life, and had three children, one of whom died young. To Arthur's great sorrow, Nell also died, at the age of forty-two, shortly before his nomination as Garfield's running mate. The triumphs which crowned his career could not be shared with her.

He nevertheless transformed the White House into an elegant and hospitable mansion, which it had not been since the days of President Buchanan. Arthur removed twenty-four wagonloads of relics which had accumulated there over the years, including the sideboard presented to 'Lemonade Lucy' Hayes by the Women's Christian Temperance Union, which ended up in a Washington tavern. The house was redecorated from top to bottom by Louis Comfort Tiffany, the fashionable New York designer, and there was now no danger of enforced sobriety at official dinners. Arthur was a portly, dignified, well-dressed man, with a tremendous pair of sidewhiskers and a fondness for good company, good food and good drink. He recruited his sister, Mary McElroy, as hostess, and his guests hailed him as one of the best fellows they had ever met.

Arthur failed, however, to establish much of a connection with the wider American public, and the Republican power brokers, still upset by his assault on the spoils system, refused to let him run for a second term. The New York Times said his presidency 'has unquestionably been more satisfactory than was expected', but he was worn out with good living, died of kidney disease soon after leaving office, and is today a forgotten figure.

GROVER CLEVELAND

Lived 1837–1908; president 1885–89 and 1893–97

Grover Cleveland rose from obscurity to the White House at amazing speed, and became the only president to serve non-consecutive terms. Joseph Pulitzer's *New York World* listed four reasons for supporting him in the election of 1884: '1. He is an honest man. 2. He is an honest man. 3. He is an honest man. 4. He is an honest man.' In the early 1880s Cleveland gained a reputation as mayor of Buffalo for his willingness to veto corrupt spending proposals, and this carried him within two years to the highest office, where this fat, stolid, unyielding figure behaved in much the same way.

Stephen Grover Cleveland was born in New Jersey, one of nine children of a Presbyterian minister, and was brought up in the western part of New York state. When he was sixteen his father died and he had to leave school. He simplified his name to Grover Cleveland and supported himself as a clerk in a village store and in other humdrum ways until he qualified as a lawyer in Buffalo, on the eastern shore of Lake Erie. By hard work he built a solid but not spectacular legal career.

In the early 1870s he served as sheriff of Erie County, in which role he carried out two public executions, refusing to delegate this disagreeable task to one of his subordinates. Cleveland pushed the lever which opened the trapdoor through which the condemned man fell to be hanged. Here was an early sign of his toughness, though it is recorded that he was 'a sick man for several days' thereafter. He is the only president to have served as public executioner, and his political opponents later attacked him as 'the hangman of Buffalo', a record which did him no harm with the voters.

Two years later he was elected mayor of Buffalo, and sprang to wider attention by vetoing crooked appropriations made by the city council. This was such remarkable behaviour, and voters were so sick of corruption, that the Democrats made him their candidate for the governorship of New York, where he swept to victory and began cleansing the Augean stables.

For the presidential contest of 1884, the Republicans nominated James Blaine, a brilliant figure tainted by shady dealings. A Republican faction called the Mugwumps said they would prefer an honest Democrat to Blaine. Cleveland, whose only claim to fame was his honesty, was nominated against the protests of the Tammany Hall Democrats, who feared, quite correctly, that if he won they would be unable to control him. He campaigned on the admirable slogan, devised for him by a member of his staff, 'Public office is a public trust.'

But the election of 1884 was vicious. The Blaine campaign cast around for some way to besmirch the supposedly spotless Cleveland, and found it when the *Buffalo Evening Telegraph* published, under the headline A TERRIBLE TALE: A DARK CHAPTER IN A PUBLIC MAN'S HISTORY, the 'pitiful story' of how Cleveland as a young man had seduced an attractive and virtuous widow, Maria Halpin, had fathered a son by her, and had then committed her to an asylum and paid for the child to be adopted.

Cleveland's appalled handlers asked him what to do. He told them: 'Above all, tell the truth.' The story, though embroidered, was essentially true, and he did not deny it. The Republicans taunted Cleveland by chanting, 'Ma! Ma! Where's my pa?' Mark Twain, however, who had joined the Mugwumps, wrote to a friend ridiculing the story: 'To see grown men, apparently in their right mind, seriously arguing against a bachelor's fitness for President because he has had private intercourse with a consenting widow!'

Blaine had serious difficulties of his own. A letter came to light in which eight years before he had asked a railroad attorney, as 'a favour I shall never forget', to 'stop the mouths of slanderers' by signing a draft statement declaring Blaine's innocence. The missive ended: 'Burn this letter!' This instruction the recipient had failed to carry out, and the Democrats soon had their own chant:

> Burn this letter!
> Burn this letter!
> Burn, burn, oh, burn this letter!
>
> Blaine! Blaine!
> The Continental liar

From the State of Maine!
Burn this letter!

A few days before the election, Blaine met a delegation of Protestant ministers in New York, one of whom declared that he was certainly not going to support the Democrats, whom he denounced as the party of 'rum, Romanism and rebellion'. The Democrats circulated this attack in New York City, where it probably cost Blaine the election by alienating the Irish Catholic vote. Cleveland proceeded to carry New York, and with it the country, by under a thousand votes. His supporters celebrated his victory with their own version of 'Ma! Ma! Where's my pa?' – 'Gone to the White House. Ha, ha, ha.' He was the only Democrat to occupy the White House between James Buchanan, just before the Civil War, and Woodrow Wilson, on the eve of the First World War.

Cleveland lived up to his reputation by vetoing an enormous number of bills, more than all his predecessors combined, including many which conferred pensions on pretended veterans and other undeserving recipients. He stood out against the spoils system, rebuking one supplicant with: 'Well, do you want me to appoint another horse thief for you?' Cleveland was a man of immense industry, who worked late into the night. He was so bad at delegating that during his first term he answered the White House telephone himself. It was said of him he would rather do something badly for himself than have somebody else do it well. For although Cleveland was unimaginative, he was his own man, and did what he thought was right rather than what other people told him to do.

He was only forty-seven when he became president, the first bachelor since Buchanan, and it was generally assumed that he would in due course get married. During his first month at the White House, he had Emma Folson, widow of his old law partner, to stay, and it was supposed, even by her, that she was going to become first lady, for he had always shown an admirable solicitude for her welfare. But at the age of forty-nine Cleveland married her twenty-one-year-old daughter Frances, whom he had known since she was born. The press and public were enormously excited by the marriage, which was celebrated in a modest ceremony held at the White House, with only a few close family friends, the Cabinet and the US Marine Band conducted by John Philip Sousa.

Infuriated by the intrusion of reporters into their honeymoon, held in Maryland, Cleveland accused the press of 'doing their utmost to make American journalism contemptible in the estimation of people of good breeding everywhere'. During the 1888 election he found himself accused of beating his wife, a slander which was hard to dispel, even though Frances issued a statement denying the story and wishing 'the women of our Country no greater blessing than that their homes and lives may be as happy, and their husbands may be as kind, considerate and affectionate as mine'. They had a happy marriage, with five children to show for it.

Cleveland would have won re-election had he not decided to push through a reduction in the tariffs which protected American industry against foreign competition, and which he said were piling up surplus money in the Treasury. As it was, he lost to an uninspiring opponent, Benjamin Harrison, but Frances told a member of the White House staff to take good care of the furniture and the ornaments: 'I want to find everything just as it is now, when we come back again.'

They duly returned in 1893, after Cleveland won a convincing victory over Harrison. The Populists, who spoke up for suffering farmers and industrial workers, achieved a strong third place. Cleveland regarded the Populists as thoroughly irresponsible, and defended the gold standard against their demand for a softer, silver-based currency. His campaign song went: 'Grover! Grover!

four more years of Grover! / Out they go, in we go; then we'll be in clover.'

They were not in clover. Two months after Cleveland was inaugurated for the second time, there was a panic, over 500 banks failed, railroads went bankrupt and millions of people were thrown out of work. At the same time Cleveland discovered he was suffering from cancer of the jaw. He thought this information would worsen the panic, so had most of his jaw removed in great secrecy on a yacht steaming slowly up the East River off New York. The President was strapped into a chair placed against the mast, and given nitrous oxide followed by ether. The public were told he was suffering from toothache, a rumour in the press of what had occurred was dismissed, the operation was a success and he lived for another fifteen years. Accurate details of his treatment only started to emerge from his doctors in 1917.

Cleveland's fortitude was not in doubt, but was an inadequate basis for dealing with the economic crisis, and before long he was deeply unpopular, which he remained to the end of his presidency. The Democrats were hopelessly divided on the tariff issue, and this inhibited him from coming down on one side or the other. He sent in federal troops to break a railroad strike, which intensified the suspicion that he was on the side of the haves rather than the have-nots. He upheld the gold standard, but had to call on the help of such kings of finance as J. P. Morgan. In foreign policy he remained resolutely non-interventionist.

At the end of his presidency, he retired to Princeton, New Jersey, where he died in 1908. Some years later his wife married a professor of archaeology. She lived until 1947, and met Dwight D. Eisenhower at a White House lunch given by President Harry S. Truman. On learning she had once lived in Washington, Eisenhower asked her where, to which she replied: 'In the White House.'

BENJAMIN HARRISON

Lived 1833–1901; president 1889–93

Benjamin Harrison, sometimes known as the Centennial President because he was elected a hundred years after George Washington, gave the impression of a small man trying to look big. His icy manner in private conversation was described as 'peculiarly repellent', and he had a handshake 'like a wilted petunia'. But he was untainted by scandal, was an excellent public speaker, and was adopted by the Republicans as their candidate when James Blaine, the darling of the convention, who was visiting Scotland with the steel tycoon

Andrew Carnegie, declined to let his name go forward and cabled: 'Take Harrison.'

The candidate was a Virginia Harrison, and in private proud of it, though in public he maintained 'every man should stand on his own merits'. His great-grandfather, also called Benjamin Harrison, had signed the Declaration of Independence and become governor of Virginia. His grandfather, William Henry Harrison, served for a month as president in 1841. His father, John Scott Harrison, was an Ohio congressman who retired to farm at North Bend and died in 1878, after which his body was stolen and sold to the Ohio Medical College, where one of his sons, John, found it while searching for another body taken by grave robbers. This scandal led to a change in the law, with the market for cadavers undercut by allowing medical schools to make use of the unclaimed bodies of paupers.

Except for his name, the Benjamin Harrison who became president bore no resemblance to his handsome Virginian forebears. He was an undersized man with small eyes and a protruding belly, and reminded people of 'a pig blinking in a cold wind'. He contemplated becoming a Presbyterian minister but opted instead for the law, attended the University of Miami in Ohio, got married at the age of twenty to a fellow student, Carrie Scott, informed her that their lives would be filled with 'quiet usefulness', and set up home with her in a three-room house in Indianapolis. They had two children, and a third who died at birth. During the Civil War Harrison raised a regiment and proved himself an able officer, rising to the rank of brigadier general.

His law practice prospered, and from 1881 he was senator for Indiana, but when he stood for re-election in 1888 he was defeated, becoming in his own words a 'dead duck'. The Republicans restored him to life by picking him as their presidential candidate. During the campaign he spoke each day from a dais erected in the park in front of his house in Indianapolis, for as he prudently observed: 'There is a great risk of meeting a fool at home, but the candidate who travels cannot escape him.'

While the incumbent President, Grover Cleveland, favoured cutting tariffs, Harrison wanted to raise them. His supporters accused Cleveland of selling out to the British and their doctrine of free trade, a charge lent some semblance of veracity by the Murchison Letter, in which the British minister in Washington, Sir Lionel Sackville-West, unwisely advised a Republican posing as a Democrat to vote for Cleveland, as being the more pro-British of the two candidates.

Senator Quay of Pennsylvania, who chaired the Republican National Committee, instructed his colleagues to 'fry the fat out of the protected industries'. These industries, anxious for high tariffs, contributed vast sums of money to the Republicans, and floaters – voters who could be bought – were recruited in correspondingly large numbers. Harrison proceeded to defeat Cleveland in the Electoral College, despite finishing 100,000 behind him in the popular vote. On hearing the news of his victory he alarmed his colleagues by muttering, 'Now, I walk with God.'

When Quay went to Indianapolis to congratulate the President Elect, Harrison told him: 'Providence has given us the victory.' But as Quay later said, 'He ought to know that Providence hadn't a damn thing to do with it.' And Harrison himself complained: 'I could not name my own Cabinet. They had sold out every place to pay the election expenses.' He was unable to control the corruption which pervaded the administration, or to counter the claim of the new Populist Party that in the 'prolific womb of governmental incompetence, we breed two great classes – tramps and millionaires'.

Harrison kept his promise to raise tariffs, but this in turn raised prices, which was unpopular, and in 1890 the Republicans lost control of the House of Representatives. His manner remained cold and off-putting. Visitors to the White House were warned he was unlikely to offer them a chair. But in uneasy collaboration with the popular and independent-minded Blaine, who had become secretary of state, Harrison settled various ticklish foreign disputes, and set in train the building of a modern navy and the acquisition of Hawaii. He also began the work, which Theodore Roosevelt was to continue on a grander scale, of protecting some of America's most famous landscapes from development by turning them into national parks.

His wife, Carrie, served as the first president of the Daughters of the American Revolution, set up in the centenary year to help preserve the nation's history. She renovated the White House, but fell ill in the winter of 1891 and died of tuberculosis at the end of October 1892, a few days before the presidential election. Harrison refused to leave her side in order to campaign. Cleveland likewise refused to campaign, but won a convincing victory. In 1896 Harrison got remarried, to his late wife's niece, which caused a rift with his two grown-up children. At the age of sixty-five he fathered another child, and four years later he died.

WILLIAM MCKINLEY

Lived 1843–1901; president 1897–1901

W illiam McKinley possessed the gentle art of not making enemies. When he turned down a request for a
job, he did so in such a way as to remain on friendly
terms with the disappointed petitioner. His unassailable nice-
ness and instinctive support for protectionism equipped him
to defend the interests of bankers and industrialists fright-
ened by the rise of the Populists. His opponent in the election
of 1896, William Jennings Bryan, one of the most brilliant orators
in American history, voiced the anger of small farmers who

suffered terribly in the depression set off by the Panic of 1893, and who blamed their sufferings on big business and the banks. McKinley never coined an original phrase in his life, but argued with success that only policies promoting business would ensure 'the Full Dinner Pail' for workers.

In 1900 he promised 'Four Years More of the Full Dinner Pail' and won a second term. He had by then led the United States through a short, victorious war with Spain, which he had opposed until the clamour for it overwhelmed him. This cautious, sluggish, vaguely benevolent figure found himself the leader of a power which had arrived on the world stage. But six months into his second term, he became the third president, after Lincoln and Garfield, to be struck down by an assassin.

McKinley was born in Niles, Ohio, the seventh of nine children. His father ran an iron foundry, while his mother, who hoped he would become a Methodist minister, taught him that virtue is rewarded with wealth and vice with poverty. He was eighteen at the start of the Civil War and enlisted as a private in the 23rd Voluntary Ohio Regiment, led by Major Rutherford B. Hayes, another future president. McKinley displayed bravery, ended the war as a major himself, and was henceforth known as Major McKinley.

After qualifying as a lawyer, he set up an office in Canton, Ohio. Here he met and married Ida Saxton, the daughter of a prosperous local banker. They soon had two daughters of their own, but Ida fell ill during the second pregnancy, which ended in a premature birth. The baby died after four months, their elder girl was not long afterwards carried off by typhoid, and Ida became a lifelong invalid, subject to epileptic fits and bouts of depression. The Major, as she called her husband, cared for her with unfailing devotion and would sit with her of an evening in a darkened room, but she was sometimes well enough to appear at his side in public. During her lifetime she crocheted about 4,000 pairs of light-blue bedroom slippers, most of which she gave to charity.

McKinley meanwhile found the time to enter Republican politics. In 1876, the year his fellow Ohioan, Hayes, became president, he was elected to the House of Representatives, where he soon became known as a campaigner for high tariffs. In 1890 the McKinley Tariff was passed, which raised import duties by an average of 48 per cent. The resulting price rises were so unpopular that McKinley lost his congressional seat.

He bounced back by forming an alliance with Mark Hanna, a Republican magnate from Cleveland, Ohio, who detected in the submissive but ambitious McKinley the imposing gaze and genial mediocrity required for a run at the presidency. The first step was to win election in 1891 as governor of Ohio. The following year McKinley made an excellent impression at the Republican convention, out of which he was carried on a chair by his supporters. He was suspected by President Harrison of trying to seize the nomination, but McKinley and Hanna were shrewd enough to start campaigning to control the convention in four years' time.

Hanna built a political machine which extended far beyond Ohio, fuelled with colossal sums of money which he raised from anxious businessmen whose interests McKinley, with his support for tariffs, promised to defend. But the contest in 1896 was transformed when William Jennings Bryan addressed the Democratic convention in Chicago, repudiating those delegates who supported the gold standard:

When you come before us and tell us that we are about to disturb your business interests, we reply that you have disturbed our business interests by your course. We say to you that you have made the definition of a business man too limited in its application. The man who is employed for wages is as much a business man as the employer . . .

The merchant at the crossroads stores is as much a business man as the merchant of New York. The farmer who goes forth in the morning and toils all day – who begins in the spring and toils all summer – and who, by the application of brain and muscle to the natural resources of the country, creates wealth, is as much a business man as the man who goes upon the board of trade and bets upon the price of grain . . .

We come to speak for this broader class of business men. We do not come as aggressors . . . We are fighting in the defence of our homes, our families, and posterity. We have petitioned, and our petitions have been scorned. We have entreated, and our entreaties have been disregarded. We have begged, and they have mocked when our calamity came . . .

You come to us and tell us that the great cities are in favour of the gold standard. We reply that the great cities rest upon our broad and fertile prairies. Burn down your cities and leave our farms and your cities will spring up again as if by magic, but destroy our farms, and the grass will grow in the streets of every city in the country . . .

If they dare to come out into the open field and defend the gold standard as a good thing, we will fight them to the uttermost. Having behind us the producing masses of this nation and the world, the labouring interests, and the toilers everywhere, we will answer their demand for a gold standard by saying to them: You shall not press down upon the brow of labour this crown of thorns. You shall not crucify mankind upon a cross of gold!

Every sentence of this speech was greeted with ecstatic applause. Bryan, who was only thirty-six, had uttered the last great cry of protest by rural America against capitalism. He believed that if silver, of which there was a plentiful supply, was minted into dollars and allowed to circulate in a ratio of sixteen to one against gold, there would be far more money around, and the plight of the farmers would be relieved. 'Free silver' was his cry.

At first Bryan carried all before him with his 'political insurrection', as the London *Times* called it. But although the impoverished farmers of the Midwest and Deep South rallied to his cause, he was less successful in reaching industrial workers, many of whom were threatened by their employers with the sack if he won. And the economy was starting to revive. In the presidential election McKinley, who supported the gold standard, came out 600,000 votes ahead, and Hanna was made, as reward for his services, senator for Ohio.

Sound money was saved, and became a bit less sound thanks to the opening of new gold fields in the Klondike and South Africa. Prosperity returned under McKinley, a president whom it was impossible to hate. His predecessor, Grover Cleveland, who during his second term had become deeply unpopular even with the Democrats, complained that McKinley possessed 'the faculty of evoking charitable judgment and kind treatment'.

In Cuba, a rebellion against Spanish rule was already under way, but McKinley promised in his inaugural address to avoid war, and added soon afterwards that 'there will be no jingo nonsense under my administration'. Pressure for American intervention nevertheless became intense. In New York the *Morning Journal*, recently acquired by William Randolph Hearst, and the *World*, owned by Joseph Pulitzer, competed to see which could strike the most jingoistic note. For a time, McKinley held out against these voices. Theodore Roosevelt, assistant secretary of the navy, was mad-keen for action and described the President to a friend as 'that white-livered cur'.

Spain tried to avert war by offering concessions which would have amounted to Cuban independence or even ceding the island to the United States. But two events forced McKinley to become bellicose. The first was the leaking in February 1898 of a letter from the Spanish minister in Washington to a friend in Havana describing McKinley as 'weak, and a bidder for the admiration of the crowd' – an accurate description published by Hearst under the headline WORST INSULT TO THE UNITED STATES IN ITS HISTORY. Soon afterwards, the US battleship *Maine*, sent to Havana to protect American citizens, blew up while moored in the harbour, with the loss of 260 American servicemen.

The cause of the explosion could have been a Spanish mine, or else, more likely, an accident on board ship. That point has never been definitively settled, but war followed. It was swift, for the American navy blew Spain's elderly ships to smithereens. McKinley was unsure where the Philippines were, but tracked them down on a map, for these were among the Spanish colonial possessions acquired by the United States after Commander Dewey's victory in May 1898 at the Battle of Manila Bay.

Several years were needed to subdue the rebels in the Philippines, for they had no desire to acquire a new master. Rudyard Kipling urged the Americans to 'Take up the White Man's burden' and become an imperial nation, though the picture he drew of that mission was discouraging: 'The blame of those ye better, the hate of those ye guard'. Cuba became nominally independent, but under American control. Hawaii, which had previously been nominally independent, became a territory of the United States.

In 1900 Bryan ran again against McKinley, this time as an anti-imperialist, but lost more heavily than before. Imperialism was popular. McKinley extended the doctrine of manifest destiny, first expounded in 1845 under President Polk, to cover it. Not long after his re-election, McKinley embarked on a tour of the west, the first president ever to go there. In California his wife fell ill and nearly died. The rest of the tour was cancelled, but six months later she was better, and he took her with him to visit the Pan-American Exposition in Buffalo, on the western border of New

York state. A few moments of jerky film, the first of a president, show him and the first lady arriving there.

The following day, McKinley went without her to a public reception at the Temple of Music, ignoring repeated warnings from his secretary, George B. Cortelyou, that this was dangerous. An anarchist called Leon Czolgosz, who was carrying a pistol hidden under a handkerchief, shot the President twice in the chest at point-blank range. Several people started beating the assailant, but McKinley, with his usual solicitude, said: 'Don't hurt him.' He also gave instructions that the news of his injury be broken gently to his wife.

He did not seem to have been mortally wounded, but one of the bullets had gone through his stomach, and could not be found. Infection set in, and a week later he took a turn for the worse and within a day was dead. He was buried in Canton, Ohio, where he is remembered with pride, though in the wider nation he is eclipsed by the more exciting personality of his successor. His wife survived until 1907 and is buried beside him.

He was the last president to have served in the Civil War, and according to John S. Wise, in Recollections of Thirteen Presidents published in 1906, was 'nothing like as unselfish a man as he has the reputation of having been', but 'a very timid, calculating person'. Vachel Lindsay wrote these words about him:

Where is McKinley, that respectable McKinley,
The man without an angle or a tangle,
Who soothed down the city man and soothed down the
    farmer,
The German, the Irish, the Southerner, the Northerner,
Who climbed every greasy pole, and slipped through every
    crack;
Who soothed down the gambling hall, the bar-room, the
    church,

The devil vote, the angel vote, the neutral vote,
The desperately wicked, and their victims on the rack,
The gold vote, the silver vote, the brass vote, the lead vote,
Every vote? . . .

Where is McKinley, Mark Hanna's McKinley,
His slave, his echo, his suit of clothes?
Gone to join the shadows, with the pomps of that time,
And the flame of that summer's prairie rose.

THEODORE ROOSEVELT

Lived 1858–1919; president 1901–09

Theodore Roosevelt is the most ebullient performer in this book and swept aside all obstacles to become, at the age of forty-two, the youngest US president. He was adventurous, energetic and lucky, and never missed an opportunity to place himself at the centre of events, often in a preposterously melodramatic way. He believed so sincerely in the act he put on that he was able to become what he was not. So the weak and fearful boy grew into a strong and courageous man, the son of east coast privilege proved himself as a cowboy, the idealist succeeded as a practical politician, the warrior won the Nobel peace prize and the world-famous hunter lent his name to a cuddly toy.

Republican bosses found him so tiresome as governor of New York they shunted him into the impotent post of vice president, only for him to enter the White House when William McKinley was assassinated. Roosevelt won the election of 1904, but in the exhilaration of victory promised he would not run again in four years' time, a decision he came bitterly to regret. In 1912 he attempted a comeback, but could not recapture the first, fine, careful rapture of his rise to power.

He was born in a brownstone house on East 20th Street in New York, one of the seventh generation of Roosevelts to enter the world on Manhattan Island, their ancestor Claes Martenszen van Rosenvelt having emigrated in 1649 from Holland to New Amsterdam, as the settlement was then known. At the table of his grandfather, a successful merchant, Dutch was still spoken at dinner. Theodore, known first as Teedy and later as Teddy, was a sickly child, plagued by asthma, but read voraciously and developed a lifelong love of natural history. His eyesight was bad, and at the age of twelve it was found he needed spectacles. His education, by tutors, included a spell in Dresden, where the oldest daughter of the house in which he stayed, who taught him German and mathematics, predicted he would one day become a great professor or perhaps even president.

His beloved father, a prosperous businessman and tireless philanthropist, encouraged him to build up his body by means of gymnastic exercises. He was admitted to Harvard where he engaged in a bewildering variety of physical sports, was elected to the exclusive Porcellian Club, wooed the beautiful and well connected Alice Lee in nearby Brookline, and started writing The Naval War of 1812, an authoritative and well-received work published when he was twenty-three, by which time he was married to Alice.

He plunged into New York politics, which gave off such a stench of corruption that most young men of his class avoided them, and was elected in 1881 as a Republican to the State Assembly in Albany. Here he was derided as a fop, but made his name by attacking Jay Gould and that mighty financier's accomplices as 'sharks' and 'swindlers', for taking control of the Manhattan Elevated Railway by manipulating its share price with the help of a corrupt judge: 'They are common thieves . . . they belong to that most dangerous of all classes, the wealthy criminal class.'

Roosevelt amassed the evidence to prove these charges with the help of journalists scandalised by the frauds which had been committed. By daring to condemn abuses which everyone suspected but no Republican considered it his business to eradicate, and by doing so in alliance with the press, he was hailed in the newspapers (except Gould's New York World) and by the public as a hero. This in turn made it hard for the party machine to ignore his claims, much though it wished to do so. He had seen how to harness the power of righteous publicity.

Alice was by now pregnant with their first child, and had moved into the house occupied by his mother and sisters, his father having died a few years before at the age of only forty-six. In February 1884 Roosevelt received in Albany the joyful news that Alice had given birth, followed by a second telegram which told him his wife and mother were both ill. He returned to New York by a train which crept through thick fog. When he reached the house he was told the two women were dying. His mother, who had contracted typhoid, expired in the early morning, and his wife, suffering from a kidney disease obscured by her pregnancy, in the early afternoon. Roosevelt placed a large X in his diary and wrote: 'The light has gone out of my life.'

Like many people who make a great show of openness, there were certain subjects he never touched on. He suppressed all mention of his dead wife, handed over the baby, who was also called Alice, to his sister and quite soon went west, to the Bad-lands in the Dakota Territory, where he began a new life as a cattle rancher. To his friend Henry Cabot Lodge he wrote: 'You would be amused to see me in my broad sombrero hat, fringed and beaded buckskin shirt, horse hide chaparajos or riding trou-sers, and cowhide boots, with braided bridle and silver spurs.'

No child could have been more thrilled by his new cowboy outfit. Roosevelt loved dressing up, getting himself photo-graphed in his finery and dashing off articles and books about his deeds so the world could learn of them, and indeed pay large sums to learn of them. His dress sense provoked mockery in the Badlands, but he soon proved he could stay in the saddle for as many hours as the other cowboys, and courted so many hard-ships and dangers that he won the locals' respect. When the boat at his ranch on the Little Missouri River was stolen by three local malefactors led by Redhead Finnegan, Roosevelt got his two employees to build another boat and they pursued the thieves a hundred miles downriver through bitter weather, captured them, and escorted them forty-five miles to the nearest sheriff, though it would have been more authentically western to shoot them dead. This adventure produced, as Roosevelt knew it would, a 7,000-word article for *Century* magazine

On a visit to New York in October 1885 he met Edith Carow, a friend of his childhood to whom he had always been close. Roosevelt felt he should remain faithful beyond the grave to Alice, but could not resist Edith, nor she him. The following month, they got engaged in secret. In December 1886, after Roosevelt had suffered a heavy defeat in New York's mayoral elec-tion, he and Edith had a quiet wedding at a fashionable church on the other side of the Atlantic, St George's, Hanover Square, in London. He was twenty-eight, she twenty-five.

They were to have five children, and Edith insisted on treating Roosevelt's daughter Alice as hers too. Alice, who was three when she was uprooted from the devoted care of her aunt, later said of her father, 'he never ever mentioned my mother to me, which was absolutely wrong . . . He didn't just never mention her to me, he never mentioned her name, to *anyone* . . . He obviously felt tremendously guilty about remarrying.' Beneath the outward show, Roosevelt was a puritan. He was horrified by any kind of decadence, disgusted by businessmen who piled up enormous fortunes by fleecing the public, and felt as a moral stain as well as a political embarrassment the decline of his handsome brother Elliott into alcoholism, adultery, lunacy and early death.

Theodore and Edith settled at Sagamore Hill, the spacious country house adorned with the stuffed heads of his hunting trophies, which he had built at Oyster Bay, the Long Island settlement where his family spent summer vacations. It seemed he might earn his living as a writer, which Edith, who was of a private and literary disposition, would have liked. But his energy was too abundant, the lure of politics too strong. In 1888 he went out on the stump for Benjamin Harrison, who on becoming president rewarded him with the unglamorous post of civil service commissioner. In that hitherto quiet office, which he held for six years, Roosevelt made a tremendous noise as an enemy of the spoils system, while revelling in the company of distinguished friends in Washington.

He returned to New York as police commissioner in 1895, and enlisted the help of skilled journalists, including Jacob Riis, author of *How the Other Half Lives*, an account of life in the New York ghetto, to report his onslaught against the corruption which permeated the force. Roosevelt took to walking the streets of New York by night in order to surprise officers who were asleep at their posts or had deserted them for all-night oyster bars and restaurants. Even more astonishingly, the new commissioner, himself of abstinent habits, waged a ferocious campaign to enforce the law closing the city's saloons for twenty-four hours from midnight on Saturday.

In 1896, Teddy, as Roosevelt was by now generally known, campaigned for William McKinley, and after that Republican's victory longed to be made assistant secretary of the navy. Lodge and many other friends lobbied hard for him to get it, but McKinley was unsure. He had heard Roosevelt was 'pugnacious'. Roosevelt promised he would be loyal to the administration and stay in Washington working through the heat of summer, which John D. Long, the navy secretary, wished to spend recuperating on the coast of Massachusetts. Long assured McKinley Roosevelt would be fine, and the president relented.

The new assistant secretary started work in April 1897 and kept his head down until June, when he delivered a bellicose speech at the Naval War College in Newport, Rhode Island, in which he began by quoting George Washington's maxim, 'To be prepared for war is the most effectual means to promote peace,' and went on to declare, 'No triumph of peace is quite so great as the supreme triumphs of war.' He used the word 'war' sixty-two times.

The speech made a nationwide impact, and Roosevelt followed it up by working with almost superhuman energy to get the navy ready for war when Long went away for August and September. Even after the *Maine* was blown up at Havana in February 1898, the President strove to keep the peace. 'McKinley has no more backbone than a chocolate éclair,' Roosevelt said, and lobbied with desperate ardour not just to ensure there would be war, but to find a way to take part in it himself.

In June 1898 he sailed for Cuba as lieutenant colonel of the Rough Riders, a volunteer cavalry regiment composed of cowboys with a leavening of New York sportsmen. He wore a wonderful uniform made for him by Brooks Brothers, offered full access to the most gifted of the war correspondents, pushed himself into the thick of the fighting, and two months later returned to America a national hero, having with conspicuous gallantry led the charge on San Juan Hill, and afterwards got his men off Cuba before they died of yellow fever.

The Republicans needed a candidate for governor of New York, and he was the obvious choice. In November 1899, at the age of forty, he was elected. Almost at once, he fell out with Senator Thomas Collier Platt, who ran the Republican machine in New York and accused the new governor of being 'a little loose on the relations of capital and labour, on trusts and combinations', and indeed on 'the right of a man to run his own business in his own way, with due respect of course to the Ten Commandments and the Penal Code'.

Roosevelt retorted that the Republicans had to oppose 'improper corporate influence' or the Populists would have a field day. Boss Platt decided to kick Roosevelt upstairs into the vice presidency. At the Republican convention in Philadelphia in June 1900 Roosevelt was enthusiastically adopted as the President's running mate, over the vehement objections of McKinley's fixer, Senator Mark Hanna: 'Don't you realise that there's only one life between this madman and the presidency?' During the presidential campaign, McKinley stayed at home, as was then the custom, while Roosevelt travelled 21,209 miles and made 673 speeches.

In March 1901 the two of them were inaugurated, and six months later McKinley was assassinated in Buffalo. Roosevelt hastened there, was sworn in as president after ordering that two dozen journalists be admitted to report on the ceremony, and sprang the first surprise of his presidency: he would 'continue unbroken the policy of President McKinley' and keep the Cabinet unchanged. Those who feared 'that damned cowboy', as Hanna called him, would usher in a period of perilous instability felt reassured. But a completely new atmosphere was at once apparent. In place of the torpid McKinley with his invalid wife came a president of abounding vitality with a wife who played the part of hostess and young children who romped through the White

House. He invited Booker T. Washington to dinner, the first time a black American had been entertained in that way at the White House, and an outrage as far as a large number of white Republicans were concerned.

In February 1902, Roosevelt sprang a greater shock. Without warning his Cabinet, he launched an anti-trust action against J. Pierpont Morgan's Northern Securities Company. McKinley would never have dreamed of taking on the mighty banker. Roosevelt knew he would earn respect for his courage, and for showing that monopolists who preyed on the public were not above the law. He was using on the national stage the tactics he had employed twenty years before against Jay Gould. Morgan visited him at the White House and is supposed to have said: 'If we have done anything wrong, send your man to my man and they can fix it up.' Roosevelt rejected the offer of a behind-the-scenes deal, and in March 1904 the Supreme Court found by one vote in the administration's favour.

Here was a president who did not drift with the current, but had a gift for pre-emptive action. He settled a coal strike which threatened to become serious. As a man with a lifelong interest in conservation, who had seen at first hand how native species and habitats were being wiped out, he created national parks which protected 230 million acres of land from logging and mining. In 1904 he set about building the Panama Canal, by supporting the secession of the isthmus from Colombia: 'I . . . started the canal and then left Congress not to debate the canal, but to debate me.' This tremendous feat of engineering – an earlier attempt by the French had ended in failure – was finished in 1914, and kept firmly under American control.

At the election of 1904 Roosevelt won his own mandate, towards which he had been working for the last three years. His critics continued to believe he would take the country to war, but he never did, and instead announced that he would not stand again in four years' time. Here again was a touch of puritan modesty beneath the swagger.

Roosevelt conducted with marvellous astuteness the peace conference at Portsmouth, New Hampshire, which in 1905 ended the war between Russia and Japan. The emperors of Russia, Japan and Germany sent him congratulatory telegrams, and the Swedes awarded him the Nobel peace prize. His touch was not always, however, so happy. Perhaps he was starting to lose it a bit, as powerful leaders do after a time. In the summer of 1906 he grossly misjudged an incident at Brownsville, in Texas, where black troops were falsely accused of running amok. Roosevelt had 167 soldiers dishonourably discharged without trial, and was heavily criticised by Congress and in the press.

Because he could not carry on as president himself, he arranged for his friend and colleague William Taft to carry on in his place. At first amity prevailed, in part because immediately after his presidency Roosevelt undertook an expedition to some of the most impenetrable parts of Africa, where he pursued his passions for big game hunting and natural history. But after receiving a hero's welcome on his return to New York, he could not conceal either from himself or from others his feeling that Taft had abandoned the true faith, and had become the tool of the pro-business Republican machine.

Roosevelt ran for the Republican nomination in 1912, but the system of open primaries was not yet extensive enough for his enormous popularity among the rank and file to sweep him to victory, and the party bosses took their revenge by sticking with Taft. So Roosevelt ran instead for the Progressive Party, telling it at its convention, 'We stand at Armageddon and we battle for the Lord.' It became known as the Bull Moose Party, for he declared, 'I feel as fit as a bull moose.' During the campaign he was shot in the chest, the impact of the bullet lessened by the steel eyeglass case and fifty-page speech through which it passed, and he insisted on speaking for an hour and a half before receiving treatment. He finished ahead of Taft, but split the Republican vote and allowed Woodrow Wilson to win. Roosevelt departed to explore the jungles of Brazil, where he nearly died.

During the First World War, he wanted to go and fight in France. The powers that be in Washington did not permit him to do so. In 1918, his youngest son, Quentin, serving as a pilot on the Western Front, was shot down and killed. Roosevelt himself died in 1919, at the age of sixty.

No president since Lincoln had made so deep an impression on his compatriots or gained such global fame. Roosevelt personified the arrival of the United States as a player on the world stage, with its armed forces at last beginning to reflect its huge national wealth. The great American strategist Alfred Thayer Mahan argued in The Influence of Sea Power Upon History 1660–1783, published in 1890, that command of the sea was decisive in becoming a world power. Roosevelt, whose own early naval studies had led him to the same conclusion, was a devout expansionist. In letters to his close English friend the diplomat Cecil Spring Rice, Roosevelt shared his subtle insights into the motives of other nations. He likewise maintained close friendships with the French and German ambassadors in Washington, and popularised, as a summary of his own policy, a West African proverb: 'Speak softly and carry a big stick.' The White House was, he remarked with relish, 'such a bully pulpit', and Roosevelt is one of the most muscular preachers ever to have occupied it.

He had a genius for borrowing other men's words and lending them new significance. In 1906 he was inspired by a line in John Bunyan's Pilgrim's Progress, 'the man with a muck-rake in his hand', to coin the term 'muck-rakers' for the investigative journalists who uncovered the horrors of the slums, child labour, adulterated food and other scandals. The Pure Food and Drug Act of 1906 was one response.

Not long after he became president, Roosevelt was taken on a five-day bear hunt in Mississippi during which no bear showed up for him to kill. One was therefore tethered to a tree, which he refused to shoot, as he could not commit such an unsporting act. *The Washington Post* carried a cartoon of the scene in which the 235-pound bear became a sweet little cub. Morris and Rose Michtom, Russian Jewish immigrants to New York, were inspired by this drawing to put a bear the size of a doll in the window of their candy shop, sewn together by Rose and labelled 'Teddy's bear'. People wanted to buy it, so they founded the Ideal Novelty and Toy Company to make, by permission, teddy bears, and to this day millions of infants hug their teddies, unconscious of the dynamic statesman whose name is thereby perpetuated.

WILLIAM HOWARD TAFT

Lived 1857–1930; president 1909–13

Illiam Howard Taft is remembered as the fattest president. He was an able, industrious, good-natured lawyer who aspired to be a justice of the Supreme Court, but before he could get there found himself manoeuvred into the White House by a combination of his wife and Theodore Roosevelt. Here he revealed to the world what he himself already knew, namely that he had no feel for politics. He got to the court in the end, becoming when he was appointed chief justice in 1920 the only person ever to hold the highest office in both the executive and judicial branches.

He was born in Cincinnati and like his father, Alphonso Taft, a distinguished lawyer, he went to Yale. In his twenties he met Nellie Herron, who ran a weekly salon devoted to politics and literature. She became, as his wife, his 'merciless but loving critic', well able to tell him when his speeches were dull, which they often were. He wanted to be a judge and took his first steps on the ladder.

In 1900 he was summoned to Washington, where he had already served satisfactorily as solicitor general, and was asked by President McKinley to become head of the Commission for the Philippines. Taft was taken aback, and said: 'I am sorry we have got the Philippines. I don't want them and I think you ought to have someone who is more in sympathy with the situation.' This reluctance pleased McKinley, who wished to avoid being seen as an imperialist. He persuaded Taft it was his duty to accept the post, and promised that if possible he would afterwards appoint him to the Supreme Court. Taft proceeded to make a success of the arduous task of bringing peace to the Philippines, but in 1901 McKinley was assassinated.

Taft was already on friendly terms with the new president, Theodore Roosevelt, who had a high opinion of his abilities and called him 'the most loveable personality I have ever come in contact with'. There was a kind of sweetness about Taft. He was enormously fat, but did not complain when people told jokes about his weight, which reached 350 pounds. On one occasion, in order to convalesce from a serious illness, he made his way to a mountain resort in the Philippines, and cabled his boss, Elihu Root, the secretary of war: 'Stood trip well. Rode horseback 25 miles to 5,000-foot elevation.' Root replied: 'How is the horse?'

Roosevelt persuaded Taft to return to Washington and succeed Root as secretary of war. Great leaders are seldom any good at picking their successors, and Roosevelt decided to pick Taft. He coached him in how to run for the presidency, urged him not to be seen playing golf, and exulted when Taft won a handsome victory over Bryan, who was running for the third and last time for the Democrats. The new president did not exult. He had accepted the presidency as a reluctant duty, and found it a severe trial, especially as Nellie, his beloved wife and adviser, suffered a stroke soon after they entered the White House.

His lack of political experience became apparent. The laborious work of managing Congress, knowing when to flatter self-important senators and when to defy them, was beyond him. He picked a fight about tariffs and lost. Nobody noticed he carried on Roosevelt's trust-busting activities, and achieved more than his predecessor in that field, for Taft was too modest to blow his own trumpet and could not remember the names of the journalists who might have blown it for him. Progressive Republicans no longer felt they had a champion in the White House, and began to dismiss the new president as an Establishment stooge. Taft, with a judge's respect for the Constitution, took a much more limited view of the president's powers than Roosevelt, who had a politician's eye for the audacious measures whose success would become their own justification.

In 1909 Taft went to inspect the construction of the Panama Canal, and four workmen were photographed sitting in the enormous bathtub installed for his use on the cruiser *North Carolina*. The president's girth was the most memorable thing about him, and to this day many Americans believe, without any satisfactory evidence, that the poor man got stuck in the huge bath which had been installed for him at the White House.

Roosevelt was distressed when one of his protégés, Gifford Pinchot, the head of the United States Forest Service, was dismissed by Taft. Progressives took this as another sign that the President was selling them out. In his 'New Nationalism' speech in 1910 Roosevelt advocated federal action to promote greater economic equality, with the rights of man placed above the rights of big business, and 'genuinely progressive' public men running the show. Having tried in vain to remain friends with his predecessor, Taft now dug in his heels and insisted on going for the Republican nomination, which he proceeded to obtain. This pyrrhic victory confirmed him as the uninspiring spokesman for an unpopular machine, and prompted Roosevelt to run against him as a Progressive. They split the Republican vote, and Woodrow Wilson came through. Taft said as he handed over the White House to Wilson: 'I'm glad to be going. This is the lonesomest place in the world.'

He retired to the altogether more congenial post of law professor at Yale. Seven years later, a new president, Warren Harding, made him chief justice of the Supreme Court. Here at last was the role for which Taft's talents suited him, and he continued to play it until a month before his death in 1930.

WOODROW WILSON

Lived 1856–1924; president 1913–21

Woodrow Wilson proved unable to practise what he preached. He proclaimed a liberal vision of a world made safe for democracy by collective security enforced by the League of Nations, but failed to persuade the United States to take part. At Versailles the great hopes reposed in him were disappointed, and the seeds of a new conflict sown.

It is possible no other president would have done any better. But Wilson's faith in his own omniscience, and preference for third-rate courtiers who did not ask how his windy idealism was going to be implemented, made him an innocent abroad when he arrived in January 1919 at the Paris Peace Conference. He had spent thirty years of his life as a university teacher and administrator, in 1912 gained the presidency because Roosevelt split the Republican vote, but soon found his domestic legislative triumphs overshadowed by the First World War and its aftermath. After a disabling stroke, he spent the last eighteen months of his second term as an invalid, his second wife hiding from the world how enfeebled he had become.

He was born at Staunton, Virginia, where his father was the Presbyterian minister. Woodrow developed a mastery of the language of moral uplift, took as his hero the British statesman William Gladstone, wanted after studying at Princeton to enter on a political career, but found it more practical to make his way as a university teacher, lecturing on and writing books about politics. He married Ellen Axson, daughter of a Presbyterian minister, who saw him through recurrent bouts of ill health, sometimes relieved by taking holidays on his own in the English Lake District or Bermuda. They were devoted to each other and had three daughters.

He was a popular lecturer and industrious author, and in 1902 was elected president of Princeton. Here he instituted a sweeping programme of modernisation, which at first went swimmingly, but after a few years created such antagonism among donors and faculty members that he was in danger of being driven out. Wilson had revealed an alarming inability to compromise. But he also caught the eye of the Democrats in the notoriously corrupt state of New Jersey, who made him their candidate for governor.

In 1910 he was elected, and at once demonstrated his independence of party bosses by pushing through anti-corruption measures of which they disapproved. He was encouraged by Colonel Edward M. House, a Texan who had acted as fixer and adviser to four governors of that state, to run for president, and on the forty-fifth ballot he was nominated. From now on, Colonel House (the title was honorary – he had no military experience) was extremely close to Wilson.

Luck favoured the Wilson presidential campaign of 1912, though with Calvinist solemnity he was inclined to think divine providence had singled him out to lead the nation. Roosevelt split the Republicans by running against Taft, and Wilson won with only 41.8 per cent of the vote. During the campaign his opponents tried to spread rumours of an affair in Bermuda with a widow called Mrs Peck to whom he was undoubtedly close and with whom he later admitted, in characteristically vague language, there had been 'a passage of folly and gross impertinence'.

Roosevelt refused to take the story seriously: 'You can't cast a man as a Romeo when he looks and acts so much like an apothecary's clerk.' There was something rather dismal, even funereal, about Wilson, who generally dressed in dark clothes and a top hat. Displays of emotion did not come easily to him, and he never acquired a nickname. Someone once shouted, 'That was a good one, Woody!' at a campaign meeting – we know this because Wilson pointed it out to a journalist – but to his regret, the name did not stick.

He started well as president by getting a remarkable quantity of legislation through Congress, including the first substantial cut in American tariffs since 1846. The banking system was put on the path to eventual stability by setting up the Federal Reserve. But in foreign affairs he never showed a happy touch. He sanctioned repeated military interventions in Mexico, a neighbour about which he knew little. In 1913, a British diplomat said to him: 'When I go back to England, I shall be asked to explain your Mexican policy. Can you tell me what it is?' Wilson replied: 'I am going to teach the South American Republics to elect good men!' One notes the assumption of moral superiority: Wilson is the teacher.

The president's beloved wife died of kidney disease in August 1914. He felt so lonely he expressed a desire to be assassinated. In March 1915 Cary T. Grayson, a junior naval doctor who had become Wilson's personal friend, physician and confidant, arranged for him to meet, as if by chance, a statuesque forty-two-year-old widow called Edith Bolling Galt, who owned a fashionable jewellery store and was known for being the first woman in Washington to drive her own car. The president, who was fifty-eight, was smitten. She returned his advances, and when Wilson left her house, the secret serviceman who was escorting him observed him dancing a jig and singing a popular song: 'Oh, you beautiful doll! / You great big beautiful doll!'

In October 1915 they announced their engagement. At the British embassy a young attaché is supposed to have said, 'When the President proposed to Mrs Galt, she was so surprised she fell out of bed.' They married in December 1915, and Grayson, of whom she approved, was soon afterwards promoted to the rank of rear admiral.

Wilson's presidency was dominated by the First World War, which broke out in August 1914. He was determined if at all possible to keep America out of the war. Edith Wilson did not approve of Colonel House, who had become his chief adviser on European affairs, and a frequent emissary to the allied powers. She described him to her husband as 'not a very strong character', a 'comfort and staff' but 'a weak vessel'. After the sinking of the British liner *Lusitania* by a German submarine in May 1915, with the loss of 1,198 passengers and crew including 128 Americans, House briefly forfeited the president's confidence by suggesting that 'America has come to the parting of the ways, when she must determine whether she stands for civilised or uncivilised warfare.' Wilson, determined to maintain American neutrality, did not wish to hear fighting talk from his chief adviser. He preferred to say, and was much mocked for saying, that America was 'too proud to fight'.

In November 1916 Wilson very narrowly gained re-election by promising to keep America out of the war. In January 1917 the Germans made it difficult for him to keep this pledge by starting unrestricted submarine warfare. This was followed by the outrage of the Zimmerman Telegram, intercepted by the British, who passed it on to Washington, in which the Germans proposed an alliance with Mexico, which would regain its lost territories in Texas, New Mexico and Arizona. In April 1917, by which time he was confident of the support of public opinion, the President declared war on Germany.

From the first, he made it clear he was waging war in order to ensure that the world was 'safe for democracy'. The fall of the Tsar in March 1917 made this an easier line to take. The United States was fighting for peace, and soon it was doing so very effectively. In 1918, its fresh troops, under the command of General Pershing, helped to halt the last great German offensive and joined in the great advance which brought victory. At home the President pandered to patriotic xenophobia by signing the Espionage and Sedition Acts, illiberal measures which he had called for as early as 1915, when he warned in his State of the Union address that there were naturalised American citizens who 'who have poured the poison of disloyalty into the very arteries of our national life'.

Wilson had already declared, with his usual fluency, the principles on which peace was to be made. He issued his Fourteen Points in January 1918, followed in February by his Four Principles and in September by his Five Particulars. In the preamble to the second of these documents, he said the eventual peace treaty should contain 'no annexations, no contributions, no punitive damages'. The Germans hoped he meant this, while the French, led by Georges Clemenceau, were implacably determined to make the Germans pay

In November 1918 the guns fell silent. When Wilson arrived in

Europe the following month, he was greeted as a saviour, and was in a powerful position, for only America could supply the food and money needed to save the European powers from starvation and from the menace of Bolshevism. But how was Wilson to translate his noble ideals into the practical provisions needed in the peace treaties? He persuaded himself that as long as he got the League of Nations, it did not matter too much if the Treaty of Versailles imposed punitive and indeed totally unrealistic reparations on Germany, which was also forced to admit its guilt for starting the war.

But it did matter. For although the Germans had no choice but to sign the treaty, they felt they had been swindled. A century before, at the Congress of Vienna, the victors of Waterloo had realised that only a peace which was in everyone's interests would endure, and had therefore taken pains to treat France fairly. At Versailles that principle was flouted, and Wilson connived in that flouting. He had, as it were, defeated himself. In his propaganda he had encouraged the highest expectations, and now here he was, betraying his ideals by putting his good name to a treaty which wise observers could see would lead to another war.

He made an unfortunate personal impression in Paris. Nobody liked him. Wilson's demeanour was cold, and he had never enjoyed the company of big, independent-minded figures. Roosevelt, the president whose achievements he wished to surpass, had always sought out the best and most stimulating company, and revelled in friendships with some of the best minds from Britain, France and Germany. Wilson spent his time with a few sycophants while posing as an Olympian figure who had descended from the clouds to bestow the blessings of peace and democracy on a shattered continent. Instead, as Colonel House sorrowfully admitted, 'When the President stepped down from his lofty pedestal and wrangled with the representatives of other states upon equal terms, he became as common clay.'

John Maynard Keynes, who attended the conference as official representative of the British Treasury, immediately afterwards published *The Economic Consequences of the Peace*, in which with wonderful clarity, charity and intelligence he explained why Wilson had failed:

> The President was not a hero or a prophet; he was not even a philosopher; but a generously intentioned man, with many of the weaknesses of other human beings, and lacking that dominating intellectual equipment which would have been necessary to cope with the subtle and dangerous spellbinders whom a tremendous clash of forces and personalities had brought to the top as triumphant masters in the swift game of give and take, face to face in council – a game of which he had no experience at all.

Faced with such wily and determined figures as Clemenceau and the British Prime Minister David Lloyd George, Wilson did not stand a chance; was indeed, as Keynes said, 'playing blind man's buff'.

Wilson could not admit even to himself that it had all gone wrong. He returned to Washington determined to get Congress to ratify what he had negotiated, including American membership of the League of Nations, which would uphold the peace. Roosevelt was by now dead, but Roosevelt's great friend, Henry Cabot Lodge, chaired the Senate Committee on Foreign Relations. Lodge riled the president by pouring scorn on his prose: 'As an English production it does not rank high. It might get by at Princeton but certainly not at Harvard.' Many of the objections Lodge had to the substance of the treaty were shared by perceptive Europeans, and if Wilson had approached ratification in a bipartisan spirit, and treated the Republicans with respect, he could probably have talked them round.

He instead reacted with his usual obduracy, and vowed to rouse public opinion on his side, to which end he set out on a tour of the country. In October 1919 he suffered a massive stroke – there had been minor ones earlier in the year – and was brought back to Washington in a desperate state, his left side paralysed.

Edith became his gatekeeper, hiding from the outside world how bad his condition was, issuing presidential instructions in her large, childish handwriting and frightening others into subservience. The Vice President, Thomas Marshall, best known for saying, 'What this country needs is a good five-cent cigar,' was a weak figure who was not prepared to take her on, and Rear Admiral Grayson refused to declare Wilson unfit to govern.

Senator Albert Fall was bold enough to complain in public: 'We have petticoat government! Mrs Wilson is President!' He was brought to the White House to 'see for himself,' and when he said, 'We, Mr President, have all been praying for you,' Wilson replied, 'Which way, Senator?' For Wilson was still capable of remaining alert for a few minutes at a time. His presidency was, however, to all intents and purposes over eighteen months before Warren Harding's inauguration in March 1921. Wilson died in February 1924 in Washington DC. His widow survived until 1961, and took part in the inauguration of John F. Kennedy.

WARREN G. HARDING

Lived 1865–1923; president 1921–23

Warren G. Harding was a malleable, vacuous, self-indulgent, handsome, warm-hearted, significant-sounding man. As he himself said, 'I like to go out into the country and bloviate,' which he defined as 'the art of speaking as long as the occasion demands and saying nothing'. Senator William McAdoo described Harding's speeches as 'an army of phrases moving over the landscape in search of an idea'.

Harry Daugherty, the insolent and unscrupulous leader of the Ohio Gang of Republicans, had spotted the inoffensive

Harding's potential as a compromise presidential candidate, and predicted in February 1920 what would happen at the convention in June: 'At the proper time, after the Republican National Convention meets, some fifteen men, bleary-eyed with the loss of sleep and perspiring profusely with the excessive heat, will sit down in seclusion around a big table. I will be with them and will present the name of Senator Harding to them, and before they get through they will put him over.'

Harding was chosen in the middle of the night by a group of fixers gathered in 'a smoke-filled room' – the expression dates from this convention – and became the most inadequate president of the twentieth century. His death at the age of fifty-seven, just over halfway through his term, spared him the exposure of the rampant corruption which flourished in his administration. But the posthumous blows to his reputation were heavy, and included the publication of the first kiss-and-tell book about a president, by a woman thirty-one years his junior who had a daughter by him.

He was born in rural Ohio, but when he was ten his father, a shiftless individual who had acquired some scanty medical training, moved to practise as a doctor in the small town of Marion. Harding left school at the age of sixteen, worked as a printer and reporter on a local paper, the *Marion Star*, gained control of it, and married Florence King, who was five years older than him and the daughter of the richest man in Marion County. They had no children, but she already had a son by another man with whom she had eloped at the age of nineteen. Harding called her the Duchess, and she proved an able manager of the newspaper.

He entered Republican politics, serving two terms in the Ohio state senate and one as lieutenant governor. When listened to his speeches had a soothing quality, lulling people into the belief that he would take care of everything. It is only when one reads the actual words that their fatuity becomes apparent. In 1912 he was chosen to propose President Taft for the Republican nomination, and claimed in his speech that there there was no difference between the official party line and Theodore Roosevelt's Progressives: 'Progression is not proclamation nor palaver. It is not pretence nor play on prejudice. It is not of personal pronouns, nor of perennial pronouncement. It is not the perturbation of a people passion-wrought, nor a promise proposed.'

Harding found alliteration worked like a charm on his audiences, and also on himself. In 1915 he went to Washington as senator for Ohio, a role in which he made no impression. This was to his advantage, for by 1920 the Republicans were in search of a pliable candidate who could be relied on to support business and had no enemies. In May that year, shortly before the convention, Harding set out his approach in a speech delivered at Boston: 'America's present need is not heroics, but healing; not nostrums, but normalcy; not revolution, but adjustment; not surgery, but serenity; not the dramatic, but the dispassionate; not experiment, but equipoise; not submergence in internationality, but sustainment in triumphant nationality.'

Here was a small-town American who offered, after the horrors of the war years and the failure of the prosy Woodrow Wilson, a return to 'normalcy'. The Republican convention, held in dreadful heat in Chicago, threatened to become deadlocked between three leading candidates, none whom had any prospect of gaining the necessary majority. During the night Republican power brokers met in Colonel George Harvey's room at the Blackstone Hotel to discuss what to do. There was an overwhelming desire to return home as soon as possible, and by the morning Daugherty had got Harding into contention. Like Grant, Hayes, Garfield, Harrison, McKinley and Taft, he had the merit of coming from Ohio, an evenly divided state which the Republicans were anxious to carry.

Harvey is supposed to have summoned Harding and asked him 'whether there is anything that might be brought up against you that would embarrass the party'. Harding said he would need to think this over, and returned ten minutes later to say there was nothing. He had presumably decided his extramarital affairs, including one with a close friend of his wife, would not become known. On the tenth ballot he came through, and the *New York Times* commented on its front page: 'The nomination of Harding, for whose counterpart we must go back to Franklin Pierce if we would seek a President who measures down to his political stature, is the fine and perfect flower of the cowardice and imbecility of the Senatorial cabal that charged itself with the management of the Republican convention.'

Denunciation by the *New York Times* is not always fatal. Harding proceeded to win a landslide victory over the Democrat candidate, James Cox. People wanted tranquility, and believed they had found it in Harding. They did not care that, as H. L. Mencken remarked after the inauguration in a column for the *Baltimore Sun* headed GAMALIELESE (Harding's middle name was Gamaliel), the new president 'writes the worst English I have ever encountered. It reminds me of a string of wet sponges; it reminds me of tattered washing on the line; it reminds me of stale bean soup, of college yells, of dogs barking idiotically through endless nights. It is so bad that a sort of grandeur creeps into it.'

Harding appointed some distinguished Cabinet ministers. The new Treasury Secretary Andrew Mellon, the great banker and art collector, cut public spending by 40 per cent. The new Secretary of State, Charles Evans Hughes, was the moving spirit in convening an arms limitation conference in Washington which established naval parity between the United States and Great Britain, with Japan in third place. Herbert Hoover, put in as commerce secretary, promoted economic efficiency by setting common standards for nuts and bolts. But Harding rewarded his Ohio chum Daugherty by making him attorney general, while Albert Fall, a senator from New Mexico with whom Harding enjoyed playing poker, became secretary of the interior. And below Cabinet level, dubious figures were installed to run various agencies, and were given important roles in the Justice Department, where they began blackmailing transgressors against Prohibition.

Two months after his inauguration, Harding signed an order transferring the navy's oil reserves to the Interior Department, where Fall proceeded to sell the Teapot Dome field in Wyoming and other valuable properties, at knock-down prices without competitive bidding. Fall himself became mysteriously rich, while in various other parts of the administration there were sudden deaths, whether from suicide or other causes it was impossible to say.

Harding felt powerless to stop any of this. He had, after all, been selected because he was weak. He played a lot of poker, and Prohibition, which as a senator he had supported and which took effect at the end of 1920, did not apply in the Harding White House. For most of his presidency he felt unwell. His doctor, Charles Sawyer, recommended to him by his wife, was a homeopathist who refused to accept that the President was suffering from heart trouble, and towards the end diagnosed food poisoning. Harding promoted him to the rank of brigadier general in the Army Medical Corps. Florence also recommended their friend Charles Forbes to run the Veterans' Bureau, where in February 1923 Harding learned that he had been selling off medical supplies at knock-down prices. Forbes fled to Europe and resigned. The following month Fall resigned.

In July 1923 Harding had a painful discussion with Daugherty's personal assistant, Jess Smith, about irregularities which had come to light in the Justice Department, and warned him he was about to be arrested. Smith went home, burned his papers and committed suicide. The following day, Harding and Florence left Washington with a large entourage on what they called the Voyage of Understanding, a nationwide tour by train and boat which took them all the way to Alaska.

Harding was exhausted, short of breath and suffering from high blood pressure, but bloviated to the best of his ability at the many stops made. On the voyage to Alaska he insisted on playing bridge from immediately after breakfast, often until after midnight. Hoover, who found himself obliged to help make up the four, 'developed a distaste for bridge on this journey'. On one occasion Harding invited Hoover to his cabin and asked, 'If you knew of a great scandal in our administration, would you for the good of the country and the party expose it publicly or would you bury it?' Hoover, by his own account, replied: 'Publish it, and at least get credit for integrity on your side.' But when Hoover enquired what Daugherty's role in the scandal was, Harding dried up.

On the return journey, the President came south via Vancouver and Seattle, collapsed in San Francisco and was taken to the Palace Hotel, where a few days later he died of a heart attack, though malicious people claimed Florence had poisoned him. Deep public mourning ensued, for the unfolding scandals in Washington had not yet affected his popularity, and a grand tomb – the last of the grand presidential tombs – was erected in Marion by public subscription for him and Florence, who died a year later.

A young woman from Marion, Nan Britton, who had for several years been Harding's mistress, applied after his death to his family for financial support for the child born to her in 1919, which recent DNA tests have confirmed was Harding's, and which she said was conceived in his Senate office. When no money was forthcoming, Britton wrote a tawdry but unintentionally comic memoir, The President's Daughter, published in 1927. According to her, Harding 'admitted that nowhere except in French had he ever read anything comparable to the love-letters we used to write to each other'. But as president, he felt himself 'in jail', had difficulty finding a private spot for their assignations, and was reduced to using a closet in the White House, where 'in the darkness of a space not more than five feet square the president of the United States and his adoring sweetheart made love'.

When Dorothy Parker reviewed the book, she said the trouble with it was that it was true. Otherwise she could have hailed 'the discovery of the great American satire, the shrewd and savage critique of Middle-Western love'.

The Teapot Dome scandal swelled into the most notorious in American politics before Watergate, and Fall, who after a long congressional investigation was found to have received $400,000 in bribes, in 1929 became the first Cabinet minister to be sent to prison. Daugherty was tried on corruption charges, but the jury failed to reach a verdict. Harding's reputation has never recovered. Theodore Roosevelt's daughter, Alice Roosevelt Longworth, bitchily remarked of him in her memoirs, published in 1933, 'Harding was not a bad man. He was just a slob.'

CALVIN COOLIDGE

Lived 1872–1933; president 1923–29

C alvin Coolidge was a living link with an older, simpler, thriftier, more upright and less demonstrative America. He was known as Silent Cal, and stories accumulated about his frugal use of words. A woman at a White House party told him she had made a bet that she could get him to say more than two words. 'You lose,' he replied.

He was a true believer in small government, cut spending and taxes, and presided with moral seriousness over the roaring twenties, a period of headlong economic growth whose manifestations included the motor car and the Charleston. The limitations of his outlook, which included a complete lack of interest in foreign travel – he honeymooned in Canada in 1905 and attended a conference in Havana in 1928, but that was it – were expressed in his declaration, 'The chief business of the American people is business.'

He was born in the remote hamlet of Plymouth Notch, Vermont, where his family had farmed for four generations. His father, Colonel John Calvin Coolidge of the militia, was a prominent local figure engaged in many different activities, including the construction in 1890 of a cheese factory which is still operating. He said of his son, 'It always seemed to me that Calvin could get more sap out of a maple tree than any of the other boys around here.' In later life, Calvin told this story of when he was eight years old:

> I remember asking Father one day for a cent to buy a stick of hoarhound candy. He refused my request and explained gravely that it looked as if the Democrats were going to carry the national election that fall and that it behooved prudent people to be exceedingly careful. But when Garfield had won and father was assured of the safety of the country for another four years, he gave me the cent out of the jar where he and mother put any spare coins.

His mother died when he was twelve – he carried her portrait with him for the rest of his life – and his only sibling, a younger sister, when he was eighteen. Calvin went to a local school followed by Amherst College, in the town of Northampton, Massachusetts, where no one spotted him as a future president. He remained in Northampton after graduation, qualified as a lawyer and set up his own practice.

One day Grace Goodhue, who had graduated from the University of Vermont and taught at a school for the deaf, spotted through an open window a man shaving while wearing long underwear and a hat. When she met Coolidge, he explained the hat was to stop a lock of hair falling over his face. They married, and rented for thirty-three dollars a month one half of a house which they kept as their residence in Northampton until 1930, a year after he stopped being president, when they found themselves obliged by increasing numbers of tourists to move.

He was elected to the town council, and in time to state positions, culminating in the governorship of Massachusetts in 1919–20. In a volume of speeches entitled *Have Faith in Massachusetts* he demonstrated his gift for coining hard but homely axioms: 'We need more of the office desk and less of the show window in politics.' 'The people who elect a man to get what he can for his district, will probably find that they have elected a man who will get what he can for himself.' But it was a third axiom, coined during the Boston police strike in 1919, which brought Coolidge to national attention: 'There is no right to strike against the public safety by anybody, anywhere, at any time.'

Governor Coolidge broke the strike by calling out the state militia and firing the strikers. The following year, delegates to the Republican convention, disgusted by the way Harding, a nonentity, had been foisted on them as presidential candidate by the party's power brokers, rebelled and voted en masse for Coolidge as his running mate.

In August 1923, Coolidge was at his father's farm in the Green Mountains of Vermont, where he was accustomed during his summer vacation to help get in the hay. The news of Harding's death in San Francisco was brought to him in the middle of the night by messengers bearing telegrams. The farmhouse had neither telephone nor electricity, but Coolidge was told he ought to be sworn in immediately. At 2.47 in the morning his father, who was a notary public, administered the oath of office by the light of a kerosene lamp, with Calvin placing his hand on the family Bible and finishing with the traditional words 'So help me God.' The new president then returned to bed.

In Washington, he stood by members of Harding's team unless and until their complicity in the Teapot Dome scandal was proven, whereupon he sacked them. Coolidge was by temperament well suited to carry on his predecessor's policy of strict economy in public spending and low taxes. He won the Republican nomination in 1924 with ease, while the Democrats made a complete mess of their convention, only managing to select their candidate on the 103rd ballot.

In the summer of 1924, the younger of the Coolidges' two sons, also called Calvin, got a blister while playing tennis on the White House court, did not tell anyone until he had developed blood poisoning, and died a few days later despite the best medical attention. Coolidge won that autumn's presidential election by an overwhelming margin, but wrote in his *Autobiography*, published in 1929: 'The ways of Providence are often beyond our understanding . . . I do not know why such a price was exacted for occupying the White House.'

In foreign policy, Charles G. Dawes devised a more realistic schedule for German reparations, and Frank B. Kellogg negotiated the Kellogg–Briand pact of 1928, which was supposed to preserve world peace. Lady Astor, a British Conservative MP of American extraction, denounced Coolidge in the House of Commons as a 'narrow-minded little beast' who was uninterested in European affairs. At home, he fed the boom by cutting taxes, refused to extend federal support to the nation's farmers, many of whom were in desperate straits, and remained faithful to the dictum he had promulgated in his inaugural address in 1925: 'Economy is idealism in its most practical form.'

The most surprising thing Coolidge did was refuse to run again in 1928. He did not attempt to explain himself. He may have suspected that the economic boom would at some point be followed by an enormous bust, or it may be that since the death of his son, and of his father in 1926, he simply did not enjoy being president.

Hoover wrote that Coolidge in private was quite different to his public image:

> With his associates there was little of taciturnity . . . He had a fund of New England stories and a fine, dry wit. After my election in 1928, he undertook to give me some fatherly advice as to how to run the White House. He said: 'You have to stand every day three or four hours of visitors. Nine-tenths of them want something they ought not to have. If you keep dead-still they will run down in three or four minutes. If you even cough or smile they will start up all over again.'

Coolidge retired to Northampton, where in 1933 he died of a heart attack, still only sixty years old. Ronald Reagan said of him: 'You hear a lot of jokes every once in a while about "Silent Cal" Coolidge. The joke is on the people who make the jokes. He cut taxes four times. We had probably the greatest growth and prosperity that we've ever known. I have taken heed of that because if he did that by doing nothing, maybe that's the answer.'

HERBERT HOOVER

Lived 1874–1964; president 1929–33

Herbert Hoover saved Europe from famine at the end of the First World War, but could not save Americans from the Great Depression. His genius as an administrator offered no answer to the Wall Street Crash of 29 October 1929, which exposed his limitations as a politician. He worked like a Trojan but could not carry people with him, and long before the end of his four-year term his high reputation lay in ruins. He considered his fall from favour unjust, and later declared: 'It was the bitter experience of all public men from George Washington down that democracies are at least contemporarily fickle and heartless.'

He was born into a Quaker community in West Branch, Iowa. His father, a blacksmith who sold farm tools, died when he was six, and his mother two years later. He went to live with her brother, a doctor, in Oregon, and became one of the first freshmen at Stanford University in Palo Alto, California, where he met his future wife, Lou Henry, who shared his love of geology. Hoover qualified as a mining engineer and displayed a remarkable gift for identifying and developing gold mines in Australia, China (where the Hoovers survived the Boxer Rebellion of 1900), Russia and South Africa, and silver mines in Burma, where he took a substantial stake himself.

The outbreak of the First World War found him in London, a wealthy man running his own mine consulting business. He drew on his own funds to make loans to stranded Americans, arranged the evacuation of 120,000 of his compatriots from Europe and organised food supplies for German-occupied Belgium. In 1917 President Wilson appointed him head of the Food Administration, charged with husbanding US food supplies without the introduction of rationing. The term 'to Hooverise' was coined, meaning voluntarily to conserve food. At the end of the war he organised with efficiency and good feeling the distribution of American food to parts of Europe in danger of starvation.

He was disgusted by the Treaty of Versailles, blamed the cynical Europeans for subverting American idealism, and intended to settle in California, within sight of Stanford, resume his business career and spend more time with his wife and their two sons. But he was by now so celebrated that the *New York Times* included him in a list of the ten most important living Americans, an accolade he enjoyed recording in his memoirs. When President Harding offered him the post of commerce secretary, Hoover accepted. He disapproved of Harding's poker – 'it irked me to see it in the White House' – but was full of schemes for making the American economy work better. Calvin Coolidge kept him on, but referred to him as the 'Wonder Boy', and on leaving office said of Hoover: 'That man has offered me unsolicited advice for six years, all of it bad.'

Hoover was, however, a very considerable administrator. In 1927 he organised help for the victims of the Great Mississippi Flood, and the following year, when Coolidge decided not to run again, he was adopted as the Republican candidate. He campaigned as 'the great engineer', a man with the practical ability to solve just about any problem, and declared, in a speech in New York City on 22 October 1928, that the choice lay between 'the American system of rugged individualism', represented by himself, and European 'doctrines of paternalism and state socialism', which 'would cramp and cripple the mental and spiritual energies of our people'. He ended with the assertion: 'We are nearer today to the ideal of the abolition of poverty and fear from the lives of men and women than ever before in any land.'

The Democrats' candidate, Al Smith, wanted 'fundamental changes' in Prohibition. He was the first Roman Catholic to run for the presidency, and faced a wave of anti-Catholic propaganda. Hoover stood up for Prohibition as 'a great social and economic experiment, noble in motive and far-reaching in purpose', rode the tide of national prosperity and won an overwhelming victory.

He did not, however, have long to enjoy it. Agriculture, mining and textiles were already depressed, and at the end of October 1929 the Wall Street Crash heralded the longest and deepest slump in modern times. In February 1930 Hoover claimed the worst was over, but it wasn't. The unemployment rate, 3.2 per cent in 1929, rose to 24.9 per cent in 1933. Shanty towns, known as Hoovervilles, sprang up to accommodate people who had lost their homes. People slept on the streets under 'Hoover blankets' – newspapers. A 'Hoover flag' was an empty pocket turned inside out, a 'Hoover wagon' a motor car pulled by horses or mules because there was no money for fuel.

Hoover himself toiled all the hours that God made. He instituted public works such as the Hoover Dam and the Golden Gate Bridge, which under his successor became part of the New Deal. But he had no idea how to raise people's spirits or sustain their morale. He had never liked giving speeches, and the first election he contested was his easy presidential victory, so he had no experience of trying to win round a sceptical public. He held endless discussions with experts, most of whom were as baffled as he was. He advocated voluntary agreements to keep wages up, but these were of no help to the thirty-four million men, women and children, over a quarter of the population, who in the depths of the Depression had no income. The great engineer faced a problem that was beyond him. The writer H. G. Wells called on him at the White House, and found him 'sickly, over-worked and overwhelmed'. The President could not inspire his Cabinet colleagues, let alone the wider nation. Henry Stimson, the Secretary of State, said talking to Hoover was 'like sitting in a bath of ink'.

The Smoot-Hawley tariff, which in 1930 increased import duties, dealt a deadly blow to foreign trade. Two years later, in a vain attempt to balance the budget, Congress insisted on tax rises. Not all the mistakes were Hoover's fault, and European governments were every bit as out of their depth, but he had promised that poverty and fear were almost conquered. Everything he did, including the suspension of First World War debt repayments in 1931, looked too little too late. From 1930–32 there were 5,100 bank failures in the United States, with catastrophic losses for depositors.

In the summer of 1932, 20,000 First World War veterans camped in Washington, demanding early payment of a bonus to which they would become entitled in 1945. Hoover refused their demand, and ordered the army to clear them out. Two veterans died, the President's reputation for hard-heartedness was confirmed, and in that autumn's election he was resoundingly defeated by Franklin D. Roosevelt, whom he detested but by whom he remains overshadowed.

Hoover's career of public usefulness was not over. During the Second World War he ran the Polish Relief Commission, and in 1946 President Truman put him in charge of the international Famine Emergency Committee. He died in 1964 at the age of ninety, and is buried at West Branch, Iowa.

FRANKLIN D. ROOSEVELT

Lived 1882–1945; president 1933–45

Franklin Delano Roosevelt was a son of privilege who became the greatest leader of the Democratic Party. He led his country through two ordeals, the Great Depression and the Second World War, and won four presidential elections, twice as many as anyone else. His well-tempered air of command resounded through his fireside chats to the nation, and extended to the denial of his own infirmity after polio deprived him, at the age of thirty-nine, of the use of his legs.

FDR had the patrician self-confidence to enjoy breaking the

rules, to feel no pang of conscience as he did so, and to condemn the rapacity of big business. A worker once said, 'Mr Roosevelt is the only man we ever had in the White House who would understand that my boss is a son of a bitch.' FDR was detested by some plutocrats as a class traitor, but persuaded most people that the federal government should pursue with the utmost energy any experiment which might relieve mass unemployment. He at length restored full employment by instituting the massive arms programme needed to prepare for hostilities in which 420,000 Americans were to lose their lives.

His father, James Roosevelt of Hyde Park, was a Hudson Valley squire who dedicated himself to a gentlemanly way of life, but also had extensive interests in railways and coal. James's much younger second wife, born Sara Delano – she was twenty-six when they married, he fifty-two – gave birth with difficulty to a son, and was advised by her doctors to have no more children. Franklin was kept at home, schooled by tutors, until at the age of fourteen his parents delivered him in their private railway car to Groton, a high-minded American version of Eton.

The following year his fifth cousin, Theodore Roosevelt – their common ancestor had landed on Manhattan Island in 1649 – came to speak at Groton about being a police commissioner in New York City, and kept the boys in fits of laughter. Franklin was invited at the age of fifteen, along with a host of younger cousins, to visit his high-spirited Cousin Theodore during the summer holidays at Oyster Bay on Long Island. He described Theodore as the greatest man he ever knew, and profited from observing and imitating his brilliant career. But the Hyde Park Roosevelts were Democrats, while the Oyster Bay Roosevelts were Republicans.

FDR went to Harvard, edited the student newspaper, the *Harvard Crimson*, and was known to some as Feather Duster, for he was seen as a bit of a lightweight. He was a handsome young man, six foot two inches tall, with a dazzling smile. His recently widowed mother moved to Boston to keep an eye on him. She was appalled when he revealed his engagement to Eleanor Roosevelt, daughter of Theodore's wastrel younger brother Elliott, but could not prevent the marriage, which took place in 1905, with President Roosevelt (as he had become) giving the bride away. Eleanor was no beauty, and worried Franklin might be too good-looking for her to hold on to. When they got engaged, she copied out Elizabeth Barrett Browning's lines for him: 'Unless you can swear, "For life, for death!" / Oh, fear to call it loving!'

In the early years of the marriage she gave birth to six children, of whom five survived. FDR dabbled in the law, decided it was not for him and in 1910 was elected as the Democrat New York state senator for Dutchess County, which included Hyde Park. Two years later, he canvassed for Woodrow Wilson, who after winning the presidential election rewarded him with the post of assistant secretary of the navy.

Like Theodore Roosevelt, who had held the same job, FDR exploited its possibilities to the full. His administrative gifts were such that after America joined the war in 1917, President Wilson discouraged him from doing what Cousin Theodore would have done, and going off to fight. FDR feared his political career would be held back by his decision not to risk his own skin, and when Groton was erecting a tablet in the chapel bearing the names of those who had served in the war, made the most of the dangers he had run while on an official visit to France in 1918: 'I believe my name should go in the first division of those who were "in the service", especially as I saw service on the other side, was missed by torpedoes and shells . . .'

While he might have been in the trenches he carried on an affair with his wife's spirited and charming social secretary, Lucy Mercer. Alice Roosevelt Longworth, daughter of Theodore, encouraged the romance: 'He deserved a good time. He was married to Eleanor.' In 1918 Eleanor discovered a packet of Lucy's love letters and offered Franklin a divorce. His mother, on whom he was dependent for funds, told him she would cut him off if he accepted the offer.

Divorce would have ended Roosevelt's career; not until Ronald Reagan in 1981 did a divorced man enter the White House. FDR promised Eleanor he would stop seeing Lucy, but from now on they conducted a political marriage, their personal relations glacial. His mother, who lived until 1941, remained firmly in charge at Hyde Park, where in the 1920s a cottage called Val-Kill was built, which was the only place Eleanor could call her own. She stayed there with close women friends, flung herself into progressive causes and journalism, and became a public figure in her own right, the most notable first lady since Dolley Madison. Relations with her husband never mended. In 1949, five years after his death, she said of him: 'I was one of those who served his purpose.'

In 1920 FDR was selected by the Democrats as their vice-presidential candidate. The party went down to a heavy defeat, but he was a rising star. The following August he was stricken, while at Campobello, the island just over the Canadian border where the Hyde Park Roosevelts spent summer vacations, with polio and found himself paralysed in both legs from the hip downwards. For a long time he hoped he would recover, and bathing in the waters at Warm Springs in Georgia made him feel better, so he developed the spa there for the use of himself and other sufferers.

There was no cure. The most he could do was learn to take a few steps with heavy steel braces supporting him instead of his legs and a son or bodyguard to hold his arm. With remarkable fortitude and self-discipline he set out to conceal from the public the gravity of his handicap. When he smiled, which was often, he looked like a man without a care in the world. Only two of the

35,000 photographs in the Roosevelt Presidential Library at Hyde Park show him in a wheelchair.

In 1924, he gave his 'Happy Warrior' speech at the Democratic convention in support of Al Smith's presidential candidacy. The reference was to Wordsworth's lines: 'This is the happy Warrior, this is he / That every man should wish to be.'

The speech was a triumph and proved that he too was a warrior. He repeated this success four years later, when he again nominated Smith, who persuaded him to run for the governorship of New York, once held by Cousin Theodore. FDR was a formidable campaigner and in 1928 won New York by the slender margin of 25,000 votes, while Smith as the Democrats' presidential candidate lost the state by 100,000 votes and went down to a heavy national defeat.

This was the springboard which could propel Roosevelt to the White House in four years' time. He set out to show he was the most dynamic governor in America, promoting unemployment insurance, farm relief and a vast electrification scheme, reaching voters directly via the radio, winning a second term in 1930 by a record margin and using state funds to fight the Great Depression by providing jobs and food.

Walter Lippmann, the famous liberal pundit, held out against the growing chorus of praise for the Governor of New York, writing in early 1932: 'Franklin D. Roosevelt is no crusader. He is no tribune of the people. He is no enemy of entrenched privilege. He is a pleasant man who, without any important qualifications for the office, would very much like to be president.' But FDR was already the front-runner for the 1932 nomination, a position he never relinquished. Doctors who watched him at work as governor testified that he was 'able to take more punishment than many men ten years younger', while Eleanor, on being asked if he was fit enough for the White House, replied: 'If the infantile paralysis didn't kill him, the presidency won't.'

A month before the Democratic convention, Roosevelt spoke at Oglethorpe University in Georgia: 'The country needs and, unless I mistake its temper, the country demands bold, persistent experimentation. It is common sense to take a method and try it. If it fails, admit it frankly and try another. But above all, try something. The millions who are in want will not stand by silently forever while the things to satisfy their needs are within easy reach.'

Once the convention had chosen Roosevelt, he flew to Chicago to deliver an acceptance speech, breaking what he called 'the absurd tradition that the candidate should remain in professed ignorance of what has happened for weeks until he is formally notified of that event weeks later'. In his peroration he declared:

'I pledge you, I pledge myself, to a new deal for the American people. Let us all here assembled constitute ourselves prophets of a new order of competence and of courage. This is more than a political campaign: it is a call to arms. Give me your help, not to win votes alone, but to win in this crusade to restore America to its own people.'

The New Deal was born. It had the advantages of being neither precise nor consistent. At times Roosevelt was accused of sounding like his opponent, President Hoover, a man wedded to more orthodox views. In the four months between Roosevelt's election victory and his inauguration there was no cooperation between him and Hoover, who loathed and despised him. This helped the President Elect to show he was a completely different kind of person. The economy continued to deteriorate, with a severe banking crisis in February 1933, adding fear of loss of life savings to fear of unemployment.

Roosevelt's first inaugural address, delivered on 4 March 1933, is famous for his declaration that 'the only thing we have to fear is fear itself', a phrase which has grown smooth from overuse.

It acquires its proper force when it is placed after the first two, somewhat platitudinous paragraphs, heard on radios across America:

> This is a day of national consecration, and I am certain that my fellow Americans expect that on my induction into the presidency I will address them with a candour and a decision which the present situation of our nation impels.
>
> This is pre-eminently the time to speak the truth, the whole truth, frankly and boldly. Nor need we shrink from honestly facing conditions in our country today. This great nation will endure as it has endured, will revive and will prosper.
>
> So first of all let me assert my firm belief that the only thing we have to fear is fear itself – nameless, unreasoning, unjustified terror which paralyses needed efforts to convert retreat into advance.

Roosevelt's success rested on his superlative ability to find the right words for every occasion. He carried Americans with him by using biblical language which would have been familiar three centuries before to the Pilgrim Fathers. 'We are stricken by no plague of locusts,' he went on to say, but have been failed by 'the money-changers', who 'have no vision, and when there is no vision the people perish'.

These exhortations would have been exposed as worthless had they not been followed by action. He put the Emergency Banking Bill through Congress in a day, and said in the first of what came to be known as his fireside chats – his radio addresses to the nation – that the legislation would only work if depositors stopped trying to withdraw their savings from the banks: 'You people must have faith; you must not be stampeded by rumours or guesses. Let us unite in banishing fear. We have provided the machinery to restore our financial system, and it is up to you to support and make it work. It is your problem, my friends, your problem no less than it is mine. Together we cannot fail.'

Roosevelt gave people hope. His clear, resonant, buoyant tones rang out across the nation, but he knew they must not ring out too often, or people would cease to pay attention. In the twelve years and one month of his presidency he delivered thirty fireside chats, each of which took 'four or five days of long, over-time work' to prepare. He had discovered how to bypass a predominantly hostile press and speak directly to the people.

His first hundred days saw a torrent of New Deal legislation, including the Agricultural Adjustment Act, the National Industrial Recovery Act, the Federal Emergency Relief Act, the Emergency Farm Mortgage Act, the Truth-in-Securities Act, the Home Own-ers' Loan Act, the Farm Credit Act, the Railroad Coordination Act, the Glass-Steagal Banking Act and the Tennessee Valley Authority Act, which sought to control floods, promote river traf-fic, generate cheap electricity and foster enterprise in a depressed area four-fifths the size of England. The results of these meas-ures were patchy, but the energy and ambition were undeniable. Unemployment did come down a bit, and FDR instilled in Ameri-cans the belief that the worst was over.

He also incurred the hatred of big business, which he assailed, in his speech accepting the nomination in 1936, for creating 'a new despotism', an 'industrial dictatorship' which destroyed small businesses and imposed 'economic slavery'. In his speech at Madison Square Garden shortly before polling day, attacking the forces arrayed against him, a touch of hubris is apparent: 'Never before in our history have these forces been so united against one candidate as they stand today. They are unanimous in their hate for me – *and I welcome their hatred* . . . I should like to have it said of my first administration that in it the forces of self-ishness and lust for power *met their match*. I should like to have it said of my second administration that in it these forces met their master.'

Roosevelt won his greatest electoral victory in 1936, and proceeded to make one of his greatest mistakes. The Supreme Court had rejected some of the New Deal measures as unconstitutional because they concentrated so much power in the hands of the president. He responded by trying to pack the court. This was a step too far, and he failed.

In foreign policy, Roosevelt was an impotent spectator of the rise of Hitler. Neither Congress nor public opinion would sanction a strong line: isolationist sentiment was too powerful. But in 1939, when war broke out in Europe, Roosevelt established communication with Winston Churchill, who had been recalled to the Admiralty. In May 1940, when Churchill became prime minister, he asked Roosevelt for the ships, aircraft, guns, ammunition and steel Britain needed to hold out against the German onslaught.

Roosevelt could not possibly do all that at once. When he informed Congress that American military aircraft production must increase from 12,000 a year to 50,000, many of his listeners declined to take him seriously. But as France crumpled under German attack in June 1940, FDR warned in a speech at the University of Virginia against 'the now obvious delusion' that America could remain 'a lone island in a world dominated by the philosophy of force', for then democracy itself would be in danger. Roosevelt employed the liberal internationalist language of Woodrow Wilson, indeed improved upon it, for he sounded less naïve.

In June 1940 he sanctioned the secret research for what became the atomic bomb. In July, in a bold attempt to build bipartisan support for American entry into the war, he appointed two senior Republicans, Henry Stimson and Frank Knox, to the posts of secretary of war and secretary of the navy. In September he agreed to swap fifty elderly destroyers for British bases in New-foundland and the Caribbean. But 1940 was an election year, so like Wilson before him, at the end of October 1940 FDR felt obliged to repeat in the most categorical terms his promise to the 'mothers and fathers' of America: 'Your boys are not going to be sent into any foreign wars.'

With such momentous events unfolding, few voters criticised Roosevelt for flouting the convention, set by Washington, that no president serve more than two terms, and they gave him a third by a convincing margin. He could now hasten to the aid of Hit-ler's remaining opponents. At a press conference in December 1940 he compared supplying arms to Britain to lending your gar-den hose to a neighbour who needed to put out a fire. A fortnight later, as the Luftwaffe subjected London to a pulverising raid which was supposed to distract attention from his speech, he said:

'The experience of the past two years has proven beyond doubt that no nation can appease the Nazis. No man can turn a tiger into a kitten by stroking it . . . We must be the great arsenal of democracy . . . There will be no bottlenecks in our determination to aid Great Britain.'

In June 1941 the war broadened with Hitler's invasion of Rus-sia. Roosevelt had already got the Lend-Lease Act through Congress, and sent his close aide Harry Hopkins, a raffish and gifted figure, to London to get to know Churchill and establish what supplies the British needed most. Hopkins went on to Mos-cow to do the same with Stalin. Hitler hoped to the end that his three main adversaries would fall out, as had Frederick the Great's at a moment of peril for Prussia in the eighteenth century. FDR never allowed that to happen.

In August 1941, on board American and British warships at Pla-centia Bay in Newfoundland, he and Churchill held the first of their eleven wartime meetings. They sang stirring hymns – 'Eternal Father, Strong to Save', 'Onward, Christian Soldiers', 'O God, Our

Help in Ages Past' – and agreed what became known as the Atlantic Charter, a Wilsonian statement of eight rather misty post-war aims, behind which could be detected Roosevelt's determination that this should be a war for democracy, not for the preservation of the British Empire.

But America was not yet in the war, and Hitler was careful to provide no provocation which would enable FDR to rout the still-powerful isolationist lobby in Washington. The Japanese were less circumspect. On 7 December 1941 they launched a surprise attack on Pearl Harbor, in Hawaii, where they destroyed or damaged eight battleships and killed 3,000 Americans. Roosevelt described this as 'a date that will live in infamy' and called for a declaration of war on Japan, which Congress immediately provided. Germany and Italy proceeded, in accordance with the axis they had formed with Japan, to declare war on the United States.

Pearl Harbor united Americans in shock and anger. Roosevelt's critics accused him of having known in advance about the attack, but could produce no evidence to support that view, nor has subsequent research revealed any. As a man who loved the navy, it is inconceivable that he would have left eight battleships tied up in port if he had known they were going to be attacked. But as soon as the attack had happened, he knew what he wanted to do. His priority was the defeat not of Japan, seen by most Americans as the aggressor, but of Hitler. FDR dramatised his role by flying to conferences with America's allies, at which they settled on a common strategy which concealed deep differences between them. He was the first president to travel by air while in power, and even his sternest critics in the American press could not help acknowledging that he possessed 'a certain vast impudent courage'.

At the same time, FDR agreed to the internment of about 120,000 people in America of Japanese descent, most of them US citizens, in clear violation of their constitutional rights but in conformity with public opinion. Roosevelt felt no qualms. He was by no means a bleeding-heart liberal.

At Casablanca in January 1943 he proclaimed the doctrine of the 'unconditional surrender' of Germany, Italy and Japan, a term which, he reminded the assembled press, had been coined by Ulysses S. Grant during the Civil War. This may have stiffened the resistance of the Axis powers, but it also reassured Stalin, who was not at Casablanca, that the western allies were not going to make a separate peace. In the summer of 1944, a year later than Stalin would have liked, the Americans, British and Canadians, along with smaller contingents from other allies, launched, under an American supreme commander, General Dwight D. Eisenhower, the D-Day landings on the Channel coast of France.

Roosevelt, learning from the mistakes made by Woodrow Wilson, was already laying the foundations for the post-war world, which would include the United Nations and the International Monetary Fund, and he decided it was his duty as well as his wish to see the job through by standing for a fourth term. In September 1944 he opened his campaign with a speech at a Teamsters' Union dinner in Washington, during which he responded to an attack on his dog:

These Republican leaders have not been content with attacks on me, or on my wife, or on my sons. No, not content with that, they now include my little dog Fala [laughter]. Well of course, I don't resent attacks and my family don't resent attacks, but Fala does resent attacks [laughter]. You know, Fala's Scotch, and being a Scottie, as soon as he learned that the Republican fiction writers, in Congress and out, had concocted a story that I'd left him behind on an Aleutian island and had sent a destroyer back to find him – at a cost to the taxpayers of two or three or eight or twenty

million dollars – his Scotch soul was furious [laughter].
He has not been the same dog since.

Brilliant performances like this, which was broadcast across the nation and can today be enjoyed on YouTube, distracted attention from questions raised in the press about whether his health was up to another term. His doctor, Admiral Ross McIntire, who was an ear, nose and throat specialist, insisted he was fine. A naval cardiologist, Dr Howard Bruenn, who examined Roosevelt in March 1944, found he was suffering from advanced heart disease and his condition was 'god awful'. Had Bruenn been asked, he would have said it was impossible for the President to run again.

But Roosevelt ran again, and won a reasonably comfortable victory, assisted by American successes on the battlefield. In February 1945 he went to Yalta in the Crimea to discuss with Stalin and Churchill the shape of the post-war world. Churchill's doctor, Sir Charles Wilson, wrote in his diary, 'the president appears a very sick man . . . I give him only a few months to live'. But Roosevelt still obtained what he most wanted, which was Stalin's assurance that when the fighting in Europe was over, the Soviet Union would enter the war against Japan, which was expected to last for a long time, at a heavy cost in American casualties. At Yalta, Stalin got a free hand in eastern Europe, subject to unenforceable promises about holding free and fair elections, but it is hard to see how Roosevelt, or any other American president, could have averted this, given the dominance on the ground of the Red Army.

Roosevelt returned to Washington, and in early April went down to Warm Springs. He was met there by Lucy Mercer, now Lucy Rutherfurd, for she had married a rich and elderly widower who was by now dead, and had rekindled her affair with Roosevelt, who was the love of her life. She was with him for most of the time after Yalta, and was present on 12 April 1945 when, as his portrait was being painted, he remarked that he had a terrible headache, and died of a heart attack. Churchill described him in the House of Commons as 'the greatest American friend we have ever known, and the greatest champion of freedom who has ever brought help and comfort from the New World to the Old'. Victory in Europe was by now imminent. On 30 April, Hitler committed suicide as the Russians stormed Berlin.

'Many books will be written about Franklin Roosevelt, but no two will give the same picture . . . He was the most complicated human being I ever knew,' Frances Perkins, his Secretary of Labour and the first woman to serve in the Cabinet, wrote in her memoir, *The Roosevelt I Knew.* 'I felt as if I knew him . . . I felt as if he knew me – and I felt as if he liked me,' a young soldier guarding the White House told Perkins on the night Roosevelt died. H. L. Mencken, known as the Sage of Baltimore, suggested by contrast that FDR 'had every quality that morons esteem in their heroes'.

Roosevelt had a devious yet open-hearted charm which baffled inquiry. Many people were so flattered to be admitted to his circle on terms of seeming equality, they were happy to contribute to his success. He had a gift for making pragmatic choices seem adventurous and morally right. When challenged to explain his philosophy, after he had denied being a communist, a capitalist, or a socialist, he replied: 'Philosophy? I am a Christian and a Democrat – that's all.'

HARRY S. TRUMAN

Lived 1884–1972; president 1945–53

Harry S. Truman was a modest but tenacious realist who
filled with aplomb the gap left by his magnificent predecessor. He gave early proof of his decisiveness by
ordering the dropping in August 1945 of atomic bombs on Hiro-
shima and Nagasaki, which ended the war in the Pacific. The
famous sign on his desk said, 'The buck stops here,' while
another, less well-known sign quoted some words of Mark Twain:
Always do right. This will gratify some people and astonish the
rest.'

Truman astonished the pundits and pollsters by fighting back from a period of deep unpopularity to win the 1948 presidential election, which they had declared this insignificant-looking man from a small town in Missouri was certain to lose. He resisted the spread of communism and in 1950 led America into the Korean War, a conflict which cost about 37,000 American lives, but which he prevented from widening into a third world war.

He was born in Lamar, Missouri, and given the middle initial S in honour of his two grandfathers, both of whose names began with that letter. His parents soon moved to the small town of Independence, where he became a good piano player and a voracious reader who devoured every book in the local library. In later life he said if he hadn't got mixed up in politics, he might have been a history teacher, and his comments on American presidents are perhaps the shrewdest of any holder of that office.

His father, a farmer who speculated in wheat futures, went bankrupt when Harry was seventeen, and there was no money for him to go to college. He hoped to go instead to West Point, but his eyesight was too bad. After several lowly jobs, he worked for ten years on his father's farm, which was always in hock to the bank. He also joined the National Guard, and in 1917, when America entered the First World War, volunteered for service as a gunner. His unit elected their officers, and chose Truman as one of them. He showed he was a natural leader who knew how to bring men with him, in part because he defended them against the unreasonable demands of higher authority. He served with distinction in France, and to the end of his days his comradeship with the men of Battery D was of the greatest importance to him.

When Truman came home from the war, he was thirty-five years old and at last managed to marry Bess Wallace, whom he had known since the age of six and had long courted, on condition that her mother, Madge Gates Wallace, a somewhat demanding woman, could live with them. This Madge proceeded to do for the next thirty-three years, expiring in the White House just before the end of his presidency. Truman never told a joke against her. He was devoted to Bess and to their daughter, Margaret, who was the apple of his eye. His favoured recreation was playing poker with old friends while drinking bourbon and telling funny stories.

Soon after the war he set up a haberdashery with one of his former comrades. It prospered, over-expanded and failed as soon as there was a slump. Truman blamed the Republicans, who were in power, for only looking after the rich. His opponents scorned him as a failed haberdasher, but his troubles gave him an authentic sympathy with the underdog, which he became skilled at communicating to voters.

His political career began in a small way in Jackson County, Missouri. He was at this stage a rotten public speaker, but when he dried up his friends from Battery D would shout, 'Three cheers for Captain Harry!' To get elected he had to became part of the Pendergast machine, run by an uncle of one of his Battery D friends. But while Tom Pendergast was known to be corrupt, Harry Truman was popular in part because he was known to be honest. The proof was that although elected to positions in which he was responsible for large road-building contracts, the family farm at Grandview remained mortgaged, and it took him fifteen years to pay off his debts from the haberdashery. He never took a cent in kickbacks, and spoke with sympathy of Ulysses S. Grant, like him a failure as a farmer and a businessman.

In 1934, by which time Truman was fifty, he was elected senator for Missouri. This entailed long absences in Washington, where he found himself insulted as 'Tom Pendergast's office boy'. He could not afford to rent an apartment fit for his mother-in-law as well as his wife and daughter, so had to leave them behind in distant Independence. He is said to have made the classic joke about Washington: 'You want a friend in this city? Get a dog.' But Truman gradually earned the good opinion of his fellow senators, and in 1940 unexpectedly won a second term, beating off a strong challenge from the Governor of Missouri.

Truman's career now flowered. He realised that defence contractors were defrauding the federal government, drove 30,000 miles to collect evidence of scandalous waste, called on the Senate to investigate this, was put in charge of the committee charged with doing so, and was lauded for uncovering the most outrageous corruption. For the presidential election of 1944, Roosevelt chose Truman as his running mate.

During the convention, the President rang Bob Hannegan, chairman of the Democratic National Committee, and asked him, in Truman's hearing: 'Bob, have you got that that guy lined up yet on that vice presidency?'

Hannegan replied: 'No. He's the contrariest goddamn mule from Missouri I ever saw.'

'Well,' FDR said, 'you tell him if he wants to break up the Democratic Party in the middle of the war and maybe lose that war that's up to him.'

Truman agreed, reluctantly, to stand, and campaigned hard in the election. But although the by now mortally ill Roosevelt won another term, he did not take the vice president into his confidence or invite him to join the hundred-strong American delegation to the Yalta conference with Stalin and Churchill in February 1945. FDR looked to Truman to control the Senate, so it would ratify whatever peace deal he struck.

As vice president, Truman played an upright piano while Lauren Bacall sat on top of it, a stunt which produced memorable photographs of him and the film star, but he was an insignificant figure for the twelve weeks until FDR's death, whereupon he became the leader of the free world. He went to Potsdam to confer with Stalin and Churchill, and realised, as the Soviets crushed freedom in Poland, Czechoslovakia and the rest of eastern Europe, that a new foreign policy was required.

In framing that policy, Truman enlisted the support of two outstanding public servants, General George Marshall and Dean Acheson. The President insisted on calling the American project to set Europe on its feet again Marshall Aid, for it was the general who while serving as secretary of state proposed it. In March 1947 the President announced in an address to Congress what became known as the Truman Doctrine: 'I believe it must be the policy of the United States to support free peoples who are resisting attempted subjugation by armed minorities or by outside pressure.'

Acheson praised Truman for not worrying about his reputation when taking decisions: 'his ego never came between and his job'. His popularity had meanwhile slumped, for the immediate post-war period saw many difficulties including strikes. Some accused him of being soft on communism, while others thought he was being too harsh towards America's long-suffering Soviet allies. In 1946 the Democrats lost control of both houses of Congress. Many in his own party had no time for him.

Truman came out fighting. In the summer of 1948 he summoned a special sitting of Congress, challenging the Republicans to do all the wonderful things they said they were going to do. They did none of them, and in that autumn's presidential election he went for them. 'Give 'em hell, Harry,' originally shouted by members of his own staff from the back of meetings on his whistle-stop tours of the country, became his slogan. The polls nevertheless indicated he was on course for a heavy defeat at the hands of his Republican opponent, Thomas E. Dewey. On the morning of his victory he posed with a copy of the *Chicago Tribune* bearing the headline DEWEY DEFEATS TRUMAN. American voters had rallied to the support of the underdog.

During his second term Truman's stand against communism succeeded in Europe, where in 1949 the Berlin blockade was defeated and Nato founded, but ran into severe difficulties in Korea, where in 1950 the communist North invaded the US-supported South. Truman responded by committing American troops under the authority of the United Nations but the leadership of the aged General MacArthur, who assured him the war would be over by Christmas. The General was wrong, and the front line swung repeatedly up and down the Korean peninsula. MacArthur argued it was necessary to attack China, which had come in on the side of the North Koreans, but Truman refused to allow this for fear of starting a third world war. When MacArthur committed acts of gross insubordination, Truman sacked him, incurring considerable domestic criticism, for to many Americans the general was a hero.

Truman was an early riser, who started the day with a brisk walk round Washington or wherever he happened to be, during which anyone who could keep up with him could ask questions. Some idea of the strain under which he was operating, and the vein of aggression in his temperament, can be gauged from a letter he wrote and posted early one morning in 1950 to Paul Hume of the *Washington Post*, after reading that critic's review of a concert given by Truman's daughter, Margaret, a soprano: 'She is flat a good deal of the time – more last night than at any time we have heard her in past years.' In his reply Truman refers to Westbrook Pegler, a well-known abusive columnist:

Mr. Hume:
I've just read your lousy review of Margaret's concert. I've come to the conclusion that you are an 'eight ulcer man on four ulcer pay.'

It seems to me that you are a frustrated old man who wishes he could have been successful. When you write such poppy-cock as was in the back section of the paper you work for it shows conclusively that you're off the beam and at least four of your ulcers are at work.

Some day I hope to meet you. When that happens you'll need a new nose, a lot of beefsteak for black eyes, and perhaps a supporter below.

Pegler, a gutter snipe, is a gentleman alongside you. I hope you'll accept that statement as a worse insult than a reflection on your ancestry.

H. S .T.

How abusive Truman could become, though mostly he kept his feelings to himself, writing many angry letters he never sent. This letter got into the press, with most people admiring him for his fierceness in defence of his daughter.

He contemplated standing again in 1952, but was dissuaded by his family and advisers, for the Korean War was unpopular and no end to it was yet in sight. Truman also proved incapable of controlling the excesses of Joe McCarthy, who had fomented an atmosphere of paranoia by making unsubstantiated allegations of communist infiltration of the American government.

Truman retired to Independence, where on the morning after his return he went for a brisk walk and was asked what he had done on returning home. 'I carried the grips up to the attic,' he replied.

He never became rich, but did raise the money for the setting up of the Truman Presidential Library in Independence. In 1956 he visited Italy and called on the famous American connoisseur Bernard Berenson, who wrote in his diary, where he was often waspish about eminent visitors:

Harry Truman and his wife lunched yesterday. Came at one and stayed til three. Both as natural, as unspoiled by high office as if he had gone no further than alderman of Independence, Missouri. In my long life I have never met an individual with whom I felt so instantly at home. He talked as if he had always known me, openly, easily, with no reserve (so far as I could judge). Ready to touch on any subject, no matter how personal. I always felt what a solid and sensible basis there is in the British stock of the USA if it can produce a man like Truman. If the Truman miracle can still occur, we need not fear even the McCarthys. Truman captivated even Willy Mostyn-Owen, aged twenty-seven, ultra-critical, and like all Englishmen of today hard of hearing anything good about Americans, and disposed to be condescending to them – at best.

A curious footnote can be added. Mostyn-Owen later became the first father-in-law of Boris Johnson, the future British prime minister, whom he described as 'rapacious'.

DWIGHT D. EISENHOWER

Lived 1890–1969; president 1953–61

D wight D. Eisenhower had the good sense not to try to be interesting. He was the first celebrated general since Ulysses S. Grant to become president, and like him enjoyed a personal popularity which was impervious to criticism. People trusted Ike, as he was known, and were determined to believe, during the prosperous 1950s, that he would keep them safe, which he did.

Unlike Grant, Eisenhower had done no actual fighting. He was a staff officer of exceptional ability, who possessed no original ideas and whenever possible avoided having rows with people. As supreme allied commander in Europe during the Second World War, this suited him for the task of keeping America and her allies united. After he had been persuaded, in 1952, to enter politics, he prided himself on not being 'stuffed shirty' and sought with success to stay above the battle, the smiling father of the nation, playing a lot of golf.

He was born in Denison, Texas, but he and his six brothers soon moved with their parents to Abilene, Kansas. Money was short, and the boys had to help with household tasks. His father had opened a general store which failed, and worked as a mechanic. His mother was pious, and in due course became a Jehovah's Witness. Dwight managed to get to West Point, where a knee injury wrecked his promising career as a footballer. He was commissioned as a second lieutenant, posted to Texas and in 1916 married Mamie Dowd, the daughter of a prosperous meatpacker. They had two sons, but the elder died of scarlet fever at the age of three.

When America entered the First World War, Eisenhower wanted to be posted to France, but his organisational abilities had already been recognised, and he was put in charge of training tank crews at Camp Colt in Gettysburg. Peace came too soon for him to see action, and he was reduced in rank from temporary lieutenant colonel to captain. From 1930 he worked in Washington and then in the Philippines for General MacArthur, whom he came to regard as 'a damn fool'. After the attack on Pearl Harbor, General Marshall plucked Eisenhower from obscurity, recognised his talents, made him head of war plans in Washington and then dispatched him to London to see if it was feasible to invade France in 1942. Eisenhower thought it was, but the British argued successfully that this would be far too soon, while accepting that the post of supreme commander for the operation would have to be an American.

There was widespread surprise when Eisenhower got the job. FDR explained to his son James: 'Eisenhower is the best politician among the military men.' After this huge promotion, Eisenhower wrote to his wife that he had to be:

'a bit of a diplomat – lawyer – promoter – salesman – social hound – liar (at least to get out of social affairs) – mountebank – actor – Simon Legree [the slave owner in *Uncle Tom's Cabin* who has Tom flogged to death, so a cruel and unreasonable employer] – humanitarian – orator and incidentally (sometimes I think most damnably incidentally) a soldier!'

Eisenhower was under enormous strain in his three and a half years as supreme commander. His burdens were eased by Kay Summersby, a former fashion model, born in Ireland, who had been assigned to him as his driver. On the one occasion during this period he returned to the United States and was able to spend a few days with his wife, Mamie, he twice by accident called her 'Kay'.

When the allies at length invaded France in June 1944, the landings succeeded, but the advance was slower than had been hoped. Alan Brooke, chief of the British general staff, complained in his diary that 'Ike knows nothing about strategy' and instead of directing operations was 'by himself with his lady chauffeur on the golf links at Rheims – entirely detached from the war'. As the allies entered Germany, Eisenhower was criticised for making no attempt to get to Berlin before the Russians.

But to the public, Eisenhower was the hero of the hour, who had masterminded the greatest invasion in history and won a glorious victory. Despite having arranged for Kay to become an American citizen, he dropped her and returned to Mamie. His position was unassailable, and people began asking him whether he would run for president. He insisted he would not, instead became president of Columbia University, and in 1949 accepted the task of setting up Nato. Three years later he decided it was his duty to avert a possible relapse by America into isolationism. It was not clear whether he was a Democrat or a Republican, but he plumped for the latter. The party devised a slogan, 'I like Ike,' which had the merit of being true. To this he added, at a late stage in the campaign, a promise to end the Korean War by going there in person. He won an enormous victory over the Democrat candidate, Adlai Stevenson, went to Korea and ended the war.

Not everyone was impressed by Eisenhower. When his fellow Republican, Senator Joseph McCarthy, assailed General Marshall as a 'traitor', Eisenhower failed to say the words he was expected to say in defence of his friend and patron Marshall, though the passage was released to the press. Although there was a pragmatic case for refusing to attack another Republican, Eisenhower's lack of moral courage disgusted the retiring president, Harry S. Truman, among others. Eisenhower grew to detest his vice president, Richard Nixon, but could find no way of getting rid of him, having missed a golden opportunity during the 1952 election campaign when Nixon was found to be operating a slush fund.

In 1954 Ike declined to give military support to the French in Indochina, where they suffered a crushing defeat at the hands of the Vietnamese communists at Dien Bien Phu, and in 1956 he refused to back the French and British when they seized control of the Suez Canal. Eisenhower did not wish to be seen supporting the old European empires, but nor did he have much idea how to replace them. Vietnam was partitioned between a communist north and a southern state reliant on American support. Eisenhower had already put forward the domino theory, which if correct, committed the United States to the defence of South Vietnam, because its loss would at once be followed by the loss of other countries: 'You have a row of dominoes set up. You knock over the first one, and what will happen to the last one is a certainty that it will go over very quickly.'

Eisenhower's health was poor – in 1949 he had suffered a

heart attack which was covered up – and his manner as president was lethargic. He played golf, bridge and poker, and in 1955 had a heart attack so severe it could not be covered up. Eisenhower made a virtue of being up front about it, in due course appearing in pyjamas bearing the words MUCH BETTER THANKS. He instituted a nationwide programme of road building, the interstate highways, and decided he was well enough to run for a second term. According to his press secretary, James Hagerty, Eisenhower reached this decision while convalescing from the heart attack: 'It was then that he faced the sheer, god-awful boredom of not being president.'

In 1956, Ike won again against Stevenson. The country was at peace, and the President kept it that way. Americans were, however, deeply worried that the Soviet Union was taking the lead in the nuclear arms race, a danger which seemed to be confirmed when the Russians put a satellite into space before the Americans, whose own satellites had crashed. Eisenhower sanctioned secret flights over the Soviet Union by U2 spy planes. In 1960 one of these was shot down, the pilot, Gary Powers, was captured, and the President was reduced to telling a series of embarrassingly obvious lies. But his cautiousness did reduce the danger of a military confrontation, and he left to his successor the question of what to do about Cuba, where the communists had seized power.

In 1961 Eisenhower, by now seventy years old, handed over to John F. Kennedy. The retiring President, who had ended one war and started no others, delivered a solemn warning to his successors: 'In the councils of government, we must guard against the acquisition of unwarranted influence, whether sought or unsought, by the military-industrial complex.' Eisenhower retired to live in the farmhouse he and Mamie had bought at Gettysburg. In 1968 he hit a hole-in-one on the golf course, and the following year he died.

JOHN F. KENNEDY

Lived 1917–63; president 1961–63

John Fitzgerald Kennedy was the most glamorous president, and the second youngest, inaugurated at the age of forty-three (Theodore Roosevelt was forty-two) and assassinated when he was forty-six. He was the first Roman Catholic to reach the White House, but although he resorted to the language of moral uplift, there was nothing churchy about him. He had a self-deprecatory lightness of touch which carried him with inspiring ease across thin ice, and he hired some of the best writers in America to compose his books and speeches. In life these courtiers tended his myth and after his death they led the veneration of him as a secular saint.

The shocking end to JFK's presidency means it will never be known to what extent he might have come to deserve their golden opinions. His successful handling of the Cuban Missile Crisis, when the world stood on the brink of nuclear war, elicited wild enthusiasm, but he also started to deploy American troops to Vietnam, and was in danger of believing he knew more than he actually did about foreign policy. His compulsive womanising, unknown at the time to the public, was not in accordance with modern norms, but has never tarnished his reputation to the extent that might have been expected.

His father, Joe Kennedy, was a rich Boston Irishman who became far richer by making astute investments in everything from the New York Stock Exchange to Hollywood films. His mother, Rose, who bore nine children including four sons, Joe, John, Robert and Ted, was the pious Catholic daughter of John 'Honey Fitz' Fitzgerald, the first Irish American to become mayor of Boston. In 1932 Joe made campaign donations to Franklin Roosevelt, who in 1934 appointed him the first head of the Securities and Exchange Commission, reasoning that here was a businessman who would understand the crooked things done by other businessmen.

In 1938 Joe obtained from FDR the ambassadorship to London, where in the early stages of the war he declared that British democracy was finished and America should send no help. His defeatism made him unpopular with his hosts, but his children were well received in London society. He was ambitious for his eldest son to go into politics, but in 1944 Joe was killed while serving as a bomber pilot.

Paternal ambition was transferred to the second son, Jack, a sickly but charismatic young man who had studied at Harvard and the London School of Economics. At the latter institution, he wrote a thesis about Britain's vain attempts to appease Hitler, which was in due course improved by a *New York Times* journalist and published, under JFK's name, as *While England Slept*.

When America entered the war, JFK joined the navy, and while serving in Washington met the love of his life, Inga Arvad, a former Miss Denmark, six years older than him, a married woman suspected unjustly by the FBI of being a Nazi spy. His father broke up the affair by getting him posted to Charleston, South Carolina, and then on active service in the South Pacific.

JFK was put in command of eleven men aboard PT-109, a wooden patrol torpedo boat which on a foggy night in 1943 was run down by a Japanese destroyer. Two of the crew were killed and a third seriously wounded. Lieutenant Kennedy rallied the survivors, who swam to an island and after five days living off coconuts were rescued. His undoubted bravery was later embellished in a book, which in turn became a film.

On returning home to Boston, he won election in 1946 as a Democrat to the House of Representatives. JFK was a brilliant campaigner, but his victories owed much to family money and influence. In 1947 he visited London, where he was found to be suffering from Addison's disease, an adrenal insufficiency, and was given less than a year to live. On the voyage home he became so ill he was given the last rites. Although he appeared handsome and healthy in photographs, he was often seriously unwell, and worsened his health by the promiscuous use of drugs supplied to him by unscrupulous doctors.

In 1952 he ran in Massachusetts for the Senate and defeated the incumbent Republican, Henry Cabot Lodge Junior. In 1954 and 1955 he underwent two dangerous operations on his back. The public were told his health problems were the result of his war service. During this period he published *Profiles in Courage*, portraits of eight heroic American senators, written for him by Ted Sorensen. It is a work of sonorous rhetoric, inspired by reverence for such great figures as Edmund Burke and John Hampden, and thanks to lobbying by Joe Kennedy won a Pulitzer prize. In the introduction Kennedy pays tribute to his young wife, Jacqueline, for nursing him through his convalescence. But theirs was in large part a marriage of convenience, arranged for him by his father, and even during the engagement JFK's womanising continued unabated.

In 1960 JFK took aim at the biggest prize of all, the presidency. There had never been a Catholic president, so he needed to show he could win in a Protestant state such as West Virginia. In Harry S. Truman's expert opinion, Joe Kennedy 'bought' the Democratic primary there, though 'he's a tight-fisted old son of a bitch; so he didn't pay any more than he had to'. When asked what would happen when the Pope moved into the White House, Truman replied: 'It's not the Pope I'm afraid of, it's the Pop.'

The election of 1960 was a close-run thing, but JFK squeaked home against Richard Nixon. Before departing for Washington, the President Elect delivered a speech at the Massachusetts General Court in which he assured his fellow citizens of the Bay State that 'this will remain my home', and quoted from the sermon preached by the Puritan leader John Winthrop on the *Arbella* when sailing from England to Massachusetts in 1630: 'We must always consider, he said, that we shall be as a city upon a hill. The eyes of all people are upon us . . . and our government . . . at every level . . . must be as a city upon a hill, constructed and inhabited by men aware of their great trust and their great responsibilities.'

In Washington Kennedy delivered a memorable inaugural address, written by Sorensen, in which he said, 'the torch has been passed to a new generation' – he was twenty-seven years younger than Eisenhower – and went on: 'Let every nation know, whether it wishes us well or ill, that we shall pay any price, bear any burden, meet any hardship, support any friend, oppose any foe, in order to assure the survival and the success of liberty.'

There was no end to JFK's spirit of self-sacrifice, or to the sacrifices he demanded from others: 'And so, my fellow Americans: ask not what your country can do for you – ask what you can do for your country.' The Peace Corps was set up in 1961 to enable idealistic young Americans to volunteer for service in developing countries.

He employed staff who were mostly as inexperienced as he was, but considered themselves the best and the brightest, and made his thirty-five-year-old brother Robert attorney general, in which role he became the president's chief adviser and enforcer. When the British Prime Minister, Harold Macmillan, returned to London after his first visit to Washington and was asked what it was like there, he remarked: 'Oh, it's rather like watching the Borgia brothers take over a respectable north Italian city.'

The first crisis arose over Cuba, where the CIA was planning an invasion by Cuban exiles whom it had trained in the art of war in Guatemala. Had Eisenhower still been president, he would almost certainly have seen, with his experience of high command, how foolish the plan was, and insisted on its improvement or abandonment. Kennedy, who was suffering from urethritis and acute diarrhoea, just insisted on diluting the part played by American forces and landing at a more remote spot, the Bay of Pigs, with the result that the Cuban exiles had no chance, and were all either captured or killed, except for a handful rescued by the CIA. This was a humiliation, and gave the Russians the unfortunate impression that the new administration was weak, but Kennedy reduced the damage to himself by admitting his responsibility for the debacle: 'There's an old saying that victory has a hundred fathers and defeat is an orphan.'

After the calm of the Eisenhower years, the Kennedy White House was fashionable, and was soon compared to King Arthur's Camelot, about which a show happened to be playing on Broadway. The Kennedys had two young children, who frolicked through the building, which Jackie redecorated. She was such a hit with the French, whose language she spoke, that the President said at the start of a press conference in Paris: 'I am the man who accompanied Jacqueline Kennedy to Paris, and I have enjoyed it.' During this visit he arranged an assignation for himself with a French prostitute.

The President led the fashion for men not wearing hats, and was blamed for destroying the American hat industry. He disconcerted the Secret Service by holding naked pool parties and sleeping with young women on the White House staff. His recklessness extended to sharing a mistress with a Mafia boss. He disconcerted Macmillan by saying: 'I wonder how it is with you, Harold. If I don't have a woman for three days, I get a terrible headache.'

He tried to recover from the Bay of Pigs by holding a summit meeting with the Soviet leader, Nikita Khrushchev, in Vienna, but instead found himself bullied and shaken. Khrushchev upped the pressure by starting to deploy nuclear missiles in Cuba, only ninety miles from Florida. An American spy plane picked up what was happening. This was an intolerable provocation, and Kennedy announced that it would not do. He rejected the advice of the chiefs of staff to bomb the launch sites, for they could offer no guarantee that all the missiles would be destroyed, and instead imposed a naval blockade. The world held its breath until the Russian ships turned back. Dean Rusk, the Secretary of State, said: 'We're eyeball to eyeball, and I think the other fellow just blinked.'

When the President emerged from the White House to give the news, a British journalist, Peregrine Worsthorne, described the effect:

the whole emergency press conference roared its admiration. I remember writing in my dispatch that it was like watching Prince Hal suddenly turn into Henry V. Kennedy had been transformed. Cynical journalists are not meant to lose their heads, not meant to go wild with enthusiasm, but this we did, fighting, almost literally, to shake his hand or touch his garments. Back in London the subeditors were also infected, heading my piece with the over-the-top words 'New Emperor of the West'. Such hyperboles were bound to turn the gods against him, as indeed, all too soon, they did.

This famous victory for Kennedy encouraged the illusion that he and his team were masters of foreign policy. But at the end of that year the President sent the first 7,000 American troops to Vietnam, and in 1963 he sanctioned a coup against General Ngo Dinh Diem, the corrupt South Vietnamese leader, who was assassinated on 2 November 1963.

The President felt bad about that. He intended to win re-election, to which end he visited Texas, on the advice of his Vice President, Lyndon B. Johnson. Jackie disliked campaigning but consented to come along too. On 22 November 1963 they drove in an open car through Dallas, where as the motorcade made its way at about eleven miles per hour along Elm Street he was shot from the Texas Book Depository by a gunman, soon identified as Lee Harvey Oswald, who was himself shot dead two days later. The killing of the President caused profound shock around the world, though also rejoicing in regions such as Latin America. Alistair Cooke noted the astonishing parallels between the assassinations of Lincoln and JFK:

> Lincoln was elected to Congress in 1846, Kennedy exactly one hundred years later in 1946. Lincoln was elected president in November 1860, Kennedy in November 1960. Lincoln had a secretary named Kennedy who advised against his going to the theatre. Kennedy had a secretary named

Lincoln who advised against his going to Dallas. Booth shot Lincoln in a theatre and ran off into a warehouse; Oswald shot Kennedy from a warehouse and ran off into a theatre. Lincoln was succeeded by a southerner named Johnson, Kennedy was succeeded by a southerner named Johnson, the first Johnson was born in 1808, the second in 1908.

The self-congratulatory element in the JFK myth is tiresome, but he was a star performer, and even now his charm is hard to resist.

LYNDON B. JOHNSON

Lived 1908–73; president 1963–69

Lyndon Baines Johnson was a ruthless, hard-driving Texan with an urge to dominate that made him difficult either to love or to advise. His genius for getting Congress to do his bidding enabled him to see civil rights reforms into law, but his presidency was wrecked by the ever-expanding horror of the Vietnam War, which created bitter divisions in America and brought protesters onto the streets chanting, 'Hey, hey, LBJ, how many kids did you kill today?'

He was born into rural poverty on a farm by the muddy

Pedernales River in the Texas hill country west of Austin. His father was ambitious to better himself, served in the state legislature and speculated in cotton futures, but periodically lost everything. Lyndon, in his teens, worked in a road gang and told his fellow labourers he would one day be president. He grew to be almost six foot four inches tall, studied at Southwest Texas State Teachers College in San Marcos, south of Austin, worked for three years as a teacher and married Claudia Alta Taylor, known since infancy as Lady Bird, a name coined by her nursemaid.

LBJ treated his wife with dictatorial boorishness, was an unrelenting womaniser, and later boasted he'd 'had more women by accident than Kennedy had on purpose'. Lady Bird was a loyal and supportive consort and suffered many miscarriages before giving birth to two daughters. Her uncouth husband possessed titanic energy and drive, and an exceptional ability to get people to do what he wanted them to do. He got a job working for a Texas congressman in Washington, and at the age of twenty-six met and impressed President Roosevelt, who made him Texas director of the National Youth Administration. Two years later, in 1936, Johnson secured election to the House of Representatives in Washington, where he won valuable contracts for his state, the Texan company Brown and Root in return providing him with the financial muscle needed to make him a Democratic power broker.

He continued as a congressman during and after brief service in the navy during the Second World War, and in 1948 won election as senator for Texas. He worked so hard that in 1955 he suffered a severe heart attack, but according to Lady Bird his twelve years in the Senate were the happiest of their lives. His gifts as a wheeler-dealer compelled respect rather than affection. He spent a staggering amount of time on the telephone, marshalling and deploying his congressional forces, and became, at the age of forty-six, the youngest Senate majority leader ever.

In the race for the Democratic nomination in 1960, Johnson

attempted to derail the front-runner, JFK, who was nine years younger than him, by describing him to the press as 'a little scrawny fellow with rickets'. The attack failed, for although Kennedy was an absentee senator and in poor health, he possessed charisma and a rich father. The Kennedys despised Johnson as a hick, but offered him a place on the ticket as vice-presidential candidate, for it made sense to recruit a crude southerner to balance their New England sophistication.

Somewhat to their surprise, Johnson accepted the offer, calculating perhaps that JFK's poor health offered a route to the White House. Johnson made a vital contribution in the south to JFK's wafer-thin victory, and then found himself consigned, like most vice presidents, to a life of insignificance, with the President determined to spend as little time as he possibly could with him. But Johnson was there in the motorcade when Kennedy went campaigning in Texas in November 1963. He and Lady Bird were two cars behind the Kennedys. After the shooting, they went to the hospital, where they learned the President had died. Johnson was sworn in as president on the flight back to Washington, Jackie standing beside him in her bloodstained suit, the coffin carrying JFK in another part of the plane.

LBJ's handling of the transition was masterly. Like Theodore Roosevelt after McKinley's assassination, he steadied the nation by announcing that he would carry on with the same team. He proclaimed that the best way to commemorate JFK was to pass the civil rights legislation which the deceased President had spent a year trying and failing to get through Congress. LBJ got it through in four months. He held out the vision of a Great Society in which poverty in its various forms had been eliminated. It became hard to object to his crudity of manner, his love of giving orders while sitting on the toilet, his desire physically to humiliate senior figures by leaning over them, when he was pursuing such noble aims.

In the 1964 presidential election the Republicans put up Barry

Goldwater, who declared himself in favour of the use of nuclear weapons against the communists. Their slogan was 'In your heart you know he's right,' to which the Democrats replied, 'In your guts you know he's nuts.' The Gulf of Tonkin incident of August 1964, when an American destroyer was said on doubtful evidence to have been fired upon by the North Vietnamese, led Congress to empower Johnson to take whatever measures he saw fit, while he promised his mission was peace. He campaigned with folksy brio, said he would not allow 'American boys to do the fighting for Asian boys', and won the election by a landslide.

He persisted with his domestic reforms, rendered more urgent by the violent response of Alabama state troopers to the civil rights marchers who made their way from Selma to Montgomery in early 1965. In Congress, LBJ delivered his greatest speech, comparing Selma to Lexington, Concord and Appomattox, a 'turning point in man's unending search for freedom'. The Voting Rights Act vastly increased the number of African Americans who could vote in states such as Alabama and Mississippi.

But LBJ avoided debate about what the United States could reasonably expect to achieve in Vietnam. He was not an easy man with whom to have a discussion, for he insisted on abject obedience. As he said of one adviser who was about to join his team, 'I don't want loyalty. I want *loyalty*. I want him to kiss my ass in Macy's at high noon and tell me it smells like roses. I want his pecker in my pocket.'

In February 1965 he ordered the bombing of North Vietnam. Over the next few years a far greater weight of explosive was dropped on that country than on Germany during the Second World War, but, like the Germans, the Vietnamese did not crack. Johnson agreed to deploy hundreds of thousands of ground troops in South Vietnam, but as casualties mounted and reports appeared in America of atrocities committed against innocent civilians, he suffered a catastrophic loss of moral authority.

A 'credibility gap' opened between what the President said was happening in Vietnam and what was actually taking place. The public no longer believed him, and those members of the administration who had survived from the Kennedy days detested him. Robert Kennedy, who had been kept on as attorney general, described LBJ as 'mean, bitter, vicious – an animal in many ways', and contrasted him with his late brother, who had been 'a gentleman and a human being'.

By 1968 the United States was trapped in Vietnam, and so was Johnson. The ruthlessness that enabled him to dominate Congress, of which he had an intimate knowledge, was of no use in south-east Asia, about which he understood nothing. The ruthless measures recommended to him by hawks were counter-productive, and meant there was no way he could demonstrate this was a just war, or at least an unjust war America was going to win. American boys were being drafted into the jungles of Vietnam, and were coming home in body bags, or maimed in body and mind. The *New York Times* lost faith in Johnson in 1966, the *Washington Post* in 1967, and by 1968 America seemed to be falling apart, with the assassination of Martin Luther King in April and of Robert Kennedy in June, riots in many cities and huge anti-war demonstrations at which veterans flung their medals away in protest.

Johnson announced in March 1968 that he would not fight a second presidential election. He devoted his last nine months in office to a vain attempt to bring peace to Vietnam without admitting American defeat, after which he retired to his ranch in Texas beside the Pedernales River, abandoned the health regime which had kept him in shape in the White House, let his hair grow long in apparent sympathy with the hippies who had been among his most vociferous opponents, and in 1973 died, almost universally unmourned, of a heart attack.

RICHARD NIXON

Lived 1913–94; president 1969–74

R ichard Milhous Nixon destroyed many enemies during his rise to power, and ended by destroying himself. By ordering that his conversations in the White House be tape-recorded so posterity could learn of his brilliant foreign policy, Nixon provided the evidence which convicted him of direct involvement in the Watergate scandal, the most ignominious episode in presidential history since the attempted impeachment of Andrew Johnson in 1868. The courage and far-sightedness which impelled this statesman to seek a rapprochement with China were vitiated by the vindictive, devious, dishonest tactics to which he resorted when taking on domestic opponents.

Nixon was a loner who rose from humble origins and even as president felt other people were looking down on him. He was born in the small settlement of Yorba Linda near Los Angeles, where his father, an irascible Irish American, tried and failed to make a living as a lemon farmer, and then opened a gas station and store. His mother, a devout Quaker who knew Latin and Greek, set high moral standards to which Nixon was guiltily aware he failed to live up. In old age he said, 'she never indulged in the present-day custom, which I find nauseating, of hugging and kissing her children or others for whom she had great affection'. He was one of five boys, two of whom died of tuberculosis, probably contracted from the milk provided by the family cow.

He showed outstanding ability at school and was told he should go to Harvard, but his family could not afford to send him, so he studied instead at Whittier, a local Quaker college, while continuing to help out at the gas station and store, after which he went on a scholarship to read law at Duke University in North Carolina. He returned home to work as a lawyer, and married Pat Ryan, an attractive young teacher. During the Second World War he served in the navy, mostly in administrative roles.

In the autumn of 1945 the Republicans in his district of southern California invited him to run against the incumbent Democratic congressman, Jerry Voorhis. This was Nixon's big break, and he seized it with a singular lack of scruple. By portraying Voorhis, quite unjustly, as 'a tool of the communists', working 'in the interests of international Jewry', Nixon came through and won.

In 1950 Nixon used the same vicious tactics to unseat Helen Gahagan Douglas, Democratic senator for California, smearing her as a communist sympathiser 'pink down to her underwear'. Douglas popularised the name Tricky Dick for Nixon but, according to him, 'Nice guys and sissies don't win many elections.' He was a rising star, and in 1952 Dwight Eisenhower invited the ruthless young attack dog, darling of hardline anti-communist Republicans, to be his running mate.

All went swimmingly until news broke of a slush fund financed by rich Californian Republicans, keeping Nixon in a style far beyond his senatorial salary. Eisenhower was running on an anti-corruption ticket and wanted to drop him, but Nixon refused to go and demanded the right to clear his name in a television broadcast. His career hung by a thread. In his speech he insisted the donations had been used entirely for campaign expenses, and had not enriched him or his wife Pat by a single cent. By going through their household finances, he made them sound like ordinary Americans struggling to make ends meet. And then he said:

> One other thing I should probably tell you, because if I don't they will probably be saying this about me, too. We did get something, a gift, after the nomination. A man down in Texas heard Pat on the radio mention the fact that our two youngsters would like to have a dog and, believe it or not, the day before we left on this campaign trip we got a message from Union Station in Baltimore, saying they had a package for us. We went down to get it. You know what it was? It was a little cocker spaniel dog, in a crate that had been sent all the way from Texas – black and white, spotted, and our little girl Tricia, the six-year-old, named it Checkers. And you know, the kids, like all kids, loved the dog, and I just want to say this, right now, that regardless of what they say about it, we are going to keep it.

The Checkers speech, as it became known, was viewed by sixty million Americans, the largest ever television audience for a political broadcast, and reduced many of them to tears. Messages flooded into Republican headquarters saying that Nixon must stay. Eisenhower was stuck with him but did not like him, and offered only tepid support when Nixon secured the Republican nomination for the 1960 presidential election. John F. Kennedy, the Democrats' candidate, was a hawkish anti-communist millionaire, so could not be smeared as a pinko. When the two candidates faced each other in the first ever television debate, Nixon looked shifty and unshaven, while Kennedy was smiling and debonair.

Kennedy won a very narrow victory. Both sides had committed electoral fraud, and Nixon decided not to plunge the country into crisis by bringing a legal action. He instead tried to recover by running in 1962 for the governorship of California. He lost, blamed the press for his defeat and told reporters when he met them the morning after: 'But as I leave you I want you to know – just think how much you're going to be missing. You won't have Nixon to kick around any more, because, gentlemen, this is my last press conference.'

That seemed to be the end of his political career. He set up as a lawyer in New York. But as the 1968 presidential election approached, he assembled a coalition of wealthy backers and offered himself as the candidate who could best unite the Republicans and lead them to victory. The party duly adopted him, after which he disconcerted almost everyone by backing the unknown and unvetted Spiro Agnew from Maryland as his running mate.

Nixon promised 'an honourable end to the war in Vietnam', but in the closing stages of the campaign was dismayed to see that Johnson, the outgoing President, might attain this goal first. Nixon dissuaded the South Vietnamese President, Nguyen Van Thieu, from accepting peace on Johnson's terms, and proceeded to win a narrow victory at the polls. He was helped by the fracturing of the Democratic vote, with Johnson's civil rights reforms rejected by much of the south, which turned instead to a candidate who advocated racial segregation, the governor of Alabama, George Wallace.

In his inaugural address, Nixon spoke the language of reconciliation: 'When we listen to the better angels of our nature, we find that they celebrate the simple things, the basic things – such as goodness, decency, love, kindness.' These qualities turned out to be in short supply during his presidency. After his victory, he told his staff, 'the press is the enemy. When news is concerned, nobody in the press is a friend. They are all enemies.' Nixon suffered from a paranoia which became self-fulfilling. The hatred he felt for the press was fully reciprocated. It really was out to get him, pretty much regardless of what he did.

Although he and Henry Kissinger, his national security adviser, knew America had to get out of Vietnam, he could not stand the idea of being humiliated by a 'fourth-rate power'. In order to force concessions from Hanoi, he began by secretly intensifying the bombing campaign. He tried to keep this even from many of his own colleagues, but was attacked as a warmonger, indeed as a genocidal war criminal who accepted no constitutional checks and balances. The feeling grew that the nation was splitting in two.

In his address to the nation in November 1969 Nixon warned: 'If a vocal minority, however fervent its cause, prevails over reason and the will of the majority, this nation has no future as a free society.' He appealed for support to 'the great silent majority of my fellow Americans'. The President calculated that if he could carry respectable opinion with him he could win, whatever the liberal press might say. This continued to be his calculation even after May 1970, when four student protesters were shot dead by the National Guard at Kent State University in Ohio, and disturbances followed at 350 other colleges and universities.

The President believed he was playing a larger and more strategic game than his opponents. In February 1972, after secret diplomacy had prepared the way, he made an official presidential visit to China. His critics were astonished, and so were his friends, for Nixon had always been a virulent anti-communist. Yet here he was making friends with the communists in Peking, calculating that this would make it easier to conclude arms limitation talks with Moscow, and to disengage from North Vietnam.

Both things happened, after a fashion. In May 1972 Nixon went to Moscow and signed agreements with the Soviet leader Leonid Brezhnev which imposed limits on nuclear weapons. And Nixon had already withdrawn most American troops from Vietnam, where they would supposedly be replaced by South Vietnamese forces. He was delighted to find himself fighting, in the presidential election of 1972, George McGovern: 'Here is a situation where the Eastern Establishment media finally has a candidate who almost totally shares their views.' In November of that year Nixon won a colossal victory at the polls.

And yet he was already in deep trouble. In June of that year White House operatives known informally as the Plumbers, for their supposed aim was to prevent leaks, had mounted a break-in which went wrong at the headquarters of the Democratic National Committee on the sixth floor of the Watergate building in Foggy Bottom in Washington. This in itself did not necessarily threaten the president. But Nixon almost at once ordered the CIA to stop the FBI from investigating the break-in, and that constituted a clear obstruction of justice. From now on he was in a precarious position, dependent on the loyalty of those of his henchmen who knew what he had done, but also inclined, if he could get away with it, to blame them in order to save himself.

His enemies in Congress and the media saw their chance to destroy him, and began to investigate what the President had known about this murky affair and when he knew it. In April 1973 he tried to extricate himself by announcing the resignation of two of his loyal servants, Bob Haldeman and John Ehrlichman, and the sacking of John Dean, who worked for Ehrlichman. In May, the Senate hearings began, and in July they learned from Alexander Butterfield, who had worked for Haldeman, of the existence of the taping system which had been installed on Nixon's orders in February 1971.

Nixon, pleading executive privilege, refused to hand over any of the tapes. He had often behaved strangely towards his staff, but now, as he fought for his political life, they wondered whether he had actually gone mad. He left foreign policy to Henry Kissinger, who was promoted to secretary of state, in which capacity he dealt as he saw fit with the military coup in Chile in September 1973 and the Arab attack on Israel the following month, sending enormous quantities of arms to the Israelis. In that same month Spiro Agnew had to resign as vice-president, unable to contest allegations of corruption and tax evasion committed while he was governor of Maryland. Nixon appointed Gerald Ford in his place.

Over Christmas 1973, Nixon ordered one last bombing campaign against North Vietnam, after which he agreed a peace deal not much different to what Lyndon Johnson had come close to obtaining in 1968. The bombing helped entrench his reputation as a warmonger rather than a peacemaker.

In April 1974 Nixon consented to the publication of transcripts of forty-two tapes, but insisted on the profanities he had uttered being replaced by 'expletive deleted'. This made it look as if he had been more foul-mouthed than was actually the case, for most of the deletions were exclamations such as 'Goddamn,' 'Hell,' 'Damn,' 'Christ' and 'For Chrissake.' The President told a member of his staff, 'If my mother ever heard me use words like that she would turn over in her grave.' She had died in 1967, but her son still wanted to appear to live up to her standards.

At the end of July 1974 the House Judiciary Committee voted by 27 to 11 to recommend that the full House vote for the

President to be impeached. On 5 August a transcript was published of the so-called 'smoking gun' tape of Nixon telling officials to stop the FBI investigation. Nixon's last congressional support fell away, it became clear that if the impeachment proceedings reached the Senate he would be convicted, and on 8 August 1974 he announced in a televised address to the nation that although he had 'never been a quitter', he would resign. He was the first president to resign, and had only done so after subjecting his country to a horribly protracted ordeal. In a final act of shameless defiance, he gave his trademark double victory sign before departing by helicopter from the White House lawn.

Nixon lived for another twenty years, during which the animus against him diminished. He wrote successful books, and his defenders hailed him as a strategic genius. He himself said towards the end of his life: 'I am a square. My values are traditional: God, country, family. I am absolutely opposed to the destruction of those values that came about during the Vietnam era. Free love, drugs, tearing down your country, denying God, selfishness and indulgence – everything I despise took root when I was president and there was so little I could do to stop it . . . I represented everything they were trying to overthrow.'

Traditional values include respect for the rule of law, and for honest dealing. By flouting those values, Nixon inflicted deep wounds on his country as well as on himself.

GERALD FORD

Lived 1913–2006; president 1974–77

Gerald Ford was a popular and trusted figure until a month into his presidency, when he pardoned Richard Nixon. The new President never recovered from this act of charity, for although his decency and moderation were undeniable, so was his dim-wittedness. His opponents ran rings round him, and in the presidential election of 1976 he lost to Jimmy Carter, which made him the shortest-serving president since Warren Harding. His wife, Betty Ford, is remembered for the courage and candour with which she faced her alcoholism.

Ford was born Leslie Lynch King in Omaha, Nebraska, but his mother immediately fled his violent and abusive father and went home with the baby to Grand Rapids, Missouri, where she in due course married Gerald Ford, a house painter, whose name her son took. The boy grew into an outstanding athlete who played centre for the University of Michigan football team, was taken on as a coach at Yale and at length managed to enrol in the law school there, from which he returned to Grand Rapids to set up as a lawyer.

During the Second World War he saw extensive service aboard an aircraft carrier in the Pacific. In 1948 he married Betty Bloomer Warren, a divorced former dancer, and gained election as a Republican to the House of Representatives, where he remained for the next twenty-four years. Ford gained respect in Congress for his honesty and hard work, and served as House minority leader, but was described by President Johnson as 'so dumb he can't fart and chew gum at the same time'. LBJ also said, 'The trouble with Jerry Ford is that he used to play football without a helmet.'

In late 1973, when Vice President Spiro Agnew was forced to step down, Nixon appointed Ford in his place, as someone who had the support of both houses of Congress. Nixon may also have calculated that Congress would be reluctant to bring impeachment proceedings, because if these succeeded, the mediocre Ford would enter the White House. But in August 1974 Nixon resigned and Ford did enter the White House, the first person to do so without being elected as either president or vice president. After being sworn in on 9 August he said: 'My fellow Americans, our long national nightmare is over. Our Constitution works; our great republic is a government of laws and not of men. Here, the people rule. But there is a higher power, by whatever name we honour Him, who ordains not only righteousness but love, not only justice, but mercy . . . let us restore the golden rule to our political process, and let brotherly love purge our hearts of suspicion and hate.'

Ford meant this more literally than his listeners realised. On 8 September 1974 he made the announcement which would colour his entire presidency:

As we are a nation under God, so I am sworn to uphold our laws with the help of God. And I have sought such guidance and searched my own conscience with special diligence to determine the right thing for me to do with respect to my predecessor in this place, Richard Nixon, and his loyal wife and family. Theirs is an American tragedy in which we all – all have played a part. It could go on and on and on, or someone must write the end to it. I have concluded that only I can do that, and if I can, I must.

Ford said Nixon had 'already paid the unprecedented penalty of relinquishing the highest elective office of the United States', asserted that the former president 'and his loved ones have suffered enough', and granted him 'a full, free and absolute pardon'.

Many Americans thought Nixon had not suffered enough, especially compared to his various subordinates who got jail sentences. Ford's poll ratings collapsed, and he was accused of doing a shabby deal with his predecessor. This he denied. It seems more likely he was manipulated by Nixon and by White House staff loyal to Nixon into supposing his predecessor was more unwell than was actually the case. Ford was surprised, after granting the pardon, to find his old boss in good health, and disgustingly impenitent.

Ford's authority never recovered. Vietnam and Watergate had discredited the office of president in the eyes of the public and the press, Congress was determined to assert control over foreign policy, and even his own staff accorded him scant respect. The

South Vietnamese government collapsed in April 1975, Congress rejecting Ford's plea to shore it up, and the evacuation of the last Americans by helicopter from the roof of the embassy in Saigon provided an indelible image of humiliation.

At least his wife was popular. Betty Ford amazed the nation with an outspoken performance on 60 *Minutes* soon after she became first lady, in which she approved of abortion, equal rights and pre-marital sex. When the interviewer suggested her own eighteen-year-old daughter was 'pretty young to start affairs', Ford replied: 'Oh yes, she's a big girl.' She was also open about her breast cancer and the mastectomy she underwent at the end of September 1974. A few years later, she was equally open about her treatment for addiction to painkillers and alcohol, and opened the Betty Ford Centre in California, where others could receive help.

Her husband lacked her gifts as a communicator. He handled America's economic troubles – high oil prices, inflation, unemployment – skilfully, but got no thanks for it. The Republicans were split, and only with difficulty did he beat off a challenge from Ronald Reagan, the former governor of California, for the nomination in 1976. Reagan's neoconservative supporters then refused to campaign for the man they derided as 'Bozo the president'.

The campaign against Carter saw the first television debates since the Kennedy–Nixon clashes in 1960. Ford asserted there was 'no Soviet domination in eastern Europe', had no idea how to correct this ludicrous assertion, and went down to a narrow defeat. The career of this honourable man demonstrated how difficult it was to play the role of president. Integrity and geniality were not enough. He retired to California, where he survived until 2006, and Betty to 2011.

JIMMY CARTER

Lived 1924–; president 1977–81

J immy Carter won the presidency as an outsider, and would
not accept the need, on entering the White House, to mas-
sage the egos of congressional insiders in order to get things
done. He was a pious, good-natured, born-again southern Baptist, who trusted in his conscientious ability to work things out
for himself. In the eyes of his critics in Washington he was a
sanctimonious fool from the sticks, while even his friends admitted he could be naïve. For the last 444 days of his term of office,
his fate was in the hands of Iranian revolutionaries inspired by

Ayatollah Khomeini who held fifty-two American diplomats hostage in Tehran, and in November 1980 he suffered a crushing defeat at the hands of Ronald Reagan.

James Earl Carter Junior was born in Plains, a small town in Georgia, where his father, James Earl Carter Senior, kept a general store and grew peanuts and other crops, and his mother, known as Miss Lillian, was a nurse. Their house had neither electricity nor indoor plumbing. Young Jimmy had never seen the sea, but set his heart on going into the navy, and in 1943 entered the naval academy at Annapolis. As soon as he graduated he married Rosalynn Smith, the best friend of his younger sister, with whom he had three sons. Carter was a solitary but competent naval officer, serving in submarines when his father died in 1953, whereupon he yielded to his mother's plea to go home to Plains and salvage the family business.

Rosalynn was horrified by his decision: 'I argued. I cried. I even screamed at him.' But on returning to the small town where she too had been born, she formed a close working relationship with her husband, helping him first to build up a successful business as a peanut farmer and then to enter state politics, in which he evinced such ability that he became a state senator and in 1970 was elected governor of Georgia.

He was so unknown at national level that in December 1973 when he appeared on the television programme *What's My Line* the panel had great difficulty identifying him. In the summer of 1974 he told his mother he was going to run for president, and she replied, 'President of what?' Few people apart from Jimmy and Rosalynn Carter could imagine him in the White House and, in any case, no southerner had been elected president since Zachary Taylor in 1848.

But Carter turned his obscurity into a plus. Becoming nationally known only after winning the New Hampshire primary in February 1976, this smiling innocent from Georgia could have nothing to do with either Vietnam or Watergate. He presented himself, not as a politician, but as 'a farmer, an engineer, a businessman, a planner, a scientist, a governor, and a Christian'. About his policies he remained artfully imprecise, so people could believe what they liked. He won the Democratic nomination, and in the election took on the sitting president, Gerald Ford, whom many Republicans found uninspiring.

Carter told the voters, 'I will never lie to you.' But in order to avoid sounding holier-than-thou, he also gave an interview to *Playboy* magazine, at the end of which he delivered 'a long, softly spoken monologue that grew in intensity as he made his final points':

I try not to commit a deliberate sin. I recognize that I'm going to do it anyhow, because I'm human and I'm tempted. And Christ set some almost impossible standards for us. Christ said, 'I tell you that anyone who looks on a woman with lust has in his heart already committed adultery.' I've looked on a lot of women with lust. I've committed adultery in my heart many times. This is something that God recognises I will do – and I have done it – and God forgives me for it. But that doesn't mean that I condemn someone who not only looks on a woman with lust but who leaves his wife and shacks up with somebody out of wedlock.

Christ says, don't consider yourself better than someone else because one guy screws a whole bunch of women while the other guy is loyal to his wife. The guy who's loyal to his wife ought not to be condescending or proud because of the relative degree of sinfulness.

Carter's admission: 'I've committed adultery in my heart' went round the world, with some people worried that his indiscretion showed he was not worldly enough to cope with the presidency, while his fellow Baptists were upset by terms like 'shacks up' and 'screws'. Few Americans were delighted by either candidate, but Carter was sharper than Ford in the television debates and gained the narrowest victory since Woodrow Wilson won a second term in 1916.

To show how modest his presidency was going to be, he, Rosalynn and their nine-year-old daughter Amy got out of their limousine and walked back to the White House from the Capitol after his inauguration. But how was he going to use his victory? He pardoned most of those who had dodged the draft during the Vietnam War, which annoyed conservatives, and failed to realise that although his party controlled both houses of Congress, its representatives would have to be wooed if he was to get substantial reforms in fields like energy, welfare and immigration. Nor did he have much idea what to do about inflation, which reached 14 per cent in 1980.

In foreign policy he set out to reaffirm 'America's commitment to human rights' but found this an inadequate guide to a world where it often seemed prudent to support an oppressive regime for fear of seeing it replaced by a more oppressive one. His most notable success came in September 1978, when he brought the leaders of Israel and Egypt to Camp David, in Maryland, and after thirteen days of talks prevailed on them to sign the Camp David Accords, under which the Israelis returned Sinai to Egypt and promised not to build on the occupied West Bank.

The Iranian revolution presented an even sterner test of statecraft, and Carter failed it. In October 1979 he allowed the Shah, who had been forced in January to flee Tehran, to come to New York for medical treatment. In narrow moral terms this decision could be defended as honourable – the Shah was a friend of America – but it placed US diplomats in Tehran in extreme peril. After the Carter administration refused Iranian demands for the extradition of the Shah to face trial and probable execution, students in Tehran invaded the American embassy and, with the approval of the spiritual leader of the revolution, Ayatollah Khomeini, took its staff hostage.

Carter was now in an agonising predicament, one which his simple-minded approach had helped to create. He tried negotiating with the revolutionaries in Tehran through shadowy intermediaries in West Germany and Algeria, and in April 1980 attempted to regain the initiative by launching a rescue mission, codenamed Eagle Claw. But of the eight helicopters deployed, only five arrived at the staging post in the Iranian desert in an operational condition. The mission was therefore aborted, but as the force withdrew one of the helicopters crashed into a transport aircraft with the loss of eight lives.

American voters, who at the start of the crisis had rallied round the President, now lost faith in him, and in the presidential election Reagan trounced Carter, who spent the last days of his presidency almost continually awake, trying to arrange the hostages' release. When he rang his successor to give him the good news that this had been achieved, he was told Reagan was asleep and not to be woken. Thus did a president who had no idea how to delegate hand over to one with a gift for remaining calm.

Rosalynn took her husband's defeat hard, for she had been so closely involved in his presidency that she attended Cabinet meetings. Together they returned to Plains, where they lived out the longest retirement of any presidential couple. Carter remained involved in attempts to promote peace and human rights around the world, continued to teach Sunday school, and at the time of writing he and his wife are still alive, honoured inhabitants of their home town, though too naïve to make a success of their four years in the White House.

RONALD REAGAN

Lived 1911–2004; president 1981–89

R onald Reagan was a professional actor who turned the presidency into his greatest role. He was optimistic without arrogance, handsome without perturbing sex appeal, patriotic without wishing to spill American blood, enjoyed telling jokes at his own expense and possessed an astonishing ability to instil in voters his own unruffled confidence. When he entered the White House the liberal Establishment feared and despised him as a trigger-happy cowboy and B-movie actor, but he became the most successful president since

Eisenhower, and the first since him to leave office in happy circumstances.

His father, an Irish American shoe salesman, was a wonderful storyteller but fought a losing battle against alcoholism. He moved from job to job in Illinois and when Ronald was born in the village of Tampico is supposed to have said: 'He looks like a fat little Dutchman. But who knows, he might grow up to be president one day.' Ronald was called Dutch by family and friends, and revered his mother, who was a staunch member of the Disciples of Christ church. He studied economics and sociology at Eureka College, flourishing as a football player and paying his way by working as a lifeguard. He loved all sports and became a sports announcer, doing radio commentaries even on games he could only follow by ticker tape.

At the age of twenty-six he broke into Hollywood, going under contract to Jack Warner. He made a total of fifty-four films, proved himself completely reliable and said of his performances, 'I was brave but kind of in a low-budget fashion.' In his best picture, *Kings Row*, made in 1942, he plays a man who loses his legs, and, on waking up in bed and seeing the flat sheets where they should be, cries out to his co-star Ann Sheridan, 'Where's the rest of me?' Reagan did the scene in a single take and used the line as the title of his autobiography. That same year he went into the army and made training films, and after the war his career faded.

His first marriage, to his fellow actor Jane Wyman, with whom he had two children, ended in 1948. She was irritated by his growing interest in politics. Reagan was deeply affected by the break-up, but in 1952 married another actor, Nancy Davis, with whom he had two more children. He did not appear to take much interest in his children, and Nancy found herself unable to get through to him on any deep level, but his performances were immaculate. He moved from films into television, changed from a Democrat into a hard-line Republican, and in 1964 delivered a speech in praise of Barry Goldwater, the Republican presidential candidate, which was so well received that party backers in California urged Reagan to run for governor.

He was an exceptionally effective campaigner, not original, but voters seldom want originality. He made things simple, sparing people the details and never talking down to them, and in 1966 was elected governor. In that era of race riots and anti-war demonstrations, Reagan stood for respectability, but in a good-natured way. When a student demonstrator shouted, 'We are the future,' through the glass of the governor's limousine, he got a bit of paper, wrote on it and held up to the window his reply: 'I'll sell my bonds.'

A run at the presidency was now on the cards, but in 1968 Richard Nixon wrapped up the Republican nomination and in 1972 he ran again. Reagan campaigned as a Cold War warrior against the moderate Gerald Ford for the nomination in 1976, narrowly failed to win, but succeeded in 1980, whereupon he faced the Democrat incumbent, Jimmy Carter, in a single television debate.

Carter launched an earnest attack on him on health care. Reagan, smiling, just shook his head and said, 'There you go again!' The economy had not prospered under Carter, and at the end of the debate Reagan turned to the camera and asked the voters: 'Are you better off than you were four years ago? Is it easier for you to go and buy things in the stores than it was four years ago? Is there more or less employment in the country than there was four years ago? Is America as respected throughout the world as it was? Do you feel that our security is safe, that we're as strong as we were four years ago?'

While casting his own vote, Reagan was asked who his wife was going to vote for and replied, 'She's going to vote for some former actor.' He had better lines than Carter, delivered them better and won by a landslide.

On taking office in January 1981, Reagan was just short of his seventieth birthday, so broke the record for oldest president set 140 years before by the sixty-eight-year-old William Henry Harrison. Not until Donald Trump's inauguration in 2017 at the age of seventy was the record broken again. Reagan was also the first divorced man to enter the White House, with Trump the second. But Reagan's graceful manners were quite different to Trump's, and he kept himself in far better physical shape. His wife, a thin woman immaculately turned out in designer clothes, stood loyally at his side.

At the end of March 1981, as the new President was leaving the Hilton Hotel in Washington after speaking in favour of federal spending cuts, a deranged young man fired six shots at him. Reagan's press secretary received a serious head wound, and a police officer and a Secret Service agent were also hit. Another bullet ricocheted off the presidential limousine, entered Reagan's body under his arm and ended up less than an inch from his heart.

He was driven to George Washington University Hospital, insisted on walking in, but was losing so much blood that delay might have proved fatal. When his wife arrived from the White House, he told her, 'Honey, I forgot to duck,' a line used by the boxer Jack Dempsey the night he was beaten by Gene Tunney. In the operating room, where the bullet was extracted, Reagan removed his oxygen mask and said to the doctors, 'I hope you are all Republicans.' The surgeon, who was a Democrat, replied, 'Today, Mr President, we are all Republicans.' While unable to speak because he had a tube down his throat, Reagan wrote a note to one of the nurses, borrowing the joke by W. C. Fields about what he would like written on his tomb: 'All in all, I'd rather be in Philadelphia.'

By playing this brush with death as comedy, Reagan soared in the public's estimation. His escape suggested fortune was now smiling on America, and his plan to cut taxes, increase defence spending and reduce other federal outlays sailed through the Democrat-controlled House of Representatives, where it might have been mauled. Reagan, unlike Carter, took the trouble to charm members of Congress, and knew how to do it.

Reaganomics, as the programme became known, did not at first appear to work, and the budget deficit ballooned to alarming proportions. Reagan just said it was big enough to look after itself. A technocrat might have taken corrective action, but he stuck to his course, and gradually the economy started to recover.

He increased defence spending in the belief that he could precipitate the collapse of the Soviet Union, which would be unable to keep up. Reagan had for decades described communism as evil, a view which commanded widespread support in Russian-occupied eastern Europe as well as in the United States. His call to 'make America great again' struck a patriotic chord with voters. Reagan might be old, but he seemed stronger than Carter, Ford, Nixon or Johnson had turned out to be, especially as he relied on economic pressure and avoided any serious fighting. In a debate with Walter Mondale, the Democratic candidate in the 1984 presidential election, Reagan said: 'I will not make age an issue of this campaign; I'm not going to exploit for political purposes my opponent's youth and inexperience.' Mondale could not resist laughing, and Reagan proceeded to win a larger victory than he had won over Carter four years previously.

Not everything went swimmingly in his second term. The Iran-Contra scandal, involving the supply of arms to Iran with the proceeds used to fund right-wing rebels in Nicaragua, indicated a propensity to law-breaking by White House staff which recalled the worst days of Richard Nixon. But Reagan, pretending to a shakier grasp of detail than was actually the case, rose above it, and few Americans wanted to believe he was a crook. At a dinner in Washington at the Gridiron Club in 1987 he played up to the idea that he was too idle to have any idea what his subordinates were doing: 'It's true hard work never killed anybody, but I figure, why take the chance?'

Like his friend the British Prime Minister Margaret Thatcher, Reagan became a hero to the subject peoples of the Soviet bloc, and sought to reach out to them rather than maintain a convenient accommodation with their oppressors. In 1987 he delivered an acclaimed speech in front of the Brandenburg Gate, on the western side of the Berlin Wall, in which he indicated that he expected concessions from the new Russian leader, Mikhael Gorbachev: 'There is one sign the Soviets can make that would be unmistakable, that would advance dramatically the cause of freedom and peace. General Secretary Gorbachev, if you seek peace, if you seek prosperity for the Soviet Union and eastern Europe, if you seek liberalisation: come here to this gate! Mr Gorbachev, open this gate! Mr Gorbachev, tear down this wall.' Reagan had placed himself on the right side of history, for in November 1989, less than ten months after his departure from the White House, the Berlin Wall fell.

Towards the end of his presidency Reagan did not always appear as alert as he had at the start. He may already have been suffering from the early stages of Alzheimer's. Five years after he left office, by which time the signs had become unmistakable, he announced in a letter to his fellow Americans that he had the disease, and went on: 'I now begin the journey that will lead me into the sunset of my life. I know that for America there will always be a bright dawn ahead.'

After his death in 2004 his wife said that for the last four years of his life he had not opened his eyes. As president he blotted out the memory of the twenty troubled years before his election, and led the West to victory in the cold war – not bad for a man once derided as second-rate actor.

GEORGE H. W. BUSH

Lived 1924–2018; president 1989–93

George Herbert Walker Bush was more ambitious than he looked. His country club manner, which he tried in vain to hide behind a populist exterior, was accompanied by a competitiveness which carried him into the White House. He handled foreign crises – the invasion of Kuwait, the collapse of the Soviet Union, the reunification of Germany – with exemplary prudence, but at home doomed himself by breaking a pledge he had given in one of his moments of bogus demagoguery: 'Read my lips, no new taxes.'

His father, Prescott Bush, was a partner in a Wall Street investment firm, Republican senator in the 1950s for Connecticut and an outstanding golfer, often invited to play with President Eisenhower. Prescott married Dorothy Walker, daughter of George Herbert Walker, a brash and prosperous businessman after whom both the Walker Cup golf trophy and the future President were named. Dorothy was described after her death by her daughter as 'an enormous athlete . . . a beautiful shot and a good horsewoman and a fabulous swimmer – and tennis, and golf, and paddle tennis. And a fantastic game player. Bridge, Scrabble, anagrams, backgammon, Peggoty, gin rummy, Sir Hinkam Funny-Duster – marvellous card game. Mother was a champ at it. Russian bank, tiddly-winks.'

The Bush family competed desperately at games, but Dorothy made sure nobody showed off about winning. When the second of her four sons took his first run at the presidency in 1979, she told him after watching him on television: 'George, you're talking about yourself too much.' The inability to blow his own trumpet had been instilled from earliest youth. Throughout his life he was inarticulate, and had trouble finishing his sentences.

Actions spoke louder than words. He volunteered at the earliest opportunity for war service in the navy, became at the age of eighteen its youngest pilot, flew fifty-eight missions over the Pacific, was shot down but picked up by an American submarine as he drifted in a dinghy towards the Japanese. His radio operator and gunner, whom he honoured to the end of his days, were killed.

At the age of seventeen Bush had fallen in love with sixteen-year-old Barbara Pierce, a distant cousin of Franklin Pierce, the fourteenth President. They got engaged before he went off to war and married when he got back. He studied like his father at Yale, but rather than follow him onto Wall Street, went west, to Midland in Texas, where he made a fortune in oil. The Bushes had six children, including a daughter, Robin, who died of leukaemia at the age of three. Barbara's hair turned white and she kept it that way.

In the 1960s Bush stood and failed for a Senate seat in Texas. He briefly represented the state in the House of Representatives, but was unable to develop a convincing political persona of his own, for though he flirted with hard-line anti-communism, it did not suit him. His rise to the White House was as an insider, working for three successive Republican presidents, none of whom he found personally sympathetic.

Richard Nixon sent him in 1970 to New York as ambassador to the United Nations, then brought him back to Washington in 1972 to chair the Republican National Committee, in which capacity he was loyal to the president until the final days. Gerald Ford sent him to China, where Bush enjoyed a close but discreet liaison with a divorcee, Jennifer Fitzgerald, whom he had appointed without obvious qualifications to his staff, before returning to Washington to become director of the CIA, where Fitzgerald's services remained important.

Jimmy Carter removed him from the CIA, and in 1979 Bush mounted his first bid for the Republican presidential nomination. He was defeated by Reagan and agreed to serve as vice president, which he did for eight years. Like his boss, he knew about the Iran-Contra scandal but avoided contamination. He and Barbara were not close to the Reagans, but nor was anyone else, and Bush earned the President's tepid support as his successor.

For the 1988 election campaign, Bush chose a dimwit, Dan Quayle, as his running mate. Quayle was capable of saying any number of idiotic things, and when he tried during a television debate to rebut the charge of inexperience by pointing out he had served as long in Congress as John F. Kennedy, his Democratic opposite number Lloyd Bentsen responded: 'Senator, you're no Jack Kennedy.'

Bush won by sanctioning a ruthless attack on the Democratic presidential candidate, Mike Dukakis, Governor of Massachusetts, who was blamed for the release of Willie Horton, a murderer who had gone on to commit armed robbery and rape. Lee Atwater, who ran the Bush campaign, said of Dukakis that he would 'strip the bark off the little bastard' and 'make Willie Horton his running mate'. Bush had shown how competitive he could be. But in order to reassure Republicans who feared he might turn out to be a wimp, he had also pledged himself not to raise taxes.

The first challenges he faced were in foreign affairs. In the second half of 1989 Soviet-backed regimes all over eastern Europe collapsed, with East Germans walking through the Berlin Wall on the night of 9th November. German reunification was suddenly in prospect, and Bush accepted this as natural and right, brushing aside the objections of the British Prime Minister, Margaret Thatcher, to whom he thought Reagan had been too subservient.

In August 1990 Saddam Hussein, the leader of Iraq, invaded Kuwait. Bush said this would not do, patiently assembled an international coalition under the authority of the United Nations, and in January 1991 threw the invaders out of Kuwait in a war which lasted a hundred hours. The President refused to carry on to Baghdad and overthrow Saddam. This moderation in victory annoyed some Republicans, but meant the United States and its allies were not faced with the responsibility of governing Iraq.

This success raised Bush to a pinnacle of popularity, but there were almost two years until the next presidential election, and in his hour of triumph he faltered. He felt depressed, the economy faltered too, and in negotiations with Congress about how to deal with the budget deficit, the President, who was by nature a conciliator, felt obliged to concede there would have to be tax rises. Reagan might have risen above such a reversal. Bush could not communicate a vision of his own, for he did not have one.

This prim and preppy figure lacked the ability to persuade ordinary Americans he was on their side: something his Democrat opponent, Bill Clinton, could do very well. Atwater had by now died at the age of forty of a brain tumour, claiming before his death that he repented of the smear campaigns he had run. In the presidential election of November 1992 a third candidate, Ross Perot, complicated matters, taking almost a fifth of the vote, and Bush was beaten by Clinton.

That was not the end of the Bushes in presidential politics. Eight years later, his son, George Walker Bush – here was a family which liked to recycle a limited stock of names – entered the White House. They referred to each other as 41 and 43, their numbers in the list of presidents. As a father, 41 could not help feeling proud, but he was also distressed to find his statesmanlike moderation lauded by critics whose sole purpose was to denigrate his son. Another son, Jeb, became governor of Florida, entered the presidential race of 2016 and was demolished by Donald Trump, who described him as 'low energy'.

In an interview given by George H. W. Bush not long before his death in 2018 he wondered whether he would be remembered at all: 'I am lost between the glory of Reagan – monuments everywhere, trumpets, the great hero – and the trials and tribulations of my sons.'

BILL CLINTON

Lived 1946–; president 1993–2001

William Jefferson Clinton made his rivals look like stuffed shirts. He had an insatiable need to connect with ordinary voters and a genius for winning their support, but was also addicted to sleazy sexual encounters, most notoriously with Monica Lewinsky, a twenty-two-year-old intern, in the White House. His opponents denounced him as a disgrace to the presidency and tried to impeach him, and even his friends found him an embarrassment, for they never knew what scandal was going to erupt next. But a large part of the

American public loved him all the more because he was not respectable.

He was born in Hope, Arkansas, the posthumous son of a travelling salesman who died in a car accident and had been married five times. His mother Virginia, ebullient, resilient, a Baptist but also fond of race tracks and gambling, endlessly proud of Bill, transmitted to him her energy, optimism, gift for having a good time and urge to get close to people, for as she herself put it: 'If I see you once, you're my friend. If I see you twice I'll more than likely hug you.' She moved to Hot Springs, Arkansas, worked as a nurse and was herself married five times, including twice to Roger Clinton, a gambler and an alcoholic who abused her and her son Bill until the boy was old enough to defend his mother.

Bill took his stepfather's surname, fell in love at an early age with politics, and on a school trip to Washington at the age of sixteen was thrilled to shake hands with President Kennedy. He studied at Georgetown University in Washington DC, as a Rhodes scholar at University College, Oxford, and at Yale Law School, where he met Hillary Rodham, serious-minded daughter of a Republican businessman. She moved to the left and to Arkansas, where she joined a law firm and married Clinton.

He ran for Congress, lost but began to make a name for himself in the Democratic Party and ascended via the office of attorney general to the governorship of Arkansas, attained in 1978 at the age of only thirty-two, which made him the youngest governor in America. Two years later the voters threw him out, but two years after that he was back in the governor's mansion in Little Rock, impressing people by raising educational standards, winning repeatedly in this state of just over two million people, but aware of the danger that if he tried to go any higher in politics, the press would take an interest in his less than salubrious private life.

In the autumn of 1991, he announced he was running for the

presidency, and would lead 'a crusade to restore the forgotten middle class'. Other candidates hung back, for the incumbent president, George H. W. Bush, remained popular thanks to victory in the Gulf War. Clinton's outstanding performance in the New Hampshire primary, his empathy with any voter who had suffered some appalling misfortune, the scandals which surfaced as soon as his bandwagon began to roll, the sordid manoeuvres and moral compromises which were needed to deal with these, the greatness and decadence of his campaign are brilliantly caught in Primary Colors, a comic novel first published during the next presidential cycle and said to be by Anonymous, though it turned out to be by Joe Klein, a Newsweek journalist.

In the real-life presidential campaign the first scandal the Clintons had to deal with was the claim by Gennifer Flowers, a singer, of a twelve-year affair with Bill. Bill and Hillary went on television and he admitted having caused 'pain' in their marriage. His wife indicated that since she was standing by him, the voters should do so too. Flowers produced tape recordings of Clinton asking her to hush everything up, but somehow the story faded, in part because it was replaced by the perhaps more damaging charge that Clinton as a young man had dodged the draft in order to avoid fighting in Vietnam.

More women appeared in due course. George Stephanopoulos, who worked for Clinton during this presidential campaign and for four years in the White House, wondered in his memoir: 'How could a president so intelligent, so compassionate, so public-spirited, and so conscious of his place in history act in such a stupid, selfish, and self-destructive manner?' Clinton impelled an odd mixture of admiration and disgust even among some of those closest to him.

But he won in 1992. Compared to Bush, he possessed a shameless authenticity. As a minor character in Primary Colors remarks, 'I didn't say fucking around is a bad thing. I think it's a good thing. It's basic. Like your position on abortion or something. You want a guy who's got juice, right? A human being.'

According to various women, Clinton had juice. But he was not well prepared to be president. The White House under him was chaotic, and leaked like a sieve. He despised Jimmy Carter, the southern governor who had entered the White House sixteen years before him, but like Carter, Clinton was out of his depth in Washington, a hick who had no idea how to persuade Congress to do what he wanted it to do.

He made a bad impression by announcing on day one, without consultation, that gay people would be allowed to serve in the military, a decision which annoyed the chiefs of staff and many members of Congress, especially as Clinton himself had evaded service. Nor was it tactful to ask his wife to devise the ambitious health care reform he had promised to introduce. Her unwieldy and over-complicated plan, produced in conditions of excessive secrecy, was crushed by the vested interests in health care which she imagined she could bend to her will.

Nothing seemed to go right for Clinton. In April 1993, almost a hundred people including many women and children were killed at Waco, Texas, when a fire broke out as the FBI, acting with Washington's approval, invaded a compound occupied by a bizarre sect, the Branch Davidians, which had stockpiled arms and sworn it would never surrender. Clinton blamed the carnage on the Attorney General Janet Reno, appointed by himself after his original choices were turned down.

In July 1993 Vince Foster, a close friend of the Clintons from Arkansas who was working for them as a lawyer in the White House, committed suicide in a park in Washington. This prompted a plethora of conspiracy theories. It was suggested Foster had been murdered in order to cover up the Whitewater affair, a murky series of property transactions in Arkansas in 1978 with which the Clintons seemed to have some connection. Reno decided to appoint an independent counsel to look into the Whitewater allegations.

In the mid-term elections of 1994 the Republicans gained control of both houses of Congress for the first time since 1954 – a slap in the face for the President, whose ineptitude had inflicted grave damage on the Democrats. But from this low point, his fortunes started to recover. The Republicans in the House of Representatives, led by the overconfident Newt Gingrich, overplayed their hand, shut down the federal government and began to be seen as a bunch of ideologues who only cared about the rich. Meanwhile Clinton, branding himself a New Democrat, pursued economic policies of a moderate Republican stamp, getting the budget deficit under control and presiding over a period of strong economic growth.

After the bombing in April 1995 of a federal building in Oklahoma City, where American terrorists who regarded the federal government as their enemy murdered 168 of their fellow citizens including 19 children on the second anniversary of the Waco disaster, Clinton was thought to have struck the right note, telling the nation via an audience of the children of his own staff: 'We will triumph over those who would divide us. And we will overcome them by doing it together, putting our children first.' His command of tone, and also of detail, in foreign policy was unsure, but he did manage to avoid any major American casualties.

The Republicans nominated an ineffectual candidate, Senator Robert Dole, for the presidential election of 1996, and Clinton won for a second time. He had shown a remarkable capacity to remain upbeat through dark days, but his second term was in many respects worse than the first. In 1997 the Supreme Court ruled that Paula Jones, who accused Clinton of sexual harassment committed while he was governor of Arkansas, could have her case against him heard while he was still president. Investigators seeking to demonstrate a pattern of sexual abuse lighted on the case of Monica Lewinsky, a White House intern who claimed to have had sexual relations with Clinton on nine occasions between November 1995 and March 1997.

In January 1998 Clinton said at a news conference: 'I did not have sexual relations with that woman, Miss Lewinsky.' Kenneth Starr, the special investigator who in 1994 had taken over the Whitewater inquiry, obtained a blue dress from Lewinsky which bore traces of Clinton's semen. The President contended that oral sex did not count as sex. This demeaning argument divided the nation. In October 1998 Toni Morrison, a black American novelist and critic who had in 1993 been awarded the Nobel prize for literature, offered this subtle but trenchant defence of Clinton in the *New Yorker*:

African American men seemed to understand it right away. Years ago, in the middle of the Whitewater investigation, one heard the first murmurs: white skin notwithstanding, this is our first black president. Blacker than any actual black person who could ever be elected in our children's lifetime. After all, Clinton displays almost every trope of blackness: single-parent household, born poor, working-class, saxophone-playing, McDonald's-and-junk-food-loving boy from Arkansas. And when virtually all the African American Clinton appointees began, one by one, to disappear, when the President's body, his privacy, his unpoliced sexuality became the focus of the persecution, when he was metaphorically seized and body-searched, who could gainsay these black men who knew whereof they spoke? . . .

This is Slaughtergate. A sustained, bloody, arrogant coup d'état. The Presidency is being stolen from us. And the people know it.

In December 1998 the House of Representatives voted to launch impeachment proceedings. The trial was conducted in the

Senate, and in February 1999 Clinton was acquitted. But his reputation took a long time to recover, in some quarters never has, and shortly before he left office in 2001 he gave his enemies further ammunition by conferring a presidential pardon on Marc Rich, a commodity trader accused of tax fraud.

In an interview Hillary Clinton gave in the summer of 1999, when she was preparing for her successful run in New York for the US Senate, she said her husband was 'a hard dog to keep on the porch', had suffered 'bimbo eruptions' such as the Lewinsky affair because of the abuse he had suffered in his childhood, and had lied about these lapses in order to protect his wife. Some people were allergic to Clinton, others could not help liking him. An upper-class Englishwoman who met the former President at a charity event, and was determined to detest him, admitted that after two minutes in a lift with him she was 'weak at the knees'.

Bill watched Hillary run for the presidency in 2008, when Barack Obama defeated her in the race for the Democratic nomination, and in 2016, when she got the nomination but was defeated by Trump. She had failed to become the first woman president because although she was a more distinguished lawyer than her husband, she was nothing like as good a campaigner. The Clintons were by now cut off from his Arkansas roots and lived among the super-rich, who funded her campaigns, but made her sound hypocritical when she said she cared about ordinary people. Nor could she claim to have risen solely on her own merits when people knew she had already entered the White House as first lady thanks to her husband.

GEORGE W. BUSH

Lived 1946–; president 2001–09

George Walker Bush was the first person since John Quincy Adams in 1825 to succeed his father in the presidency. But while the second Adams was a man of outstanding intellect and scant ability to get on with ordinary people, the second Bush had few ideas of his own and scant ability to take an intelligent interest in anyone else's, but could get on well with ordinary people.

In order to distinguish him from his father, Bush the younger was often known as Dubya, a Texan pronunciation of W, his middle initial. After the attack on the World Trade Center in New York on 11 September 2001, in which almost 3,000 people were murdered, he proclaimed the need to invade Iraq and overthrow Saddam Hussein, although there was no evidence the Iraqi regime had been involved in this crime. Bush believed he was being more resolute than his father, but it turned out he was being more reckless and, quite soon, as Iraq descended into civil war, he found himself paralysed, unable either to retreat or to make a success of the occupation. His patriotism won him a second term, but he was out of his depth, an impression confirmed by his feebleness in 2005 when Hurricane Katrina struck New Orleans.

Bush grew up yearning for his high-achieving father's approval, while fearing he lacked the ability to earn it. The oldest of six children, he was bad at academic work and also at sport, was not allowed to grieve properly for his three-year-old sister who died when he was seven (his parents had not told him she was mortally ill), and only got into Yale because his father and grandfather had gone there and done extremely well, an embarrassing credential in the increasingly egalitarian and meritocratic 1960s.

He was tapped for – selected for – Skull and Bones, most exclusive of the student societies, to which again his father, by now a congressman, and his grandfather, until recently a senator, had belonged. We catch a glimpse of him as a rebellious student, doing something his inhibited forebears would not have done: 'On a Sunday morning, at five a.m., I saw him raving drunk, holding on to the back of a garbage truck in a three-piece suit, singing and carrying on and helping the garbage guys put the garbage on the truck. He was known in those days as an affable drunk.'

He went on drinking until he was forty, when he became a teetotaller, for his wife, Laura, a librarian, told him she would divorce him unless he sobered up and started being a proper father to their twin daughters. At around this time he came to Jesus in an evangelical kind of way, recounted with artful imprecision in order to gain the votes of believers while not putting off unbelievers. He had attempted to make money in the Texas oil business, but less systematically than his father, and failed to emulate his success. Nor had an early run for congress worked out.

In 1988 he acted as enforcer on his father's presidential campaign, approved of the character assassination of his father's opponent, and at last won a measure of paternal approval. Four years later, he reckoned his father lost for lack of ruthlessness. The younger Bush had by now achieved success in business by putting together a consortium of rich men which took over the Texas Rangers baseball team, and had also caught the eye of Karl Rove, a political consultant who perceived in him the makings of a successful candidate.

Rove was right. In 1994 Bush ran for governor of Texas and won, for he was good at getting down with the folks, totally unpretentious and relaxed, his inarticulacy suggesting he was one of them. In 1998 he won again, and won well. A run for the White House followed, with Bush profiling himself in the 2000 presidential election as the sober, respectable, monogamous alternative to the priapic Bill Clinton.

Clinton was coming to the end of his eight years, but his vice president, Al Gore, who won the Democratic nomination, could be treated as complicit in Clinton's scandals. Neither Bush nor Gore ran an exciting campaign, and they ended up in a dead heat, with the national result turning on Florida, where Bush's brother Jeb was serving as governor. A few hundred votes separated the two candidates, and it was evident that for various reasons, including voting machines which malfunctioned, there were grave inaccuracies in the first count and deep uncertainty about which votes were valid for the recount.

Not since 1877, when Rutherford B. Hayes only learned he had won while on his way by train to the inauguration, had a presidential election been marred by such conspicuous errors. This time the trouble took thirty-six days to settle, with the eventual Supreme Court verdict going by five votes to four in Bush's favour. Gore conceded defeat, but the new President started off without a proper mandate.

He had no very clear idea of what he wanted to do, except be more decisive than his cautious, temporising father. This was the younger Bush's way of showing the world he was not a wimp. At home he gave speeches about compassionate conservatism, and used the full treasury left behind by Clinton to put through a tax cut which relieved the heavy burden on the rich. It is easier to look decisive in foreign policy, and here he had a team of neoconservatives which not just helped him, but seemed to many observers to run him. Bush knew next to nothing about foreign affairs, and had seldom been abroad except to Mexico, just over the border from Texas. His Vice President, Dick Cheney, was an expert, and became the most powerful holder of an office dismissed by one of his predecessors as 'not worth a bucket of warm piss'.

In September of his first year came the attack on the twin towers of the World Trade Center in New York. When the news was brought to Bush by one of his staff, he was reading a story to some schoolchildren in Florida, and was seen on television unable to take in the magnitude of the news. He went on reading the story, and then, instead of returning at once to Washington, allowed himself to be flown for his own safety to Omaha, Nebraska.

He recovered from these fumbles with a display of martial vigour, declaring at his first press conference that the attacks were 'more than acts of terror, they were acts of war', and America was now engaged in a 'monumental struggle between good and evil'. The Secretary of State, Colin Powell, was appalled, and said later that Bush had 'cowboy instincts', but Cheney and the Secretary of Defense, Donald Rumsfeld, approved of such rhetoric. They wanted to take the chance not just to hunt down the mastermind of the attack, the al-Qaeda leader Osama bin-Laden, in Afghanistan, where in the event they failed to get their man, but to invade Iraq, the operation Bush Senior had refused to sanction in 1991.

The son rushed in where the father feared to tread. His most conspicuous ally in this venture was the United Kingdom, led by the messianic Tony Blair. The French incurred American opprobrium for holding out against the enterprise, as did the Germans and the Russians. American troops entered Baghdad in April 2003. Bush soon afterwards landed on an aircraft carrier, not in the waters off Iraq but more conveniently off the coast of California, and paraded in front of a banner bearing the words MISSION ACCOMPLISHED. His father had been a hero of the Second World War; the son had avoided service in Vietnam, but here, belatedly, was his victory.

It emerged that there was no plan about what to do next. The occupiers disbanded the Iraqi army and the country collapsed into sectarian strife between Sunni, Shia and Kurds, and against the occupiers. Bush had allowed himself to suppose he was bringing democracy to the region. He had instead unleashed a hellish civil war, which corrupted the occupiers too, found to have tortured Iraqi detainees at Abu Ghraib prison.

And yet in the presidential election of 2004 he won a second term. His opponent, John Kerry, had served with distinction in Vietnam but did not know how to defend himself when doubt was cast upon that service. Bush proved himself more ruthless as an electioneer than his father, but less astute as a president. Hurricane Katrina, which killed almost 2,000 people when it struck the coast of Louisiana in August 2005, saw him at his most hapless, incapable of mobilising the federal relief effort which was obviously needed. He was instead filmed peering out of an aeroplane window at the devastation below.

Bush was a poor advertisement for the hereditary principle.

He strutted and boasted in order to conceal his insecurity. None of the neoconservatives who urged him on to Baghdad can now be heard defending him. At the end, even Wall Street lost confidence, and crashed shortly before he handed over to his successor. Bush retired with relief into a dignified obscurity from which even he perhaps wishes he had never emerged.

BARACK OBAMA

Lived 1961–; president 2009–17

B arack Hussein Obama was a brilliant orator, a master of the sublime tone who could also tell jokes. His name carried an unfortunate echo of Osama bin-Laden, the terrorist who masterminded the attack in 2001 on the twin towers. But Obama worked out how to turn his origins, unusual for a presidential candidate, to his advantage, stepping before the public as an exemplar of the generosity of the United States, an affirmation of the ideals expressed in the Declaration of Independence, a rebuke to the politics of character assassination. As the first African American president, he embodied the hope that racial divisions could be healed, and gave his adoring supporters the chance to be nice to each other.

This rebuke to the rougher side of American life did not go unanswered. In 2016 Henry Kissinger, grand old man of American realpolitik, criticised Obama for pursuing too 'passive' a foreign policy, designed 'to keep the insensitive elements of America from unsettling the world'. And in that same year Donald Trump won the presidency in part by giving voice to those insensitive elements, and repudiating everything Obama stood for.

Obama's mother, Ann Dunham, a white woman born in Kansas, was studying at the University of Hawaii when she met a black African student, Barack Obama, whom she married when she was three months' pregnant. Their son, also called Barack, was born when she was eighteen. The marriage did not last, Barack returning, after a spell of study at Harvard, to Kenya, where he was killed in a car accident in 1982.

Ann contracted a second marriage, to an Indonesian, so Barack junior spent part of his childhood on the island of Java, a formative experience which may have contributed to his serenity of manner. He later wrote of his mother, to whom he was very close: 'She taught me to disdain the blend of ignorance and arrogance that too often characterised Americans abroad.' When he was ten, he returned with her to live with his beloved grandparents, who had settled in Hawaii. He was a gifted student, who attended Punahou School in Honolulu, followed by Occidental College in Los Angeles, Columbia University in New York, a spell as a community organiser on Chicago's South Side, and Harvard Law School, where he was elected the first African American president of the *Harvard Law Review*.

The publicity attending that distinction led to a contract to write a memoir, *Dreams from My Father*, published in 1995. Unlike the campaign biographies of other presidents, this book was composed by Obama himself before he was well known. He tells with care, emotion and wit the story of his search for his father, who had come to see him only once, in Hawaii, when he ordered his ten-year-old son to stop watching television.

Obama married Michelle Robinson, a black woman from Chicago who when he met her was like himself an upwardly mobile lawyer, though neither of them could bear to stay on that treadmill. In 1996 he won a seat in the Illinois legislature and in 2002, by which time he and Michelle had two daughters, he opposed the Iraq War before it had even started: 'I am not opposed to all wars. I'm opposed to dumb wars.'

In 2004, he won the Democratic nomination for a seat in the US Senate, and in July that year he burst upon the national scene by giving the keynote speech at the Democratic National Convention for John Kerry and John Edwards, the party's presidential and vice-presidential candidates. Obama started with his own story, the dreams of his parents, the belief that in America you don't have to be rich to achieve your potential, and went on:

> Yet even as we speak, there are those who are preparing to divide us, the spin masters and negative ad peddlers who embrace the politics of anything goes. Well, I say to them tonight, there's not a liberal America and a conservative America – there's the United States of America. There's not a black America and white America and Latino America and Asian America; there's the United States of America. The pundits like to slice-and-dice our country into Red States and Blue States; Red States for Republicans, Blue States for Democrats. But I've got news for them, too. We worship an awesome God in the Blue States, and we don't like federal agents poking around our libraries in the Red States. We coach Little League in the Blue States and have gay friends in the Red States. There are patriots who opposed the war in

Iraq and patriots who supported it. We are one people, all of us pledging allegiance to the stars and stripes, all of us defending the United States of America.

In the end, that's what this election is about. Do we participate in a politics of cynicism or a politics of hope? John Kerry calls on us to hope. John Edwards calls on us to hope. I'm not talking about blind optimism here – the almost wilful ignorance that thinks unemployment will go away if we just don't talk about it, or the health care crisis will solve itself if we just ignore it. No, I'm talking about something more substantial. It's the hope of slaves sitting around a fire singing freedom songs; the hope of immigrants setting out for distant shores; the hope of a young naval lieutenant [Kerry] bravely patrolling the Mekong Delta; the hope of a mill worker's son [Edwards] who dares to defy the odds; the hope of a skinny kid with a funny name who believes that America has a place for him, too. The audacity of hope!

Even before he won election, by a landslide, that autumn as senator for Illinois, he was being talked of as a presidential candidate for the next race, in 2008. Hillary Clinton had the machine required to win that nomination, Obama had the voice. He attracted worldwide admiration for his oratory, and my newspaper in London sent me to America to see if he was as good as he was said to be.

My wife was already an ardent supporter of his, and one morning in April 2008 I rang her from Philadelphia to boast I was on the same train as Obama. She demanded that I get him to write the following inscription in my copy of his autobiography: 'To Sally, Lots of love, Barack.' The train made its first stop, at the scruffy suburban station of Wynnewood. Obama dismounted and addressed a wildly enthusiastic crowd in the station car park, with people hanging out of trees to hear him. There was then a delay, and I saw a volunteer carrying some copies of *Dreams from My Father* into the waiting room. I placed my copy on the top of the pile, together with a note about the preferred wording.

Obama went in and signed the books, including some volumes which did not look like any known work of his, over which he laughed. As he came out, I stepped forward, shook him by the hand, told him my name and newspaper, and offered the only connection between us which occurred to me: 'Your grandfather and my grandfather were both with the British army in Burma during the Second World War.' Obama's grandfather had gone to Burma with the British army as a cook.

Obama smiled. He was being ushered towards his train, but gave the impression he had all the time in the world to talk to this strange Englishman. 'That's pretty impressive,' he said, 'coming from different angles' – here he raised one of his hands high and pointed diagonally down at his other hand – 'in the British Empire.'

'You're partly British,' I said, emboldened by his friendliness. For his father, born in what was then a British colony, spoke English with a British accent and while in America attempted to drive on the left-hand side of the road. Obama laughed in the most engaging way, but was not going to admit to being the British candidate in an American presidential election.

He defeated Hillary Clinton by a narrow margin for the Democratic nomination, and John McCain, the Republican candidate, by a somewhat wider margin in the presidential election. After he had won, he and his wife were soon on the warmest terms with the Queen. Though not actually British, Obama at least had British affinities.

As president, he needed to deal with the crash which had just shaken the entire economy to its foundations. He took the measures needed to stabilise the financial system and save the American car industry from collapse. These policies were not glamorous, but they worked.

It was impossible for Obama to be as glamorous as president as he had been on the campaign trail. He ordered the closure of the military prison at Guantanamo Bay, used to hold terrorist suspects without trial, within a year, but failed to achieve this during his eight years in the White House. He did get the Affordable Care Act through, and that health reform has so far survived as a major legislative achievement, one which eluded Bill Clinton. In 2009 he was awarded the Nobel peace prize, which struck even Obama's admirers as premature. In 2011, American special forces tracked down Osama bin-Laden in Pakistan and killed him, with Obama watching the operation from the White House. But he was altogether less gung ho than George W. Bush had been, and more inclined to give conciliatory speeches. His critics said that once he had delivered a thoughtful speech on a difficult subject, he imagined he had dealt with it. The uncomfortable truth was that many of the issues he faced were so intractable that no president could solve them.

In 2012 he won a second term by defeating Mitt Romney. After various terrible shootings in the United States, including an attack on Sandy Hook Elementary School in Connecticut in December 2012 in which twenty children aged six and seven were murdered, he said he would make gun control a 'central issue' of his second term. Connecticut passed a gun control law but action at federal level failed. In 2013 Obama incurred criticism for failing to punish the Syrian dictator, Bashar al-Assad, for using chemical weapons. In 2016 he paid the first visit by an American president to Cuba since Coolidge in 1928, part of a diplomatic strategy which sought to normalise relations with that country.

He was not able to remove the wild partisanship from American politics. His mere presence in the White House enraged some people, and prompted the circulation of wild rumours on the Internet, including the ludicrous accusation that he had not actually been born an American at all. This so-called birther controversy was fomented by Donald Trump among others. At a White House correspondents' dinner attended by Trump, Obama revealed that a video of him being born had come to light, had a clip played from *The Lion King* of Simba's birth, and remarked: 'I want to make clear to the Fox News table that was a joke.' In 2017, graceful to the last, the Obamas and their daughters left the White House. But although he had retained his dignity, his presidency was clouded by a faint but unmistakable sense of anti-climax.

DONALD TRUMP

Lived 1946–; president 2017–

D onald Trump was the first reality TV star to become president. His opponents considered him a sleazy, unstable, self-obsessed fantasist, and watched his ascent with astonishment and dismay. They believed they could stop him by proving him a liar, and collected mountains of incontrovertible evidence to convict him of this charge. But it would be more accurate to describe Trump as a bullshitter, uninterested in whether his stream of boastfulness bore any relation to the truth. He knew the value of putting on a performance, and dominated the theatre of politics by flouting the canons of good taste which inhibited his rivals. The more he scandalised high-minded liberals by appealing to emotions such as fear of Mexicans and of Muslims, the more he became the chosen instrument of revenge for voters who worried their jobs were going abroad and were fed up with being ignored by the political class. In his way, Trump was every bit as democratic as Andrew Jackson, president from 1829 to 1837, and every bit as barbarous.

Trump was born in the borough of Queens, in New York City. His grandfather, Friedrich Trump, had emigrated from the village of Kallstadt, in Palatinate in south-western Germany, origin also of the H. J. Heinz tomato ketchup family. The future President's father, Fred Trump, was a hard-driving businessman who built up a successful real estate business in the suburbs of New York. He married Mary Anne Macleod, born into rural poverty on the Isle of Lewis in the Outer Hebrides, who spoke Gaelic as her first language, emigrated to the United States in 1930, when she was seventeen, and worked initially in domestic service. Donald was the fourth of their five children and professes to this day his love for Scotland, while showing scant interest in his German roots and for many years claiming his father's family were Swedish. He went to New York Military Academy, a private boarding school sixty miles north of the city, avoided service in Vietnam by pleading bone spurs on his heels, studied at the University of Pennsylvania and entered the family real estate business.

Like Barack Obama, Trump published his autobiography well before becoming a presidential candidate. *Trump: The Art of the Deal* is a vainglorious account of his first twenty years in the real estate business. He proclaims the importance of 'gut feeling' in making decisions, and says: 'I wasn't satisfied just to earn a good living. I was looking to make a statement. I was out to build something monumental – something worth a big effort.' Of his apartment in Trump Tower, his headquarters on Fifth Avenue, he claims: 'What I'm doing is about as close as you're going to get, in the twentieth century, to the quality of Versailles. Everything is made to order. For example, we had the finest craftsmen in Italy hand-carve twenty-seven solid marble columns for the living room. They arrived yesterday, and they're beautiful.'

The book came out in 1987, spent almost a year in the *New York Times* bestseller list, and established his reputation as a tycoon. He drew a veil over his many high-profile projects which had not worked out, and his dependence for financial support on his altogether more prudent and prosperous father. From 2004 he honed his gifts as a showman by presenting *The Apprentice*, a reality TV show in which contestants competed for a one-year, $250,000 contract to run one of his companies.

Trump has been married three times, first in 1977 to Ivana Winklmayr (née Zelnickova), a Czech model, with whom he has three children; next in 1992 to Marla Maples, an American actress from the state of Georgia, with whom he has a daughter; and since 2005 to Melania Knauss, a model from Slovenia, with whom he has a son. He has also belonged to three political parties, first the Republicans, next the Reform Party, for which he considered making a presidential run in 1999, and thirdly the Democrats. In 2009 he rejoined the Republican Party, and although in 2011 he said he would not be running for president, four years later, in June 2015, he announced his candidacy at Trump Tower, under the slogan MAKE AMERICA GREAT AGAIN.

Trump was the oldest runner in a crowded field, one of seventeen contenders for the Republican nomination, and unlike all previous presidents had served neither in the military nor in any federal office, so conventional opinion was inclined to dismiss his chances. Conventional opinion was wrong. He was a brilliantly unconventional candidate, with more experience on reality TV than all his rivals put together, and he realised that by waking very early in the morning, for he did not need much sleep, he could set the news agenda by posting some tweet so outrageous it cried out for correction.

Senior Republicans called him 'a pathological liar', 'a race-baiting, xenophobic, religious bigot', 'utterly amoral', a 'narcissist at a level I don't think this country's ever seen' and a 'terrible human being' who has made 'disgusting and indefensible' comments about women. None of this held him back. He had no need of the hierarchy because he had a direct connection via Twitter to millions of disappointed Americans who felt their standard of living under pressure, thought excessive immigration had something to do with it, sensed that only Trump understood their desperation, and liked his proposal to erect a wall along the Mexican border.

After winning the Republican nomination, he took on Hillary Clinton – 'Crooked' Hillary as he dubbed her on Twitter. She was incautious enough to say at one of her fundraisers that you could put half Trump's supporters in 'the basket of deplorables', people who are 'racist, sexist, homophobic, xenophobic, Islamophobic – you name it'. That was the problem about condemning Trump: how did you avoid implying that his supporters must be terrible people too?

Tony Schwarz, who had ghostwritten *The Art of the Deal* and been paid half the royalties for his trouble, said in the summer of 2016: 'I put lipstick on a pig. I feel a deep sense of remorse that I contributed to presenting Trump in a way that brought him wider attention and made him more appealing than he is. I genuinely believe that if Trump wins and gets the nuclear codes there is an excellent possibility it will lead to the end of civilisation.' The note of hysteria in that belated repentance is perhaps one reason why it bounced harmlessly off Trump, or may even have done him some good.

Shortly before the election the *Washington Post* published some remarks Trump had made in 2005, when he said of a married woman he was about to try to seduce, 'I don't even wait. And when you're a star, they let you do it. You can do anything. Grab them by the pussy. You can do anything.' Trump rather unusually apologised for that remark, while claiming 'Bill Clinton has said far worse to me on the golf course.' But more often Trump enjoyed scandalising the mainstream media, whom he accused of printing 'fake news' about him whenever it suggested he was an atrocious liar, or was otherwise in the wrong.

On polling day Trump came second in the popular vote but finished ahead in the Electoral College. To the surprise and consternation of the American Establishment, he was now president. His administration was staggeringly chaotic: he kept firing senior people, one of whom, James Comey, the head of the FBI, responded by comparing him to a New York Mafia boss. The wall he was going to build along the Mexican border – see the epigraph at the start of this book – remains at the time of writing almost entirely unbuilt, with the Mexicans naturally declaring they will not pay for it and the US Congress also reluctant to provide the necessary funds, though 27.5 miles of new wall have been constructed at El Paso and 76 miles of the existing fence have been reinforced.

But Trump did make strenuous attempts to implement his programme. He put through tax cuts, greatly increased the bureaucratic obstacles to entering the United States, attempted in particular to keep Muslims out, started a trade war with China, was for a time on suspiciously good terms with the Russian leader Vladimir Putin, withdrew American troops from Afghanistan and Syria, withdrew the USA from the 2015 nuclear deal with Iran, withdrew also from the 2016 Paris climate accords, recognised Jerusalem as the capital of Israel, and as soon as he arrived in the White House began campaigning for a second term.

Trump failed in his attempt to scrap Barack Obama's health reforms, but no one could accuse him of seeking to emulate his predecessor's wonderful manners. Trump remained Trump, thriving on controversy though in private capable of charming people when it suited him to do so. He had members of his family around him in the White House, including his daughter Ivanka and her husband Jared Kushner, and took many of them on a successful visit to Buckingham Palace, for he revered the Queen and loved being entertained by her, and she knew how to make this strange guest feel welcome.

The president was still for much of the time setting the agenda, and for much of the time driving his opponents so crazy with personal loathing that they just wanted to destroy him, and became incapable of understanding why some of his measures were popular. When evidence emerged that in the summer of 2019 he had threatened to withhold the payment of $400 million in military aid to Ukraine unless that country investigated one of his potential Democratic opponents in the 2020 presidential election, the House of Representatives began impeachment proceedings against him, but there seemed no prospect of the Senate voting him out of office.

Few of Trump's opponents had much idea about Andrew Jackson's bloodthirsty career. They knew too little history to make comparisons with the Mexican War waged by James K. Polk in the 1840s, or Andrew Johnson coming within one vote of impeachment in the 1860s, or the corruption which flourished under Ulysses S. Grant and Warren G. Harding. The licentiousness of JFK, the horrors of the Vietnam War under LBJ, the lies of Richard Nixon, the attempt to impeach Bill Clinton, the disasters in Iraq under George W. Bush: these painful episodes tended to be forgotten or downplayed by commentators determined to condemn Trump as the most embarrassing president ever. That charge has been levelled at many of his predecessors too, and one cannot yet be confident Donald Trump is any worse than they were.

AFTERWORD

Should you wish, despite having seen from this book how many presidents have come to grief, to run for that office, and should you fulfil the requirements of being a natural-born American citizen and at least thirty-five years of age, you will have to consider which of the following ways of reaching the White House is most in accordance with your character and abilities:

1. Have a good war. Washington, Jackson, Grant and Eisenhower are among those who attained, thanks to their military exploits, an almost impregnable popularity.
2. Produce sublime words. Jefferson and Lincoln are the outstanding examples.
3. Promise change. Nothing in America is as old as the idea of change, understood as the return to a primal state of innocence.
4. Promise mediocrity. That way you will annoy fewer people.

Successful candidates have sometimes combined elements from all four approaches, but there can be no doubt that, from a statistical point of view, the last option has been the most successful.

Eminent observers have long been struck by the low quality of American presidents. Alexis de Tocqueville, who visited the

United States in 1831–32, remarked in the first volume of *Democracy in America*:

> On my arrival in the United States I was surprised to find so much distinguished talent among the citizens and so little among the heads of the government. It is a constant fact that at the present day the ablest men in the United States are rarely placed at the head of affairs; and it must be acknowledged that such has been the result in proportion as democracy has exceeded all its former limits. The race of American statesmen has evidently dwindled most remarkably in the course of the last fifty years.

The election in 1828 of Andrew Jackson, described by de Tocqueville as 'a man of violent temper and very moderate talents', heralded the change. The first six presidents were cultivated men who could hold their own with the best in Europe. Jackson was a ruthless brute, who represented the ruthless and brutish strain in American life and ushered in a long succession of mediocrities, nominated by their parties not because they were the most distinguished figures in public life, but because they could win a tawdry presidential election and be counted upon to distribute the spoils of office to their followers.

Of the seventeen presidents between Jackson and Theodore Roosevelt, only Lincoln can be described as a statesman, and most have passed into obscurity. So too have a number of more modern presidents: who now remembers Warren G. Harding? And although it would be wrong to describe such recent figures as Lyndon B. Johnson, Richard Nixon, Gerald Ford, Jimmy Carter, Bill Clinton and George W. Bush as devoid of talent, each of them found himself involved in transactions which at the time seemed just as bad, albeit not in quite the same way, as anything which has occurred in the last few years.

In a chapter entitled 'Why Great Men Are Not Chosen President' in *The American Commonwealth*, published in 1888 and revised in 1910, James Bryce examined why 'this great office . . . is not more frequently filled by great and striking men'. He suggested that

> eminent men make more enemies, and give those enemies more assailable points, than obscure men do. They are therefore in so far less desirable candidates. It is true that the eminent man has also made more friends, that his name is more widely known, and may be greeted with louder cheers. Other things being equal, the famous man is preferable. But other things never are equal. The famous man has probably attacked some leaders in his own party, has supplanted others, has expressed his dislike to the crotchet of some active section, has perhaps committed errors which are capable of being magnified into offences. No man stands long before the public and bears a part in great affairs without giving openings to censorious criticism. Fiercer far than the light which beats upon a throne is the light which beats upon a presidential candidate, searching out all the recesses of his past life. Hence, when the choice lies between a brilliant man and a safe man, the safe man is preferred.

It is all too often safer in politics to say next to nothing, to hold no deep convictions of your own, to look the part and be ready to do your party's bidding.

From Jackson onwards the question was how to win elections, not how to govern the country. An ideal candidate might be able to do both, but how often does an ideal candidate come along? The party hacks who from the 1830s selected presidential candidates were intent on getting their hands on the patronage at the disposal of the victor, and that meant choosing third-rate figures they expected to be able to control.

It is no good denouncing this system as immoral. Moral indignation impedes understanding of how people actually are. And yet of course there is a moral, indeed a spiritual thread in the American idea of politics. Washington often used the word 'sacred', as have many of his successors. American democracy is regarded by some of its staunchest supporters with the veneration befitting a religion.

The difficulty of writing about American politics – perhaps all politics – is the difficulty of holding contradictory thoughts in one's mind. High ideals and low machinations, nobility and demagoguery, the sublime and the tawdry are mingled together, and have been from the earliest days, with neither element able to obliterate the other. In this book Jefferson, one of the noblest presidents, can be found describing Washington as an apostate and a heretic who has gone over to 'the harlot England'.

Donald Trump is regarded by his critics as a profaner of the temple of democracy. They feel his presence in the White House as a stain on the 'sacred honour' pledged in 1776, and are in no doubt that he deserves to be excommunicated. But when one reads the lives of his predecessors, one finds American democracy has always been both sacred and profane. It encompasses gentlemen and hucksters. It encompasses Washington and Trump.

21. Chester ARTHUR (1881-85); 22. Grover CLEVELAND (1885-89); 23. Benjamin HARRI
26. Theodore ROOSEVELT (1901—09); 27. William TAFT (1
    30. Calvin COOLIDGE (1923—29); 31. Her

32. Franklin D ROOSEVELT (1933-45)†; 33. Harry S.TRUMAN (1945-53); 3
36. Lyndon B. JOHNSON (1963—69); 37. Richard M. NIXON (1969—74
41. George H.W. BUSH (1989-93); 42. Bill CLINTON (1993-2001); 43. George W. BUS